A Century of Swindles

Ponzi Schemes, Con Men, and Fraud

Railey Jane Savage

LYONS
PRESS

Guilford, Connecticut

An imprint of Globe Pequot, the trade division of
The Rowman & Littlefield Publishing Group, Inc.
4501 Forbes Blvd., Ste. 200
Lanham, MD 20706
LyonsPress.com

Distributed by NATIONAL BOOK NETWORK

British Library Cataloguing in Publication Information available

Library of Congress Cataloging-in-Publication Data available

Names: Savage, Railey Jane, author.
Title: A century of swindles : Ponzi schemes, con men, and fraudsters / Railey Jane Savage.
Description: Lanham, MD : Lyons Press, [2021] | Includes bibliographical references and index.
Identifiers: LCCN 2021020482 (print) | LCCN 2021020483 (ebook) | ISBN 9781493053681 (paperback ; alk. paper) | ISBN 9781493053698 (epub)
Subjects: LCSH: Swindlers and swindling—United States—History. | Fraud—United States—History.
Classification: LCC HV6695 .S28 2021 (print) | LCC HV6695 (ebook) | DDC 364.16/30973—dc23
LC record available at https://lccn.loc.gov/2021020482
LC ebook record available at https://lccn.loc.gov/2021020483

To Chuck—
the real McCoy

"Once you give a charlatan power over you, you almost never get it back."

—CARL SAGAN, *THE DEMON-HAUNTED WORLD: SCIENCE AS A CANDLE IN THE DARK*

"Shut up and take my money!"

—PHILIP J. FRY, EVERYMAN, *FUTURAMA*

Contents

INTRODUCTION

Dear Reader:

The conspirators in the following pages were all guilty and, for the most part, received generous helpings of their just desserts. The crimes are fascinating and, once upon a time, diverting. I wrote the majority of this book in 2020 while under COVID-19 lockdown and was glad for the distraction from the world around me. But as I became more familiar with the scammers' modes and methods, the distraction faded; for all the reports of pain and suffering these baddies were inflicting, their overarching response was, "Don't believe the press." The swindlers' true enemy is information, and by undermining the Fourth Estate they are better able to direct the narrative and, therefore, interrupt the flow of objective information. When there is no longer a consensus on "fact" then the border abutting "fiction" becomes increasingly fuzzy. This is dangerous territory.

The dogged journalism that helped unmask each of the confidence tricksters in the following pages was not the end of the story, by any means—the victims still had to admit to being bamboozled, which was no small feat—but the louder the con men cried to ignore the pesky reporters, the hollower their words became. I remember being a young girl and hanging out in the kitchen where an aging boombox constantly blared NPR. The late great Cokie Roberts told a story of *New York Times* reporter Charles Mohr covering the Goldwater campaign in 1964 when a woman ran from the rally with frantic tears in her eyes shouting, "Stop them! Stop those reporters! They're writing down every word he's saying!" I let out a short, sharp laugh when I heard this because it was so absurd, so backward. But the tearful woman was not alone and probably not even malicious in her intent. I have thought of this story many times since

I first heard it in the 1990s. When truth is devalued and rejected, the architects of fiction prevail.

I have only examined con artists working in America—the Land of Opportunity—and only those working the pre-internet era (1850–1950). I saved myself from wading into the opaque waters of email scams and modern-day catfishing, but I have passed judgment on the characters in these chapters and have developed fully formed, 2020-based opinions of them. However, their stories do not require editorializing but, rather, retelling. I have kept myself out of these narratives because you, dear readers, can reach your own conclusions based on the evidence before you. Worry not, though, for the writing is energetic and colorful, but the facts are there. The haunting echoes of these long cons still ring today, which made writing this . . . challenging. To ignore and reject history only imperils the future, and the 2020 present was proof. Of course, I hope that readers will not look through the wrong end of the telescope here— this is not an instructional manual—but instead, I hope you come away from these stories with a renewed appreciation for The Truth.

Railey Jane Savage

CHAPTER ONE

They Call Me ... Gordon Gordon

THE TIME: 1868–1874
THE PLACE: Edinburgh, Scotland; Minneapolis, Minnesota;
                 New York, New York; Manitoba, Canada
THE TAKE: $37,000–$1,000,000, jewels, baubles, endless
                 streams of champagne
THE PLAYERS: Rev. Simpson, Forfarshire, Scotland
                 Thomas Smith, of Marshall & Sons Jewelers, Edin-
                 burgh
                 Howard Paddison, Esq., Lincoln's Inn, London
                 Colonel Loomis, Land Agent Commissioner,
                 Northern Pacific Railway
                 William Belden
                 Horace Greeley
                 Jay Gould
                 Boss Tweed
                 Merriam, Fletcher, and Hoy
                 Hubert Hamilton, Lord Glencairn, Lord Gor-
                 don-Gordon, George H. Hamilton Gordon, and
                 the Pretender to the Earldom of Aberdeen—
                 referred to as "GG'" in this narrative

The Reverend Simpson lived quietly at his rectory of the Free Church Manse in Forfarshire, Scotland. The mid-nineteenth century was bucolic but hard in rural Britain. The landed gentry had their estates, and the clergy had their housing, but class mobility was rare and always hard-fought. In the summer of 1868, an affable young man leased a small plot for shooting and quickly became friendly with Rev. Simpson, his neighbor. This pleasant neighbor—to all appearances a gentleman—was familiarly known as "Hamilton." And, as Simpson described, "There was much surmising as to who he was, but as he paid his bills punctually, lived quietly and had the manners of a gentleman, no one could find anything against his character or conduct." Hamilton went away but returned the following season as "Lord Glencairn," (we'll call him "GG") and sought an introduction to those who could help elevate his furnishings and dress to match his recently elevated bearing. Rev. Simpson obliged and took him to a jewelry firm in Edinburgh, Marshall & Sons, of which Simpson was a regular client. And though Simpson had been curious about the apparently upstanding young man, "as he continued to behave in a gentlemanly way and had friends from England with him who were men of standing and respectability, and especially as he was certified to be a man of rank and wealth by his lawyers, a well-known firm in Lincoln's Inn, I was willing to think the best of him, and at least to wait until he discovered himself before I judged him."[1]

Simpson's attitude was representative of nearly all those who came to know GG; there was no real reason to question claims that the man never explicitly made; he never claimed to be a lord but never balked when others presumed. Presumption, assumption, and inference were his currency, and in this way, GG was wealthy beyond measure.

GG was described as "about five feet eight or nine inches high, of light build, with short black hair, black side whiskers, a bold, overhanding forehead, small features and small grey eyes. He dressed quietly and in good taste."[2] But also, he was "about forty years of age, of medium stature, rather stout, dark hair, mutton chop whiskers, prominent forehead, blue eyes and lots of cheek. A noted detective states that his hair is dyed, and: judging from his eyes, fancies the hair must be light."[3] And, he was also described as "impressive but of medium height (5' 10"), small, well-formed hands and feet, curling brown hair, side whiskers, eyes of blue or grey, finger nails manicured, full or protuberant forehead, erect form, peculiarly stiff and set way of holding his head up and back, nervous and restless manner."[4] The overall impression was generally consistent among the describers, but they differed in small ways; given that the devil is in the details, it was in these consistencies and gaps that GG allowed his reputation to grow organically.

His suggestions—both stated and implied—toward his bearing were supported by his associations with a legal firm out of Lincoln's Inn, London, and a powerful bank in Dundee, Scotland. Mr. Howard Paddison of Lincoln's Inn had so fully embraced him as a client that he allowed GG to use the rooms above his law offices. And with the Dundee banker, GG deposited a few thousand pounds on which to draw for general expenses, but he also had "implied that the income was £40,000 to £50,000 a year" for the peerage.[5] Of note: The Scottish banker had unwittingly acted as confirmation by association, but he never extended GG an overdraft; whether forethought or frugality drove this decision matters not, for, in the end, he was practically the only person from whom GG could not get more out of than he put in.

The Dundee banker's caution notwithstanding, GG had set it up that the responsibility of vetting and legitimacy fell to the firms. With respected outfits vouching for him, GG was able to deflect all questions of his character and honesty to his banker and lawyer: Dundee, Scotland, and Mr. Paddison in London were positioned to answer any challenges to GG's claims. With only these two firms, GG had begun spinning his web of not-so-much plausible deniability but plausible confirmation. This method was risky, though, and generally considered shady, at best: "In the absence of other recommendations, to rent a country-house with shootings, and keep an account with a banker in the nearest town, are usually accepted as an unchallengeable passport to good society in Scotland. It is a cheap way of making character, not very nicely scrutinized."[6]

In the same way GG leveraged his association with the banker and lawyer, he used ostensibly noble objects to signify his standing. Dress, accessories, and trappings all had to support GG's unspoken claims while he maintained "that kind of placidity of countenance and dreamy indifference which are considered to be marks of high breeding."[7] After receiving confirmation from Dundee and London that GG was, in fact, a known client, Marshall & Sons must have felt eager and lucky to have such an esteemed client with such magpie urges in their good graces, and in them, GG had found an ideal partner.

He had fittingly taken rooms at the Royal Hotel in Edinburgh. He wrote notes and scores of letters on printed stationery bearing a fancy coronet over the monogram "H.G.," all of which he signed "H. Glencairn." He kept a "tiger," a squire-like attendant dramatically outfitted in buckskin breeches, top boots, and a cockade to indicate his master's military commission under the Queen. His dresser set and small boxes were all monogrammed with "Right Honorable Lord Glencairn." As he allowed others to fill in the blanks of his lineage, so, too, did he tacitly encourage a royal reputation through his things.

GG paid special attention to a Dresden dinner plate, painted with a portrait of Napoleon's mother. GG said this marvelous dish had been coveted by former Emperor Napoleon who, he told Mr. Thomas Smith of Marshall & Sons, had offered £10,000 for it. But GG was restrained and would not part with his treasure! That is until he offered it to the jewelers for display in their front window to entice and inspire potential customers. How lucky for them that GG's largesse was so flexible! He brought them the priceless treasure two days later, wrapped in brown paper, and it was put in a position of power in the display window at once.

Trivial though this one plate might seem, it revealed GG's preternatural sense for social manipulation. Through peddling this relic, his fancy but generic stationery, and his superficial tiger, GG maximized the goodwill the shops and banks extended him.

His claim to the peerage of Glencairn was to mature upon his twenty-seventh birthday, which was March 25, 1870. This, he claimed, would give him full access to the estate's coffers. The shops and firms were happy to extend credit to that date, expecting the payoff to not only settle accounts but also secure a lifelong customer with deep pockets. In many ways, it was brilliant for GG to set a deadline, for it gave him a window of time in which to freely operate while setting a firm date for him to flee.

A photo of Lord Gordon Gordon looking extraordinary in his trademark tam and sporran.

Before disappearing, though, he tried to glean and gain as much stuff as he could to act as evidence for future flings. He leaned into Marshall & Sons's good graces and commissioned a great number of baubles and trinkets of his own design. All of them bore his monogram. His sketches were careful and fastidious such that "no one could have imagined him to be naught but a gentleman of refined tastes and habits."[8] His familiarity with the shop was so complete that upon seeing one of the partner's sons one morning, he took a knee and earnestly addressed the lad and "benevolently gave him some good advices regarding his conduct through life, especially recommending him to be diligent, truthful, and always to keep in mind that 'honesty is the best policy.'"[9]

The scene in the jewelry shop is revealing; GG knew proscribed signifiers of title and rank, so he knew just what to ask for in order to look the part. And *how* to ask for it by *playing* the part. GG's sage, idiomatic advice would have been received like a blessing by these grateful merchants, more of his same magnanimity that he'd graced them with by generously lending them his £10,000 Dresden plate. "Honesty is the best policy," but not always the most lucrative.

Smith's initial inquiries into GG's standing reveal the wheels-within-in-wheels of plausible deniability and plausible confirmation that GG had so expertly designed. After GG had been haunting the jewelers for only a few weeks, Smith called on Paddison to establish how much—if any!—credit should be extended GG, given the delay in payment for items already procured.

"I had better see his Lordship," said Smith after seeing GG's trademark Tam O'Shanter lying on one of the tables in Paddison's office.

"I am surprised you think the Lordship should be here!" replied Paddison with false amazement. Paddison left his office to go upstairs.

When he returned, he bade Smith follow him as GG had "agreed to grant an audience," so he ushered Smith up the stairs to an elegantly furnished room GG dubbed his "audience chamber."

GG welcomed Smith, "What a pleasure to see you, Mr. Smith. You are quite right to see me and make an inquiry. You are quite right to make all the inquiries!" But, gesturing to Paddison, who had entered the chamber but stood silently, GG said, "I leave all my money matters entire to my solicitor, dear Mr. Paddison. I leave it to you to take up the matter with him."

Paddison returned to his office. GG kept Smith a moment longer in the chamber to call attention to the bookcase filled with beautifully bound volumes and the detailed plans for his estates that lined the walls.

Smith had come for restitution on delinquent accounts so he was not satisfied with being fobbed off to Paddison, who seemed an accomplice, no matter how unwitting. Wanting as few feathers ruffled as possible, Paddison assured Smith that he would retrieve some of the goods his Lordship had purchased and write a check for the remaining balance. "But," Mr. Paddison added, "if I do this, it would give great offense to his Lordship."

Weighing the risk of slighting GG against being taken to court by Smith, Paddison gave Smith a written guarantee for the full amount due and that it would be paid on March 25.[10]

— —

On March 9, 1870, though, GG disappeared from the British Isles, leaving a trail of debts, unpaid notes, and memories of stolen baubles. On March 25, Smith wrote to Paddison, reminding him of the promise. Paddison's reply: "The whole of us have been duped."

GG had absconded, leaving the solicitors of his mythical estates in the lurch to the extent of over $25,000 and several unsettled bills with the leading shopkeepers of London and Edinburgh, and doubtless there were many others who were too embarrassed, or too ruined, to make themselves known.[11]

A small, though strangely endearing, twist was that many of the unpaid-for items were recovered as GG had made gifts of them to his friends, family, and business associates. Once the bills were due and merchants began to "follow the money," much of the gifted contraband was returned such that GG's financial destruction was somewhat mitigated. Paddison returned the gifts he had received, thereby decreasing his own financial liability as GG's guarantor, and sometime later, the Dundee banker sent to Marshall & Sons a gold chain and locket GG had given a bank clerk.[12]

Whether Paddison and the banker had vouched for GG before or after receiving these gifts was not discussed.

———

There were multiple and differing reports on when and where GG landed on the North American continent. Some said Nova Scotia. Some said Boston. One report told of an English gentleman who moved elegantly through Portland, Maine's social scene: "With a fine personal appearance, and courtly dress and manner, he soon made many acquaintances, who, dazzled by his wealth and splendid equipage, believed him to be and English nobleman traveling *incog.*"[13] This person made overtures toward buying vast tracts of American land on which to house his purportedly hundreds of tenant families. However, this person of interest left the area without finalizing the deal. Or paying.

GG's whereabouts were confirmed that winter, 1870, in Minneapolis, Minnesota. Somewhere between Edinburgh and Minnesota, he'd become heir to the Earldom of Aberdeen and a fully landed lord: Lord Gordon Gordon.

In Minneapolis, he swanned through the social circles, wined and dined by the effete, all while talking of his grand plans to bring his people to American land—tenants of his vast estates in Scotland and England. "The coronet upon his livery and the insignia of nobility on his papers gave strength to his assertions,"[14] as did the endless stream of letters on impressive stationery he received from impressive-sounding people. These stories and his just-so, put-together air made him the cream of the Minnetonka set in the 1871 season. He was partial to patent leather shoes, a silk hat, and gloves. He was the darling of hungry investors and their wives.

The promise of tenants, and the influx of the $5 million it would take to get them there, piqued the interest of Colonel J. Loomis, Land Commissioner of the Northern Pacific Railway, who quickly made available 50,000 acres of Northern Pacific land, just in case.

Northern Pacific's interest in GG's whale of an investment was not a surprise, but their extravagance to court him, fueled by desperation, was. Just two years prior, Northern Pacific's president, Jay Cooke, had sold immigrants and farmers on the "atmospheric Gulf Stream" that moved through the upper Midwest, warming the air and cultivating a natural "second Garden of Eden. . . . One thousand bushels of potatoes are reported to have been raised on a single acre; the pears and cherries are in season from three to seven months, and grain ripens into a magnificent crop, no matter what time of the year it is put into the ground."[15] This was, of course, not true; Cooke had sold them a false promise of real estate in America's Garden of Eden. A promised interest rate of 7.75 percent, coupled with the immigrants' tens of thousands of dead livestock and their crippled farms after a typical Minnesota winter that brought temperatures of 30 degrees below zero, nearly destroyed Northern Pacific and made its directors vulnerable and desperate. Did GG know this? Had he just *happened* upon a powerful railroad magnate desperate for a too-good-to-be-true investment?

At one point, GG was asked of his intentions in Minnesota, to which he charitably offered: "Yes . . . I do covet a few thousand acres of your beautiful lands: not for myself—I have more than enough for the remnant of my poor life—but for my beloved sister, for the gratification of her benevolence. She would like to present to some of my old tenant lands in your free republic, where they may rear their families in peace and plenty; and to gratify my beautiful sister I would like to buy a few thousand acres—not many thousands, you know—say—say—say—say about—about 50,000 acres or so—just a little for my poor people."[16]

He needed the land for his tenants . . . his sister . . . any party at least one degree of separation removed. Wheels within wheels: plausible deniability, plausible confirmation.

What the Americans didn't know—and wouldn't have understood, probably—was GG's promotion to "Earl" while sailing for America. What could have prompted this? And why move from "Glencairn" to "Gordon"? Stranger still, "Gordon Gordon"? As a contemporaneous historian surmised: "[H]is choice of name was chiefly to the possession of note-papers with the earl's coronet, and the monogram H. G, or G. BL, just as you chose to read it. Possessing a quantity of these note-papers, his lordship needed to make no change. He was Hamilton, Lord Gordon, or, if you like, George Hamilton Gordon, Earl of Aberdeen." GG's name changed depending upon the stationery he was using that day. Somewhere in the Atlantic, between a single Dresden dinner plate and a stack of fancy stationery, GG had found his calling.

It would be a full year before anyone in America thought to question GG's supposed coat of arms. Being generally clueless to the workings of the British realm—a safe bet and security blanket for GG—his American marks did not know "that the bearing an earl's coronet over a monogram was an irregularity unknown to the laws of arms."[17]

Northern Pacific didn't want to lose this kilted boon, so Colonel Loomis quickly arranged a grand survey of the lands for GG. The introduction/survey/claim party Loomis put together to parade Gordon around Minneapolis was the stuff of local legend. A description from the then editor-in-chief of the *Minneapolis Tribune* demonstrated just how grand that expedition was: teams of horses, wagon trains, manual laborers, a French cook, white silk be-gloved waiters, full table service for every meal, bottomless potted grouse, and endless streams of champagne. A land surveyor rode alongside to point out the "tastiest spots" to GG for his settlement. The Stars and Stripes marked their camp, but the "banner of the Gordons" was always fluttering outside GG's well-appointed tent. "Meantime [Loomis] studied the sphinx Milord, and concluded that he was a queer cross between the lofty and the lowly; he was half lord and half lackey; perhaps his father was an English earl and his mother an Irish chamber-maid."[18] Loomis was about half right.

By the end of the storied trip, Gordon had laid claim to upwards of 50,000 acres with the promise of one hundred Scottish families reaching Duluth by the spring of 1872. Northern Pacific's imaginative and hard-working publicist fed the Associated Press a $7,000 bribe for the November 22, 1871, headline: "Lord Gordon, a wealthy Scotch noble who had purchased two townships of land from the North Pacific Railroad Company, on which tracts his countrymen are settling. The vast and fertile fields of the great Northwest offer extraordinary inducements to the thrifty denizens of overcrowded Europe."[19] GG's baseless claim had been legitimized with an ill-gotten headline. The layers of deception were stacked, exponentially increasing with each claim to plausible confirmation.

However, as the *Times* reported: "In November they came back half frozen. Milord had selected his 50,000 acres in Otter Tail and Beaver Counties. The Northern Pacific Railroad Company footed the bills—$50,000 for two months. The absurd farce was at an end. Milord Gordon did not buy the land for his poor tenants, and he never again mentioned his benevolent sister to anyone."[20]

Embedded in these layers was GG's genius for psychological manipulation. For as desperate as Jay Cooke was for cash, so, too, was Col. Loomis for fame. On their storied tour, GG staked many lots along Pelican Lake, which the rail line abutted, 150 miles northwest of Minneapolis. There were detailed maps of his plans for this new, idyllic city, which he planned to call "Loomis."

The stacked layers of deception also allowed for GG to move more fluidly from one mark to the next. Though he had spent two months touring Northern Pacific's land in Minnesota, laying claim to favorable tracts and happily riding in the sumptuous dining car, GG did not make any real purchases. Money never officially changed hands. Why Loomis did not know this, or take care to know this, was a mystery. Perhaps he was blinded by the sparkling waters of Pelican Lake and the glittering shores of his namesake fantastical city.

Whatever the case, GG left Minneapolis around New Year's Eve 1871 and made for the Eastern seaboard, armed with a mountain of letters of introduction to New York's cream. Loomis traveled eastward alongside him while scribbling multiple letters on GG's behalf, including one to Horace Greeley. What plans Loomis and GG must have made for the utopian city along Pelican Lake! The *New York Herald* noted GG's generosity and grace—and speech patterns!—when laying out his new city:

Everybody was struck with the magnificent ideas of this philanthropic noble who was possessed of such fabulous wealth, and when in conversation, he remarked to one gentleman, "Aw, my deaw fellah, as a fwend, I will let you have one cworner of a stweet." Lord Gordon . . . paid a "VISIT TO PROVIDENCE" and was there received and fêted in magnificent style. General Burnside and other distinguished gentlemen were asked to meet him at dinner. Lord Gordon was delightful in his manners and affable beyond measure and became so overcome with gratitude at the kindness of his host that before leaving he sold a few "cworner lots" in the city of Loomis, on Pelican Lake, to the son of the above gentleman.[21]

It was a few short months after GG was so warmly welcomed that a lengthy bio/speculation piece published in the *New York Herald* revealed GG's layers were crumbling in real time. The future landholders of Loomis grew uneasy after reading the article, so they checked on their "cworner lot" claims with the Northern Pacific. Whatever degree of shock the deed-holders experienced at being told their claims were worthless, the Northern Pacific officials were even more bewildered for, as they informed the distressed deed-holders, GG did not own any Northern Pacific land. Not one single acre.

"In the meanwhile these anxious inquiries came to the ears of His Lordship, and as he had other FISH TO FRY of a more important nature the purchasers of the 'cworner lots' were returned their money, with the information from Lord Gordon that he had discovered the title was not good."[22] How laughable, nigh impressive, it was of GG to accuse Northern Pacific of selling him bum deeds (more plausible deniability). Though the fact that his friend Loomis had been recently fired as Northern Pacific's land agent gave GG a ready scapegoat. One can only picture what a confrontation between a swindled General Burnside and darling GG might have looked like: a bewhiskered battle between fury and feigned fury.

So, by April 1872, GG's tapestry of lies was actively fraying. As the *Herald* brilliantly noted, though, GG had other "FISH TO FRY." Enter: Jay Gould, Fish.

In the course of swanning through Minneapolis society, GG had made fast friends with the Beldens. While impossible to confirm, GG *must* have known Bill Belden's recent history as a central member of the New York cabal that had, only two years prior, tried to corner and short the gold market. With Diamond Jim Fisk and Jay Gould his co-conspirators, Belden's notoriety as a business associate of the day's preeminent robber barons, and co-architect of the Black Friday of 1869 run to corner the gold market, was certain. Perhaps GG specifically positioned himself to rub elbows with Belden, a uniquely well-positioned mark. Perhaps he saw the writing on the wall for Loomis, who was still scribbling introductory notes on GG's behalf. The Northern Pacific "cworner lots" wouldn't be revealed for a few weeks yet, so GG's social capital still had outsized spending power. Whether based on forethought, or fueled by happenstance, GG found himself steaming westward on the same train as Mrs. Belden, all but assuring his entrée into New York's railroad society.

Boss Tweed manipulated and abused the markets with a sharp stick, honed with Jay Gould's ready cash infusions.
THE "BOY OF THE PERIOD" STIRRING UP THE ANIMALS; CURRIER & IVES CARTOON OF JAY GOULD POKING BULLS AND BEARS, 1869; LIBRARY OF CONGRESS, PRINTS & PHOTOGRAPHS DIVISION, LC-DIG-PPMSCA-11784 (DIGITAL FILE FROM ORIGINAL PRINT), https://www.loc.gov/item/90712364/.

Of note is that Diamond Jim Fisk—preeminent robber baron, scandal of society pages, beloved figure of New York's working poor, and partner of Jay Gould—had been gunned down in the lobby of the Grand Central Hotel on January 6 of that year by his mistress's jealous lover, mere days before GG's arrival in New York. Fisk had weathered the financial furor of 1869 and had continued to hold sway with Boss Tweed and President Ulysses S. Grant. His murder set the city agog and had a profound effect on Jay Gould. Gould was wracked with grief and beset by violent coughing fits brought on by consumption. It was a scant two months after Fisk's ignominious death that Gould met GG.

The economic and psychological turmoil Gould had lately experienced made him a prime mark for GG. There was already trouble afoot in the Vanderbilt–Gould dispute over control of the Erie Railroad, so GG's inflated—nay! Fantastical!—claims of lands and tenantry were perfectly suited to float dreams of expansion and lust for control. GG's calculated claims were set in motion such that he secured an introduction to Loomis, to an introduction to Horace Greeley, to an introduction to respected railroad manager Colonel Tom Scott, to an introduction to Jay Gould.

GG's boast of 60,000-share ownership of Erie stock was effective and pricked Gould's ear. With Gould's term as president of the Erie Board under fire from Greeley's Southmayd Bill, he was only too eager to secure means—by hook or by crook—of retaining his control of the railroad.

Gould would also have been worried by a suit brought against him by London firm Heath & Raphael, taking him to task for defrauding Erie's English stockholders. Under assault but steeled, Gould was not about to cede the controlling interest in Erie to Cornelius Vanderbilt, and he jumped at the chance to acquire Gordon's supposed mountain of controlling shares and his supposed connections to powerful people in England. He did not think to distrust GG's references.

With a supposed $50 million worth of shares under his control ($30 million his, $20 million from rich English parties), GG—an exotic and esoteric millionaire lord with expensive tastes and grand designs—seemed tailor-made to soothe and save Gould. It's impossible to say if Gould had always been GG's intended prey or even whether GG's deceptions were pathological or calculated. Unethical? Certainly. Immoral? Unclear. What was certain, though, was his commitment to his persona. His self-aggrandizing lies were impressive and consistent. These outlandish claims would have seemed so anachronistic and unbelievable from someone in plain clothes, or otherwise unremarkable, that his engraved goatskin sporran and gilded rings and stickpins would at once suggest and confirm the illusion. Did his lies inform his dress and carriage, or was he always predisposed to shiny things? A kind of delusional magpie? Either way, he jumped at the chance to whisper and suggest at his impressive status: He had been the youngest member of the House of Lords at age twenty-two, his landholdings spanned the British Isles, and the Queen had appointed him a special emissary because he was the only one who could outsmart Bismarck. He proudly wore a solid-gold stickpin she had gifted him. It *definitely* wasn't something he'd swindled from an Edinburgh jeweler.

GG positioned himself as Gould's only hope for salvation, strange alliances notwithstanding—Gould and Greeley were well-documented enemies. William Belden had been a co-conspirator with Diamond Jim Fisk and Gould, by extension, in the gold market scandal of 1869, but his affinity for GG currently outweighed his loyalty to Gould. Horace Greeley and his rallying cry of "Go West, young man!" were in principle and in practice diametrically opposed to Jay Gould and his manipulative industrialist aims. Still, "the enemy of my enemy is my friend" was persuasive logic, however fallible.

As GG massaged his connections and refined his image, he made inroads to Gould. GG installed himself (in style, naturally) at the Metropolitan Hotel, Room 110. His suite of well-appointed rooms was at the top of the staircase on the drawing-room floor and cost him $150 per week, not including his lavish meals and healthy drinks bill. He was generous with the staff—the hotel's bookkeeper proudly wore a set of diamond studs GG had given him—and they attended to his every, noble need. His time and attention were well-guarded, with only a sacred few allowed to call on his lordship unannounced. One of these rarefied few was Greeley. One of their more significant tête-à-têtes was later described as the following:

> *Mr. Greeley had dropped in, as was his custom, to discuss an omelet and immigration with his Lordship. Immigration and colonization of study agriculturists from old countries at that time were Mr. Gree-*

ley's hobbies. Lord Gordon had heard the story of "Go West, young man," and he knew that an introduction to Horace Greeley would lead to a close friendship, and didn't he, Gordon, have something of a hobby of that kind himself? And if he didn't, wasn't it easy to acquire one? To the subject of the management of the Erie Railway Company, "[Gordon] intends to control the next election for directors. These are glad tidings to the editor of the Tribune, *and he at once enlists in 'the Gordon reform movement' against the alleged corrupt control of the great railway. It was a great breakfast for Greeley."*[23]

The arrangements it took to get GG and Gould in the same room were intricate and convoluted. Letters of introduction and appointment cards flew across the city. GG's reputation preceded him, and he leaned into the impression that his time was precious and jealously guarded. Even more carefully than his seemingly bottomless pockets.

On March 2, 1872, at the Metropolitan Hotel, Room 110 was thick with power and pomp. GG's rooms were impressive, as were his wardrobe, and his prominently displayed collection of items—boxes, maps, silver—denoted a noble bearing. He presented himself as just the type of well-heeled investor toward which the American tycoons would flit. "The Americans, with all their republicanism, are the most arrant title-hunters. They run after persons with a title, and, as has just been observed, a number of them are eager to get hold of any one who will buy large lots of land in the western part of the States."[24] GG and Gould each had their part to play.

With appointment card in hand, Gould arrived at the Metropolitan Hotel in time for his 3 p.m. appointment with GG, as had been arranged through Col. Tom Scott. Gould was intimately familiar with the place as his rotund peer, Boss Tweed, held Room 112.

Gould sent his card to GG and, upon acknowledgment, was summoned up the stairs to Room 110. The door opened to an extravagantly furnished scene, GG at the center.

"I presume I am addressing Lord Gordon," said Gould, simultaneously confirming and challenging GG's title.

"Yes, sir," answered GG with all the gravitas he could muster standing in his decadent room, wearing his sartorial kilt. "Do come in. There is likely much for us to discuss."

Mr. Greeley, a scant twelve months before his fateful breakfast with GG at the Metropolitan Hotel.

"Yes, Lord Gordon. I believe there is." With that, Gould entered GG's cloister and sat down to what both men hoped would be a productive meeting.

"Now, Mr. Gould. I am in my own right possessed of upward of 60,000 shares of the capital stock of the Erie Railway Company and am in addition thereto interested in, and represent, a much larger amount of this stock. If I am to help expedite the immigration of my ruddy-cheeked Scotch tenants to these golden shores, I must insist that your Erie Railway Company, Mr. Gould, come to grips with the financial piece."

GG wasted no time getting to the heart of the matter: Erie's status of "good standing" was in question. As he controlled $50 million worth of Erie interests, GG had taken it upon himself to investigate how Erie might be saved. There was no question that a reorganization was needed. And while others were happy to make Gould the accused—and actual— offender, GG would help Gould retain his power after the shakeup. So, to make good with the shareholders and their controlling interests, a change in leadership was needed. And quick.

"My fellow Lords had entrusted the entirety of their interests to me to handle, my dear Gould. I was in Parliament, taking my seat in the House of Lords not ten years ago—a callow youth!—and though the youngest member by far (I had barely finished my twenty-first year, don't you know), I held sway in that body, dear Gould. If I can help set right the management in Parliament, surely I can help you with your American road, sir."

The walls were lined with framed maps and plans of the future city of LOOMIS, the shelves lined with impressive boxes and objects. GG's words ricocheted off their gleaming surfaces and pinged around the room, assaulting Gould and making it impossible to think of anything other than GG's grand claims whizzing through the air.

Gould was shrewd, though. Undeniably. He was also ill and grief-stricken. And he was likely more than a little desperate.

"Milord, what you describe sounds [like] a coup, more than a restructure. How am I to be guaranteed that infernal [Southmayd] Bill won't sink you? I refuse to fight wars on multiple fronts, sir; I shall not be divided and conquered."

THE MODERN COLOSSUS OF (RAIL) R

While Vanderbilt and Gould focus their attentions toward pulling
strings on the ground, they are at once propped up and controlled
by the true puppet-master: Horace Greeley.

"THE MODERN COLOSSUS OF (RAIL) ROADS," KEPPLER, JOSEPH FERDINAND,
ARTIST. NEW YORK: PUBLISHED BY KEPPLER & SCHWARZMANN. PHOTO-
GRAPH. RETRIEVED FROM THE LIBRARY OF CONGRESS, https://www.loc.gov/
item/2014645351/.

"Gould! You misunderstand, my American friend! Just as Her Majesty—the Queen, don't you know—entrusted only me to negotiate with Bismarck and the Prussians—I have him made, you see; no other man can cope—I shall deliver to you, and the world, a more honest and open Erie road. There shall be a reckoning, you shall once again be made President, I am assured, and the Board will represent yours, mine, and all our best interests." GG took a moment to sip coffee from his monogrammed china cup. "After all, you know Southmayd is mine? I had to get my bearings on your financial situation, don't you know? With me you needn't worry about the Bill. Or the [Heath & Raphael] suit, dear Gould. I will glean what I need and then make them go away. Faith, dear Gould!"

"Negotiations" continued like this for some time. If Gould offered up his resignation, GG would ensure the Board would do the same and the new Board would have members specifically appointed by Gould, GG, and Horace Greeley. GG would make the legislation and pesky lawsuit disappear at his own expense. According to GG, this was all because Gould had guaranteed him that Erie's financial standing was much rosier than the books, stocks, and press would have people believe. Things were running smoothly! Everything was *fine*.

Gould had convinced a fake Lord to help him avoid a hostile take-over by convincing him with fake financial claims. Truly, Room 110 was home to an ouroboros of scammers that day.

"It is helpful, is it not? That I should have such elevated friends in the print business, Mr. Gould? Certainly, this might further distance the Sword of Damocles from hanging over your Erie offices? A good word from me to my good friends in the press might be just the ticket. Greeley has certainly made mention of you to me, Mr. Gould."

"I do not regularly see Mr. Greeley, Lord Gordon," Gould replied somewhat scornfully. "Though I hear he has ready access to you."

Knock, knock, knock.

"Mr. Greeley here to see you, Milord."

GG had, once again, expertly manipulated a mark—for it is hard to label Jay Gould "victim"—into trusting a façade and a faulty impulse. This was a full month before his Northern Pacific scam was revealed, so

GG was able to massage his layered, round-robin deception as leverage; GG leveraged fake claims to one American railroad into a takeover of another.

GG's account of that same meeting was later labeled "verbose, bumptious, and toplofty . . . [A] consummate sample of a No. 1 perjury adulterated with a mixture of truth."[25]

The following five days were a flurry of negotiations between the two men. Gould's control of Erie was under siege from multiple parties—Greeley, Cornelius Vanderbilt, the legal proceedings out of London—and this angel investor presented not only a way out but also claimed to hold sway over those who would wish Gould harm. GG said Greeley's Southmayd Bill, actively being pushed through the legislature, was actually his own doing. Similarly, the London lawsuit was really just GG trying to discover more about Erie's workings. GG claimed both the legislation and the lawsuit, thereby positioning himself as the lynchpin to Gould's empire and his only salvation.

To ensure his future, Gould wanted the lawsuit gone. And what better way to solve a problem than to throw money at it? GG said he'd already spent nearly $1 million controlling the machinations of the Southmayd Bill and the suit; Gould quickly and readily offered to make good. He would reimburse the Lord for costs incurred.

Comprising this reimbursement package were:

500 shares of the National Stock Ward Company

500 shares of the Erie & Atlantic Sleeping Coach Company

200 shares of the Elmira Rolling Mill

200 shares of the Brooks Locomotive Works

20 bonds of $1,000 each of Nyack and Northern Railroad Company

500 shares of the Jefferson Car Company

4,722 shares of the Oil Creek and Alleghany Valley Railroad Company

600 shares of the Erie Railway Company

$160,000 in cash

GG accepted the parcel but quickly found a $40,000 error. He was willing to let this slight go uncharged, out of dignity. Upon hearing of this, though, rather than quibbling, or investigation, or arithmetic, Gould promptly assembled the cash and brought it to Gordon in utter deference: "And though there was no error, not wishing to raise any questions, and supposing that the money was safe in his hands, [Gould] took $40,000 more and deposited it with him, making in all, the securities mentioned, and $200,000 cash." GG, ever magnanimous, rejected the cash. Gould took the greenbacks as far as the door before placing them on the floor and then walking through the door without a word. GG's conflagration was so complete he had made his mark—one of the world's definitive robber baron tycoons—literally drop his cash at GG's feet.

Gould was desperate and assailed at that moment, which GG knew and banked on. The day before the GG deal was made and money changed hands, Gould wrote to GG that, "There is an important movement on foot, I think, entirely outside of your plan. During my absence today the parties sought to give me the matter shape by calling a Board meeting. The effort miscarried, but may be brought forward at any moment. If there shall be anything urgent I shall come to your rooms this evening. All Albany matters shall be suspended. If any litigation is required it shall be such as we agree upon, and as may prove beneficial to the property." Gould was grasping at straws and paying for them through the nose.

On March 9, 1872, GG held (literally) the power of Erie: Gould's stocks and greenbacks were tucked in a parcel neatly tied with a brief note on top:

"I hereby resign my position as President and director of the Erie Railway Company, to take effect upon the appointment of a successor. Yours, &c., Jay Gould. New York, March 9."

As Gould's attorney later wrote, "Marvellous as it may appear, it is nevertheless absolutely true that on the 9th or 10th of March, 1872, this arrant knave was not only possessed of the entire confidence of Jay Gould, the admiration and respect of Thomas A. Scott, the trust and affection of Horace Greeley, but he had half a million of Gould's securities and greenbacks in his trunk and Gould's resignation as a director and President of the Erie Railway Company in his vest pocket. Gould admitted that he had given his resignations to Gordon simply to induce his co-directors to do the same thing."[26]

Gould's greed and desperation were a dangerous combination and at risk of producing combustible results. Added to this volatile mixture were Gould's and GG's overlapping deceptions, as well as Gould's spiteful vengeance, which quickly rendered the compound unstable.

The proceeding two weeks, March 10–22, were wracked with strife for Gould: his resignation had been happily received but not mirrored by his board of directors, many of whom had been appointed by Gould himself. Armed with bribes and an unabating dissatisfaction with Gould's tumultuous leadership, they voted him out. Gould's shock at his underhanded play being outplayed by other underhanded parties provoked a standoff.

On Monday, March 11, Gould presented his resignation, got voted out, recanted his resignation, and then holed himself in his corner office of the Opera Palace. He called in reinforcements, led by infamous West Side gang leader Tommy Lynch and composed of hired (at $25 a head) ne'er-do-well plug-uglies. As Horace Greeley's *Tribune* gleefully noted the following day, the lobby of the Opera Palace was brimming with mercenaries "from alleys and cellars, from vile salons, thieves' dens, and the resorts of the poorest prostitutes," with "the odor of the gutter." The New York Police, with multiple precincts reporting over two shifts, fought the ruffians from Monday afternoon to 2:30 the following afternoon, at which point Gould surrendered.[27]

By Friday of that same week, the *New York Herald* had gotten hold of Erie's books and published excerpts, revealing to America some of the first glimpses of inner corporate workings. The books revealed that, in 1867, Erie's market capitalization was valued at $25,000,000. Whereas, in 1871 alone, Gould had printed and sold $51 million worth of stock. The income for these transactions, however, appeared nowhere in Erie's books.[28]

Gould's future looked dim as he had lost his presidency, authority, integrity, and well-guarded shady dealings in the span of a week. GG remained at the Metropolitan Hotel drinking champagne, Gould's greenbacks burning a $200,000 hole in his tartan pocket.

Gould's terrible, no-good, very bad week left him reeling, but somehow his trust in GG remained intact. Not until the morning of March 22, while reading the paper, did Gould connect the dots. Reading the Philadelphia stock quotes for the day, he saw a sharp decline in the market price of Oil Creek and Alleghany Valley Railroad stock, of which he had given GG 4,722 shares. Disturbed by the devaluation and sell-off, Gould telegraphed that the sale be stopped, and he leaped into action.

As deeply as he had trusted GG, Gould equally committed to his suspicions. Without delay, he secretly posted up in the neighboring room to GG's suite at the Metropolitan Hotel—a sting!—so he could readily and efficiently communicate with the intermediaries he'd hired to confront GG about his financial duplicity. Gould called on Belden, who was still in GG's thrall, but also knew on which side his bread was buttered and so had a vested interest in keeping Gould in the black.

On Saturday, March 23, 1872, after learning he'd been duped (by reading the paper, no less), Gould met Belden in the billiards room at the Metropolitan Hotel. They shared quick, furtive words before Gould hastened upstairs and Belden to the front desk. Though he liked him very much and had hoped to suspend judgment, Gould put the pieces together for Belden such that it was clear that GG was not exactly what he seemed. If nothing else, Belden knew better than to further flame Gould's already inflamed ire, so he did his best to at least diffuse things.

Belden told a room clerk that GG was a fraud and to keep the staff alerted to his comings and goings. Belden hastened to GG's room moments later. He was welcomed into his Lordship's sanctum, gleaming with royal-looking artifacts.

"Jay Gould is satisfied you have fooled him, and he has got [Police] Superintendent Kelso and a detective here with a warrant for your arrest. They have a carriage at the door and they will take you off before you can get any one made aware of your position . . . and, under a search warrant which they have, will take possession of all your papers, unless you instantly give up all the stocks and things you received from Gould."[29]

In the neighboring Room 112 were Boss Tweed, Judge Edward Shandley, and New York City Police Superintendent James Kelso. In Room 110 were nearly a half-million of Gould's dollars and securities.

The tittle-tattle between Rooms 110 and 112 was tense but almost comical in its physical setup and cast of characters. Imagine Jay Gould and the superintendent of New York Police leaning against a set of French doors, water glasses pressed between the door and their ears as they strained to eavesdrop on their little sting operation. Sitting imperiously on his couch with his prodigious belly more imposing than his mean twinkling stare and outsized sideburns was boss of bosses, Boss Tweed, scion of graft and cutthroat industrialism. Within twenty feet of each other were NYC's most infamous thieves: No. 1 fat cat, preeminent railroad robber baron, and GG.

GG's spree at least had panache, while Gould and Tweed seethed at being on the receiving end of deception, for once.

"Send Jay Gould here if he wants anything from me!" GG loudly demanded.

"Gould refuses to come in," replied the beleaguered Belden. "They will have you immediately locked up, and seize what they please; your surrendering by compulsion does not deprive you of any rights you have."

"As you extort them from me, I give them up." GG handed over the parcel of cash and stock.

Ferrying the booty from GG to Gould, Belden, an unhappy interlocutor, continued the negotiation: "That won't satisfy Jay Gould; you must give up the Alleghany and Oil Creek share."

GG explained that the shares had been tied up and complicated, but under threat of seizure and extortion, he agreed he would telegraph his brokers in Philadelphia to stop the sale at once. He promised to resolve the Oil Creek shares snafu and return them to Jay Gould later that night.

As Belden returned to Room 112, he handed the parcel to Gould, who handed it to Tweed, who immediately started counting the money therein.

"Now, I hope you are satisfied Gordon is a gentleman," hissed Belden.

To which Tweed bellowed, "That's nothing. It only shows he has got bigger game on hand!"[30]

Maybe it takes a thief to catch a thief.

Belden still believed in GG, though. He returned to GG's room shortly after quitting Gould and Tweed and offered GG some not-so-subtle advice. As GG put it, "Belden referred to the parties in the adjoining room, called them the Ring and said there was a conspiracy formed by them to do for me; that it was not the first time they had done for others, some having disappeared altogether, while others were so injured that they never recovered. . . . He advised me that I should have some person always in attendance upon whom I could rely." Belden then invited GG to spend the night at the Belden family home because he was welcome there and because he would be safe from the clutches of the Ring. And given that no formal charges were filed against GG, he was "free" to go with.

The two weeks following saw slings and barbs and legal threats fly between the parties. GG testified that, upon retaining representation for himself, Belden visited many times as emissary from Gould. Through Belden, Gould had wanted to settle, and how much would GG like to make this all go away? "I declined to interfere and referred him to my counsel, John H. Strahan. From that date to the present I have been subjected to many annoyances; parties watch my rooms at the hotel and I am watched and followed wherever I go."[31]

Three points: First, GG's impulse to keep litigious gatekeepers was still at work, just as he'd used Paddison back in London. But this time, his response of "talk to my lawyer" was girded with the haughtiness and vindication that comes with being falsely accused. Second, the implication that Gould remained chiefly interested in keeping his dubious hold on power through a payoff, rather than seeking justice, made him even less sympathetic to a public already frustrated with his graft. Third, GG's history of making fantastical claims notwithstanding, he was correct to

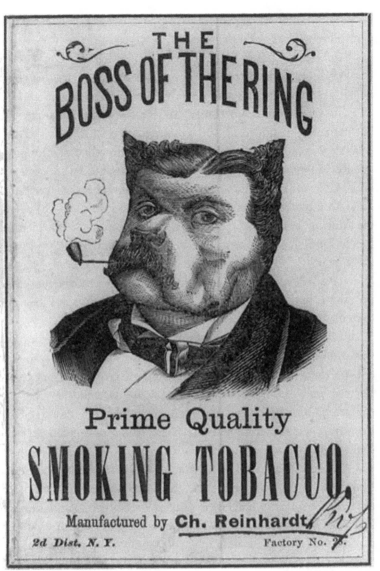

A pipe tobacco advertisement that profited from Boss Tweed's likeness—but to increase his appeal, they turned him into a bulldog.

"THE BOSS OF THE RING PRIME QUALITY SMOKING TOBACCO" ADVERTISEMENT FEATURING BOSS TWEED AS A SMOKING BULLDOG, 1869; LIBRARY OF CONGRESS, PRINTS & PHOTOGRAPHS DIVISION, LC-USZ62-31130 (B&W FILM COPY NEG.), https://www.loc.gov/item/2001697770/.

be paranoid of retribution from Gould and Tweed, as his being "watched and followed" was not a delusion.

To this third point, though, there was a catch.

While it is likely true that GG had reason to fear for his safety, ducking around corners and keeping out of sight served another purpose: no photographs. Of course, his dress was distinctive in New York, but perhaps GG hoped his foreign bearing would align with Americans' stereotypes and render him impossible to distinctly describe?

Regardless that his flamboyance and refusal to be identified were at odds, GG was masterful at stymying photographers at every turn. One New York photographer positioned his tripod on the building opposite the Metropolitan Hotel, but "Gordon took care never to keep his head steady for a single moment. He kept it constantly shaking as to defeat the operator."[32] Even in court, the resident artist was chided by the judge after GG balked at having a Lord's likeness so crudely captured. With no photos and no drawings, confirming his identity was going to be a difficult and lengthy process.

Because, of course, timing was tricky—immediate communication was still relatively newfangled and imprecise. GG's integrity and supposedly personal details had been plastered on nearly every front page on the Eastern seaboard. Even though he was able to avoid his likeness being captured, GG's trail of victims retained indelible memories of him and his ways; their search for restitution and justice dovetailed perfectly with Gould's thirst for vengeance.

A friend-of-a-friend, -of-a-friend, -of-a-friend had received a letter from Edinburgh, "intimating that the description of Gordon tallied with that of a person who had been guilty of confidence swindles on a smaller scale in Great Britain."[33] There followed a flurry of correspondence, as well as the trade of photographs and handwriting samples, all in hopes of matching GG with the British scoundrel. From this exchange was a final cable from New York to Marshall & Sons on September 30, 1872:

Same man. Send best witness.[34]

Six months before Edinburgh and New York were on the same page, on April 9, 1872—a month since Gould and GG had met, and two weeks since their falling out—GG was arrested in his suite at the Metropolitan. His lawyer, A. F. Roberts, was present and ready to put up the bail, but there was a back-and-forth over how bail may be secured. After being held in his rooms with the arresting officers until midnight, GG was able to call on another party to come at once to act as the second bailpiece. And whether he was truly credulous of GG's claim or acting out of spite matters not, for after midnight, Horace F. Clark jumped out of bed and came to GG's rescue by providing the second half of GG's $37,000 bail. That Clark, the son-in-law of his archenemy, Commodore Vanderbilt, leaped to aid GG would have surely chapped poor Gould.

The city's papers seized on the latest chapter in GG's continuing saga, and the ever-growing trend of frauds and hucksters, reporting that "the Earl of Aberdeen has taken Jay Gould for $30M." Reporters clamored for interviews and swarmed the lobby of the Metropolitan Hotel. But GG had, indeed, kept wholly out of sight; only one *Sun* reporter caught a glimpse of GG in this time. He approached GG's tiger to ask, "Your master is, I believe, the Earl of Aberdeen?"

The valet's answer was plastered on the *Sun*'s front page: "Oh, no, sir. Not by any means, sir. He never claimed to be such, sir."[35]

GG was on the hook for stringing Gould down the line, and the wolves were at the door.

Though GG was out on bail (thank you, Mr. Roberts and Mr. Clark), the suit had come to trial, and Gould and GG would both have to appear for their parts in the convoluted story that had so rocked New York's headlines. While testifying on the stand and to the New York public, GG only further endeared himself to them by acting coy and unflappable.

Gould was almost universally reviled in the city; while recounting how he'd been duped, the court gallery literally laughed at him.

GG's deft parrying and deflecting on the stand impressed everyone but Gould and his attorney. Though he appeared in Judge Brady's courtroom without his trademark kilt and feathered hat, GG stood proudly with an oversized ring on his finger and an ostentatious gold fob chain in his waistcoat. His testimony was as follows:

Question: What is your name?

Answer: Gordon Harcourt Gordon.

Q: Who was your father?

A: I never knew my father.

Q: Have you any idea who he was?

A: I have an idea.

Q: And you are not willing to tell?

A: Certainly not to you.

Q: Did you deliver your card with the name Right Honorable G. Gordon?

A: Yes, sir. I have that right by courtesy, being a lord by courtesy.

Q: What rank in the peerage do you claim to be?

A: [*impatiently*] It would be unnecessary for me to give an explanation, if you don't know the title of "lord by courtesy."

Q: You had better answer the question, and not discuss the matter. Is "Right Honorable" a title of lords by courtesy?

A: It is used everywhere by them, when they do not wish to use the term "lord."

Q: Whether they are lords or not?

A: It is used by commoners as well as lords.

Q: [*handing GG an envelope to examine*] What does the coronet at the head of that note signify?

A: It signifies nothing more than a crest.

What brilliant irony that GG was telling the truth!

Gould's attorneys continued in their questioning, trying to corner this wiliest of defendants into a discomfiting confession:

Q: By what right do you claim the title of Lord Gordon?

A: I never claimed anything of the kind.

Q: Do you mean to say that you have never represented yourself as Lord Gordon?

A: I never have; people in America have given me this title, but I never assumed it.

Q: Be good enough to look at this note and say whether it is in your handwriting.

Mr. Field, Gould's counsel, handed the witness a sheet of stationery emblazoned with an Earl's coronet with the monogram "G.H.G." The document read as follows:

Lord Gordon presents his compliments and begs he acknowledge receipt of pass over the Erie road, of which he will be happy to avail himself in the event of his passing over the line.—Westminster Hotel

A: In February last Mr. Gould addressed me as Lord Gordon, enclosing an annual pass over the Erie Railway for Lord Gordon, and I acknowledged it as Lord Gordon; perhaps I ought not to have done so. If I had known as much as I do now I would not have done so.

Q: Are your parents living?

A: No, sir, but my stepfather is still living.

Q: Who is he?

A: The Count Charles Henry de Crano.

Q: Where does he reside?

A: At 9 Place Vendome, in Paris.

Q: Have you any brothers or sisters?

A: I have a sister and a brother-in-law, the Baron and Baroness Charles Henry Thurl.

Q: And where, may I ask, do they reside?

A: In Berne, Switzerland.

Q: Any uncles or aunts?

A: My uncle, Charles Gordon, resides at Notting Hill, in London.[36]

GG remained composed and unflappable through all this; his levity was tolerated, but Gould's testimony had them rolling in the aisles. Gould did not try to hide how he'd been swindled, but his earnest testimony was met with roars of laughter as his credulity and naiveté were utterly absurd given his well-earned reputation as a hawkish businessman.

GG remained staid until Gould's team made their final lunge: "One other question, Mr. Gordon," said Mr. Field. "May I ask to which of the three noble Gordon families of England you belong?"

For whatever reason, GG did not have a ready answer to this most predictable of questions. So, ensnared, GG feigned indignance and hurled at the judge, "Is it possible, your Honor, that an English gentleman who had been guilty of no greater crime than of having had an unfortunate business transaction with Jay Gould [*with a sneer*] is to submit to having his entire family history inquired into in an American court of justice? Do your courts afford a stranger no protections against such an outrage?"[37]

The judge was moved by this outburst and ordered the line of questioning stopped at once. All parties acquiesced and agreed to return the following day with a commission taking testimony, rather than the counsel. At eleven o'clock. On the dot.

GG's well-oiled demeanor had faltered only when Gould's attorneys began questioning the Gordon family line. What was GG's lineage, exactly? Plenty of society who's whos had vouched for him, but who *was* Lord Gordon Gordon really? Court was adjourned for the day, which gave GG a night's reprieve, but also allowed time enough for the prosecution to wire Europe for verification of his reports. A long, dark night of the soul for GG, it seemed.

Overnight, Gould and his counsel sent out a stream of telegraphs to London, Paris, and Berne to confirm GG's testimony. Well after the incident in Room 110 on March 2, and while his trial was actively underway, Gould (finally) undertook an extensive investigation into GG's claims. Why they did not vet him earlier, like, *before* handing over sacks of cash and a president's resignation, remains a mystery, though assuredly a feather in GG's Tam O'Shanter

The cables confirmed GG was *not* the Earl of Aberdeen, nor a member of the House of Lords. What delight Gould must have felt with vindication, and what humiliation at confirming he'd been taken by a huckster.

Gould and his hungry prosecutors were champing at the bit at the courthouse the next morning. They were prepared to kick up a terrific fight now that they were armed with international confirmation of Gordon's chicanery. But their thirst would not be slaked that day. For, in the night, out of fear, desperation, and a healthy dose of resourcefulness, GG had hightailed it to the border: the Canadian border. He had fled and was gone. He had packed a bag of loose jewels, diamonds, and baubles, paid his hotel bill ($174.50), and scarpered.

Poor Gould. His elation upon receiving confirmation of GG's deception was immediately replaced with rage when he learned that GG was truly beyond his reach; he was a stone's throw over the northern border, yet utterly untouchable.[38]

There were rumors that placed GG in Toronto following his flight from New York. He became friendly with a family that owned a boat that trafficked trade between Canada and America. GG was said to travel with a black box that he kept under a watchful eye. There were implications of jewel theft, not the least of which because Mr. Thomas Smith of Marshall & Sons had been in pursuit of GG since his sudden departure from the United Kingdom three years prior. These less-than-glowing reports notwithstanding, GG's whereabouts were undeniably confirmed in 1873: Winnipeg.

In the summer of 1873, GG was spotted. George N. Merriam and the Honorable Loren Fletcher happened to be in Winnipeg on business. They were in from Minnesota to sell pine logs when Merriam saw GG walking casually down the street. GG was known to the law and was well-known to be known by the law, so Merriam reported GG's whereabouts to the mayor of Minneapolis, George A. Brackett, a good friend to New York's A. F. Roberts. As blissful as GG must have been strolling the Canadian summertime streets, Gould and Roberts had remained sore, and they were committed to bringing him to justice for his elaborate schemes.

Canada was far, but New York attorneys examined an exemplified copy of the bailpiece ("an attested copy of a document under official seal") and determined that GG was within grasp. His lawyers armed Roberts with an interpretation of warrants law that rendered GG reachable, even across the border. Roberts consulted with Mayor Brackett and planned for an immediate seizure.

"The peculiar advice was given that a warrant could be issued in the United States for Gordon's arrest on the ground that wherever common law prevailed, regardless of national boundaries, such a document was effective. It was compared to a situation where a parent could follow and take possession of his child, or a master an apprentice without any process of law. This argument was later presented by a letter of United States Consul Taylor in the newspapers of Winnipeg."[39]

On June 26, 1873, Policemen Hoy and Keegan departed Minneapolis for Fort Garry, where they had orders to apprehend GG and then deliver him to Winnipeg into the hands of Loren Fletcher, "who was a member, and later Speaker, of the House of Representatives of Minnesota, and still later a member of Congress."[40] A week later, on July 2, Hoy and Keegan arrived in Fort Garry and promptly met with Fletcher in the office of one L. R. Bentley, a former Minneapolis resident and current Canadian businessman. Also, he was the current landlord to GG's office, which was above Bentley's store. In this meeting, they laid out the plans for GG's capture, no matter how questionable the legality of their actions.

Later that night, around 8 p.m., GG was visiting the home of his friend Hon. James McKay. McKay being out, GG was awaiting him. In his absence, McKay's staff and farmhands all "became incapacitated" (i.e., drunk), likely alongside GG, so when Hoy and Keegan burst in and bound Gordon's hands and feet they were met with no resistance. They spirited GG into a carriage and quickly moved him south through Fort Garry and onto the ferry to the Pembina trail.

Meanwhile, Fletcher's excitement got the better of him, and he let the cat out of the bag in Winnipeg that GG was being hastily transported to the border. GG's solicitor in Winnipeg, along with the province's attorney general, telegraphed the customs official at Pembina, one hundred miles south, who intercepted the kidnapping party at the border. Gordon "laid an information" against the party—Hoy, Fletcher, Bentley, Merriam, and Keegan—who were promptly arrested and taken back to Winnipeg.

Though heavily implied, it is understood that these men's designs were not of their own making but rather those of A. F. Roberts, who was still out for his part of GG's $37,000 bail, and Jay Gould. What strange bedfellows GG had made of the New York elite!

With the entire band in irons, Winnipeg's Governor Morris cabled Prime Minister Sir John A. Macdonald the next day that a "man known as 'Lord Gordon' was last night kidnapped by some Americans near here, a reward of $10,000 being offered for his apprehension in States. They were, however, arrested this morning by Bradley, Custom's House Officer at Pembina who, I am informed, has them in custody."[41]

The cabal had made provisions for communicating the status of the kidnapping and, if all went to plan, Fletcher would telegraph Mayor Brackett in Minneapolis with "O.K., return today." In case the mission was scuppered he would write, "Too high; can't purchase; have written." It was this second message that reached Bracket around July 5—the transmission was delayed a few days because Fletcher was in jail. At the same time, though, Fletcher managed to send a second telegraph that impressed upon Bracket the severity of the situation and got him on a train, speeding northward to Winnipeg that same day: "I'm in a hell of a fix. Come at once."[42]

That same day, though, the preliminary hearings for Fletcher, Hoy, and Keegan began. Bail was refused. Proceedings were adjourned until July 8, at which point the trial began.

For two weeks, the trial raged in Winnipeg. The law prevented America's Consul Taylor from acting as a defense lawyer, so he did what he thought was the next best thing for his clients: he went to the press brandishing his opinions on the validity of the US-issued warrant. This so incensed Attorney General Clarke that he spent a full day in court railing against Taylor's impudence and impropriety—an attack on justice!

contempt of court! improper act!—and then telegraphed the Minister of Justice to demand that Washington be pressed to recall Consul Taylor.

What followed was tittle-tattle over law and jurisdiction of the highest order. Which is to say, tedious. Within days, Mayor Brackett, Minnesota's district attorney, and the US Acting Secretary of State had all arrived in Fort Garry, ready to champion the cause of the imprisoned Americans. GG's "innocence" was not discussed; how strange that a notorious, documented swindler be the only party not at fault in this international imbroglio.

Acting Secretary of State J. C. B. Davis acknowledged a telegram from J. W. Taylor, Consul of the United States at Winnipeg, on July 9 by writing, "Two detectives from Minnesota attempted to arrest a person 'Lord Gordon' in New York on proceedings by Jay Gould. Did not consult me. I have not seen their papers. Detectives arrested near Pembina for kidnapping and just arrived here."[43]

Days later, Minnesota Governor Horace Austin wrote Consul Taylor of his outrage that Americans were being held prisoner, without due process, under lock and key and manacle, and that the real villains were those (i.e., the Canadians) who had the temerity to stop the American party. This stance was reflective of the attitudes in Minnesota at the minute, though those attitudes were hardly justified. His message was clear, though: do not test Americans, for they are rabid for justice and sensitive to slights. Prime Minister Macdonald quickly directed his representatives to stop all communication with the Americans as all correspondence—revealing just how quickly the incident was being spun into a rallying cry—must move through official Washington, D.C./Ottawa channels.

By August 1, the *St. Paul Pioneer* ran the headline, "Our People Should Make Ready," denouncing the actions of the Canadian authorities and explicitly recommending staying out of the way of the Fenians, an Irish Brotherhood that attacked British posts in Canada from 1866–1871. Moreover, the article suggested to Minnesotans that matters could be taken into their own hands, but it would have to be quick. Whatever the plan, "It should be swift, silent and terrible."

Except for Merriam, the Americans were denied bail and sentenced to forty days and forty nights laying in the common jail. America did not like this, and the August 2 edition of the *Minneapolis Tribune* quotes the *New York Tribune* that the refusal of bail would be considered by America as a purposefully offensive subversion of justice and went on to agree with *Chicago Tribune's* labeling the case a flagrant violation of judicial decency.

For six weeks, the letters, telegraphs, and negotiations flew between Minneapolis and Winnipeg; D.C. and Ottawa; president and prime minister. Political pressure and legal precedent were at odds, and the Americans and Fenians at the border both seemed restless and antsy. The governors and consuls debated bail and costs. Rumblings of dissent aside, there was always time enough for political penny-pinching.

In early September an alternative was floated: have the prisoners plead guilty and receive light sentences, thereby "serving justice" and easing tensions. The governors, ministers, consuls, mayors, and prisoners all consented.

Finally, on September 16, 1873, a special court term was held to "serve justice" to the American prisoners. Their guilty pleas came with perfunctory sentences, and all court costs—except for representation—were shouldered by the Dominion. A brief stay on someone else's dime . . . how very Gordon-esque this arrangement was. The governor of Minnesota was in attendance and smiled from the gallery as the twenty-four-hour sentence was handed down. The peace between Minnesota and Manitoba was restored.

. . . some time later . . .

The Manitoba attorney general had become familiar with GG and the (known) details of his past. Therefore, when he stumbled upon GG himself while on a hunting trip, he did not hesitate to issue a warrant to have GG detained then and there in Touchwood Hills, nearly 600 kilometers away from Fort Garry. GG, it seemed, was trying to make his way to British Columbia and away from Manitoba, Minnesota, and Jay Gould.

There was a flurry of barbs and accusations traded between GG and the attorney general, which "provide material for a comic opera"[44] as GG claimed the AG was blackmailing him. He wrote to the lieutenant governor to register his complaint with the executive council, as well as to demand that his complaints also be shared with the minister of Justice.

GG was much distraught—feigned indignance was one of his strong suits, after all.

Gould was not satisfied, though. And Roberts was still out for his part of the $37,000 bail he had floated years prior. Being not so easily thwarted, in October of 1873, they brought to Toronto Thomas Smith of Edinburgh's Marshall & Sons, one of GG's original marks. Smith's testimony and evidence, with assistance from Gould, Roberts, and New York, earned GG a warrant for arrest but this time from the British Court. Canada being under its auspices, the warrant was issued in Toronto. Winnipeg's magistrate countersigned the 1874 warrant, and the officers and representatives made their way to Headingley to the home of Mrs. Abigail Corbett, GG's landlady.

For a year, GG had flown under the radar, his escapades firmly behind him. Headingley seemed so remote a place that even Gould's troubles wouldn't find him. At the country house in which he roomed, GG had found cheerful company in his landlady, Mrs. Corbett, and her nephew, Thomas Pentland, who came to be GG's de facto valet. He enjoyed shooting, riding, and hosting lavish parties for his friends. Like his time as "Glencairn" in Forfarshire, GG's affability and generosity were embraced within the community. He was kind and well-liked.

On August 1, 1874, GG was at home in Headingley. He was in his rooms, his attendant nearby. Mrs. Corbett answered the knock on the front door and was met by policemen. Asking for GG, she bade them come in.[45]

GG was confronted by the imposing party. The jig was up, and GG knew it. The law was at the door, with agents from three countries he'd offended. The writing on the wall was clear to him and his servant, Pentland. Together, they were calm and collected, and neither Pentland nor GG blubbered.

"I've come to arrest you," said the arresting officer.

"Is this to be another kidnapping?" GG asked out of curiosity and spite.

"Not at all, sir—everything regular. I can shew you the warrant." The officer's familiar tone and language might have put someone more honest at ease, but GG was no fool and concluded that his journey with the officer would not be to police headquarters but another vengeance-fueled spiriting across the border into the hungry jaws of Jay Gould.

GG only glanced at the paper but called it "all right" before coolly announcing, "I'm ready to go."

The officer and the gentleman started to make for the door, Mrs. Corbett's tear-filled eyes searching GG's face for comfort, or confirmation, or a wink. But he betrayed nothing.

When they reached the front door, they both donned their outer clothes; the officer his hat and woolen coat, GG his boots and fur-lined jacket.

"I'd like my tam," GG said plaintively, referring to his iconic Scottish cap. "It's just at the top of the stairs."

The two went to GG's bedroom, where the Tam O'Shanter was laying on the bed. GG made to reach for it but then stuck his hand atop the wardrobe and pulled down a loaded pistol. His eyes remained calm and steely as he raised the gun to his temple.

"I will not move another step," he announced. The officer lunged toward GG with his hands outstretched.

BANG!

GG crumpled to the floor at the officer's feet, his tam still on the bed.

So passed GG: his charges, his exploits, and his true identity dying with him.

The scene was grim, and an inquest was held. The arresting officer was severely reprimanded for his part in the failed kidnapping/successful suicide. Mrs. Corbett also gave lengthy testimony, including a tantalizing lead that was not pursued: weeks before his death, GG had packed some belongings, records, and correspondence and mailed them to "Canada." What became of these things, or where they went, or what secrets they contained, were never revealed.[46]

———❦———

On February 12, 1879, the *Manitoba Free Press* ran a headline, "Gordon Gordon, a Mystery Probably Solved at Last—Who and What he Was." There were two parts to the story: the first coming from the personal investigation from one Dr. Chambers, of *Chambers' Journal;* the second

An illustration of Lord Gordon Gordon looking extremely ordinary without his trademark tam and sporran.
CROFFUT, W.A. (JAN. 1910). "LORD GORDON-GORDON: A BOGUS PEER AND HIS DISTIN-GUISHED DUPES." *PUTNAM'S MAGAZINE* 7(4): 416–28: P. 423, ILLUSTRATION OF GG.

from a letter, apparently vouched for by the newspaper's editor, that claims that the identities of GG's father and sister had been established. Their reputations were that of a cultured, well-spoken, and well-traveled gentleman and lady . . . who happened to also be the leaders of a group of international smugglers operating out of the Isle of Jersey.[47]

As to GG's true identity? Many and varied theories were floated. Perhaps his father and sister gave him up after their smuggling ring was found out; perhaps he was a wretch who had been raised by a pair of spinster sisters; perhaps he was the illegitimate son of a respected English clergyman. Whoever he really was, GG's legacy is fittingly, tragically his grandiose exploits and over-the-top lifestyle, not his identity; he is remembered for who he chose to be.

CHAPTER TWO

Diamonds in the Rough

THE TIME: 1871–1872

THE PLACE: San Francisco, CA

New York, NY

somewhere between Arizona, Wyoming, New Mexico, and Colorado

THE TAKE: $200,000–$250,000,000, uncut gems, geologists' scorn, near ruin of American economy

THE PLAYERS: Asbury Harpending

J. F. Berry

Clarence King

Samuel F. Emmons

Henry Janin

William F. Ralston, President, Bank of California

William Lent

Horace Greeley

George D. Roberts

Holdsworth

Philip Arnold

John Burchem Slack

The Field

WHILE THEIR NUMBED FINGERS SCRATCHED IN THE DIRT AND STRUGgled to work their pencils, a figure appeared above the gulch. His short, curly hair and fussy waistcoat were entirely out of place on that remote, windswept mesa. He poked his head over the lip of the gulch to smile cheekily at the group of weather-beaten geologists below.

"Found any carats?" he hollered in a shockingly familiar fashion. The dusty men below him stared in stunned silence. Their expedition had been secret, and they'd taken special care to cover their tracks. To be found by an impish man in the middle of nowhere and be interrogated on their true intentions was, well, startling. Clarence King and his surveyors stared at the unwelcome city slicker.[1]

The aptly named, cartoonish fellow was J. F. Berry, a New York City diamond dealer who had just recently taken an interest in Utah mines. To check them out, he had hired engineer Henry Janin. Berry was both well-informed and unscrupulous, so he did all he could to pump Janin for information about the secretive field of diamonds that had been keeping newspapers and speculators in a vice grip of suspense. Perhaps to shut him up, or perhaps to impress him, Janin told Berry that "King had surveyed the claims," referring to Malcolm Graeme King, who had taken over for Janin when he pulled out a few months prior. But Berry thought he meant Clarence King, head of the US Geological Survey, who was currently standing beneath him in a dusty gully in barely charted territory.

Berry and a band of brigands had tailed King for three days through the howling mountain passes of Wyoming, peering at them through spyglasses from hilltops and hiding behind trees. Finally, he approached them as they were scratching in the dirt. Berry's greeting had thrown them off-guard but only for a moment. King quickly intimated that Berry was wasting his time and should move along.

But upon hearing the bad news, Berry jovially replied, "You say it's a swindle? What a chance to sell short on the stock!" This was not the response the careworn geologists had expected, and it was the opposite of what they'd hoped.

As Berry was clearly ready to make trouble, King wasted no time. He needed to meet with Janin and the San Francisco set immediately to convince them to immediately reveal the hoax to the bubbling world. The economic fallout might be terrible, but King was acutely aware that winter was coming, and the prospecting suckers who had been taken in by the scheme wouldn't be prepared in the slightest. Time was of the essence, so King took the quicker, more dangerous route back to Green River City.

⸻

The California Gold Rush poured tens of thousands of hopeful prospectors into the American West between 1848 and 1856. The Comstock Lode silver strike was made public in 1859 and sparked an equally fervent silver boom in what would become Nevada. Americans were digging and scraping at the ground, exposing deep veins of ores and riches; the American earth seemed indiscriminate in its bounty.

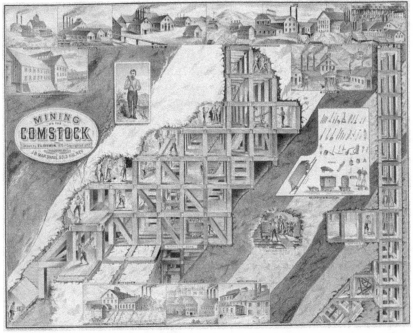

The gargantuan scope of the Comstock Lode would have skewed any man's estimation of the riches he felt the good earth owed him.

"MINING ON THE COMSTOCK," DRAWN BY T. L. DAWES ; ENGRAVED AND PRINTED BY LE COUNT BRO'S., SAN FRANCISCO, LIBRARY OF CONGRESS, PRINTS & PHOTOGRAPHS DIVISION, LC-DIG-PGA-01999 (DIGITAL FILE FROM ORIGINAL PRINT), https://www.loc.gov/resource/pga.01999/.

As the land of opportunity gushed forth, prospectors, miners, and investors all seemed to benefit; "Go West, young man, and grow up with the country!" was a rallying cry and one whose impact was gilded and gilt when wealth and notoriety became part and parcel to Manifest Destiny.

The 1850s veritably boomed in the American West, and stories of prospectors' strikes and luck became household fare. Everybody won. Tales of unrewarded hardship and predatory investors were neither inspirational nor fruitful for the boom economies, so sad stories were harder to come by. Why discourage the man who would brave the rugged lands to bring untold wealth to himself while lending a spur, boom, and boost to the Gold Standard–based economy?

Americans were lusty for growth, adventure, and competition. Opportunities were everywhere but so, too, were opportunists. While hundreds of thousands of men were braving the unknown, a canny few took advantage of what was well-known; man is greedy and will not deeply interrogate *luck*.

The Gold Rush tempted thousands. John Burchem Slack of Elizabethtown, Kentucky, just thirty years old, was so tempted and took the Santa Fe Trail to California in 1849. He had been honorably discharged as a veteran of the Mexican–American War and quietly foundered until applying his love of carpentry to the loudly booming mining economy. He was quiet and methodical, and his apparent distaste for the limelight made him a valuable employee to a series of successful mines in the Arizona Territory in the 1860s.

Meanwhile, his cousin, Philip Arnold, nearly ten years Slack's junior, had married his Elizabethtown sweetheart and moved his family to San Francisco in 1855. Arnold was as ambitious as Slack was retiring, and he quickly made a name for himself in mining circles as a shrewd operator. He cleverly linked himself with some of the most aggressively enterprising investors, and meanwhile, he honed his prospecting skills and credentials.

Arnold had established himself as the right-hand man to a particularly proactive investor—and fellow Kentuckian—Asbury Harpending.

A man of great confidence, Harpending had gained notoriety through wildly successful mining ventures in Mexico and then as the man who tried to capture a Northern ship for the South's cause at the order of Jefferson Davis. Harpending was both clever and astute so could accurately read the worth of a vein of ore, as well as the make of the man hoping to profit from it.

As the Civil War was raging, Arnold continued to make himself instrumental to mining operations out West. Around 1864, he began working for Harpending and the Lincoln Gold Mining Company in California and was "familiarly known as the Banker of Harpending mine."[2] A few years later, in 1867, a prospectus on the mine was published that raved about the untold and untapped riches the Lincoln Company might produce, and that stockholders would be wise to jump at the chance to invest. Shortly after being put on the London market, however, Harpending and his friend (and sole sitting member of the Lincoln Gold Mining Company Board of Directors) George D. Roberts tried to quell the excitement and return the investors' initial capital as, "the gold was there, but it was so fine the washing of it yielded nothing beyond the expenses."[3] They claimed this as new information, but the London financial world was suspicious and accused the operation of less-than-honorable practices and that their whole operation bore the distinct odor of salting; which is to say, London believed the riches had never been there in the first place and had, instead, been planted. Harpending backed down and tried to quiet chatter about his Lincoln mine.

With an ocean and a continent between them, London's apprehension could not keep Harpending down for long and he was soon back to investing and ingratiating. The founder of the Bank of California and one of the richest men in San Francisco—if not the whole country—William F. Ralston had, according to Harpending, sent a letter of introduction to Harpending after which they became real estate partners and confidantes.[4] Ralston was wealthy and enthusiastic, both of which made him a welcome partner for Harpending, whose thirst for venture, gains, and bluster was endless.

Diamonds were discovered in South Africa in the late 1860s. There was a surge of excitement and investment from the London market, but Americans were not convinced. Even though Americans wouldn't have known a South African diamond when they saw one (*hint hint, wink wink, nudge nudge*), somehow there were rumors that the fields in South Africa were a sham and had been salted with Brazilian diamonds. As London was still smarting from the Lincoln Gold Mining Company unpleasantness, they did little to dissuade or convince the shady Americans that the fields were genuine and so kept mum as the Americans' suspicions (stemming from their own recent bad behavior!) kept them from getting in on the ground floor of the new South African market.[5]

The fervor was not lost on America, though, and played into a long history of American fascination with diamonds. Famed mountain man Jim Bridger had spun a particularly juicy tall tale of "the most wonderful fruit—diamonds, rubies, sapphires, emeralds, etc., as large as black walnuts," well-known and oft-repeated in the fur-trading community by 1860.[6] And his contemporary, Kit Carson, had gleefully talked of a Yellowstone-area diamond so brilliant and so giant that it could be seen from fifty miles. Unlike word from London, or South Africa, or even Brazil, America was happy to take the unlikely tales from two of their most strapping examples of manliness as gospel.

Americans' predilection for shiny things, plucked from their own land, did not go unnoticed by Arnold.

Roberts was itching for an investment. He took a shine to the Pyramid Range silver deposits after a dusty prospector's finds had been underscored by a report from the surveyor general of Arizona Territory. In the summer of 1870, an investigative party, including Arnold and Slack, made their way to the claim site and quickly set up shop. The Pyramid Range Silver Mining Company was well underway when Harpending made a personal visit later that fall. At this point, Arnold had been made superintendent of operations, and Slack was busy handling the logistics of the claims and mining infrastructure, so both were on hand when Harpending arrived.

Arnold, Slack, and Harpending kept close, private company while the surveyor, assayer, and inspector completed their work at the mine. Harpending returned to his home base in San Francisco after just eight days at the mines, his work apparently completed for the moment, while Arnold and Slack stayed on for an additional two to three weeks.

The Pyramid Range prospectus was presented to the London market in January of 1871 with a capitalization of $2,500,000. The public offering was immediately seized upon by *The Times* in London, which had not so quickly forgotten Harpending's last bum steer on their market. Nor had *The Times* failed to notice that George Roberts was a player in both schemes and that he and Harpending seemed the sole managers of a new venture that bore a striking resemblance to an unsuccessful one (Lincoln) they'd managed less than five years before. "[T]he means of testing the degree of faith to be placed in the prospectus just issued would seem immediately at hand."[7] Harpending and Roberts were both indignant over the (warranted) affront, but despite their pleas and protestations and claims of reform, they could not outrun the stink still lingering from the Lincoln Mine episode. One short week after the Pyramid's introduction, *The Times* bluntly reported, "It is understood that the foundation of the Pyramid Silver Mining Company will not be proceeded with."[8] Harpending was livid and immediately went to London to demand legal satisfaction—not so much over the content (which was accurate) as the tone (which was haughty) and the recovery of his own sterling reputation, which appeared to be made from failed Pyramid Silver.

But in the short period when the Pyramid Range was gaining steam (before summarily deflating), Arnold had cozied up to James B. Cooper, an assistant bookkeeper for a diamond drilling company in San Francisco. It was through Cooper that Arnold acquired his first passel of diamonds, which he promptly mixed in with a collection of garnets, sapphires, and rubies he had picked up in his travels. Harpending later wrote that Cooper, "admitted, with noble candor, he was the author of the whole scheme . . . he suggested the 'salting' of a diamond field as a pleasing variation [on salting gold or silver mines] and told how small diamonds, such as those used for drills, could be readily obtained."[9] Once

Arnold seized the idea, he had no further use for Cooper and grabbed Slack to move boldly forward.

This small collection of found and procured stones was all Arnold needed to excite the San Franciscans' appetite for booty, and stones would have been an exciting, welcome change from humdrum silver and gold. The stones were confirmed genuine by San Francisco jewelers. Arnold took his treasure to Roberts but made him swear to keep it a secret, which was tantalizing, to say the least. Arnold was no dummy and knew the treasure-hungry man wouldn't keep quiet: "Harpending then being in London, Roberts was very much elated by our discovery and promised Slack and myself to keep it a profound secret until we could explore the country further and ascertain more fully the extent of our discoveries. So, we made a second trip to the country."[10] Arnold had guessed correctly, and Roberts's excitement came bubbling out his big mouth; there were fish on the line, and they were biting for more bejeweled bait. Arnold generously offered himself and Slack to return to the field to better understand the scope of the score, so they lit out in the summer of 1871.

With only a small sack of gems—some found, some bought—Arnold generated a buzz in San Francisco that had some of the most powerful backers in the city clamoring for a piece of the diamond action.

With only a small sack of gems, Arnold sold Slack's eighth of the total "interest" for $50,000.

With only a small sack of gems, Arnold ultimately pyramided his way to a multi-million-dollar scam that nearly destroyed the American economy.

—◦—

The Transcontinental Railroad connected the United States in 1869, opening up broad swaths of the country as-yet-uncharted by white men. Prospectors and miners and loggers were thrilled, but their happiness was predicated upon promising words from the men with boots on the ground—the surveyors and the geologists.

Clarence King was one such geologist. In February of 1867, before the railroad was completed, King had presented to Senator John Conness the idea of surveying the fifty miles of land to the north and south of

A young Arnold, looking defiantly unbothered.
PHILIP ARNOLD, https://alchetron.com/Philip-Arnold#philip-arnold-6b730d11-a4b8-43fc-b2d5-ef1c6a9a22c-resize-750.jpeg.

the railroad's planned route: the Fortieth Parallel Survey. Conness tacked King's proposal onto an appropriations bill to help secure it. Thus, the formation and funding of the United States Geological Survey were in place, and King was appropriately named its first head geologist.[11]

Surveying work began immediately and continued into 1872—the paperwork lasted until 1879—and was managed by some of the best geological minds in the country.

Enter: King, his trusted survey party leader Samuel F. Emmons, and chief topographer James T. Gardner.

It is unclear how invested, per se, Slack was in the scheme. He was a dyed-in-the-wool carpenter and had spent much of his life in mining encampments working with his steadfast compatriots: lumber and infrastructure. There is little doubt that his cousin, Philip Arnold, was the brains of the operation. Though nearly ten years younger, Arnold's drive and cunning had been on full display his whole life and how lucky for him that his reserved cousin's manner was so meager and his mining skills so great. Whatever Slack's misgivings may have been, blood was thicker than water, and Arnold correctly guessed that Slack was not about to sell out his Kentucky cousin and Confederate brother. Had it not been for their shared lineage, though, the two men would not have been compatriots; Slack was bound by responsibility, and Arnold knew it. They were bonded with a wedge between them.

On July 7, 1871, an unlikely pair visited jewelers Leopold Keller & Company in London. They were frumpy and rumpled and curious about wholesale lots of rough stones. For anyone outside of the jewelry business, this would have made for a strange and noteworthy purchase. The clerks at Keller took note but transacted all the same. That day, and over three subsequent trips in the following two weeks, nearly $20,000 worth of rough stones were sold to "Aundle and Burchem." Clumsy pseudonyms aside—Phillip Arnold and John Burchem Slack's talents lay elsewhere, but *sheesh*—the pair took their purchases and returned stateside while curiously failing to declare said purchases on any customs forms or international documentation.[12]

In addition to failing to declare the stones to customs, Arnold and Slack failed to mention their transatlantic jaunt to their slightly dubious, though decidedly frothy, investors. When the backers expressed doubt and aired their second thoughts, Arnold was already two steps ahead; as a show of good faith, he and Slack would return to their site—as yet unrevealed—to return with "a couple of million dollars' worth of stones."

Arnold and Slack ostensibly returned to their claim as the San Francisco set waited breathlessly. Harpending had oh-so charitably returned from London to act as an intermediary between Arnold and Slack and the potential investors. Certainly, he was out to make money, but from whom, and by what means, is at best unclear and, more likely, questionable.

Apparently returning from their diamond field, Arnold and Slack were weather-beaten and clearly worn out. They'd telegraphed from

Reno, and when Harpending met them as they arrived at the station at Lathrop, California, they were dusty and dirty. Mountain and mining types were ubiquitous in any western port of call, but these two were picture-perfect representations of hardship and grit. Slack was slumped and sound asleep from, likely, the trip itself but also the stress of the subterfuge; he was a legitimately gifted mining man whose talents were being spun into an illegitimate play. Next to him, Arnold sat, "grimly erect, like a vigilant old soldier, with a rifle by his side, also a bulky-looking buckskin package." Whether or not Harpending was in on it, Arnold and Slack's appearance and hard-luck tale were a complete package, and Arnold spun for Harpending a harrowing narrative that was at once outlandish and fairly plausible. He told of hardships on their journey to "The Field"—weather, Indians, lions, tigers, and bears, oh my!—and the great luck they'd had prospecting. So successful was their mission that they each had left with a full sack of diamonds and precious stones, estimating the worth at $2 million between them. With a sack apiece, they headed home, taking care to keep their quarry safe. But, alas, "on their way home they found the water in a river they had to cross extremely high and, for purposes of safety, had constructed a raft, had nearly been upset, had lost one of the bags of diamonds, but, as the other contained at least a million dollars' worth of stones, it ought to be fairly satisfactory." What drama! What luck![13]

How privileged and how confident of Arnold to make such a bold play. It was convenient (and intentional) that the location of the purported field was still a secret and that the investors had such tunnel vision that they failed to fact-check for rivers—raging or otherwise—on the route to/from the site or in the general area, for there were none. Had they encountered the fantasy river, one could imagine Roberts diving in headfirst for diamonds, no matter the cost.

Harpending took receipt for the sack of stones that hadn't been swallowed by the mythical river and quickly made for his well-appointed San Francisco home, where Ralston, Roberts, and eager investor William Lent were waiting on tenterhooks. Harpending had been both savvy and lucky in the real estate game, and his home reflected as much. In a sumptuous study, he spread a cloth on his expansive billiard table and upended the bag, glittering gems landing casually in a glorious heap. The uncut South African diamonds, purchased in London, and sister stones of garnets, rubies, emeralds, and sapphires Arnold had amassed combined into an impressive consortium of far-flung precious stones—a "greatest hits" of mined treasures. The men blinked in amazement and began planning on the spot; they could barely contain themselves.

This pile of treasures was convincing enough for the men in the room, and plans were promptly drawn to formalize and legitimize (hah!) the venture.

There had to be rules. Everything had to be aboveboard. There could be no lingering doubts if they were going to seize on this incredible windfall. So Harpending, Roberts, General George S. Dodge, and William Lent drew up provisions:

1. A large sample of the stones would be sent to noted jeweler Charles Lewis Tiffany in New York City for examination and appraisal.

2. A mining expert, of their choosing, would accompany Arnold and Slack to their site once it became accessible in the spring, assuming Tiffany's appraisal was positive.

3. Lobby for the amendment of mining laws such that their claim would be not just legal but saleable on the New York market and beyond.

No time was lost; Harpending and Dodge immediately made for New York City and quickly retained the legal services of Samuel Barlow. A longtime friend of Ralston and connection to General McClellan, Barlow quickly set up a meeting in his home to introduce the stones to some of New York's cream of society. In attendance: Charles Lewis Tiffany, General McClellan, General Benjamin Butler, a banker from a prominent New York house, and Horace Greeley, who had boldly declared the "Age of Gold" in the 1850s and might well see fit to declare an "Age of Diamonds." Harpending being no stranger to bad press, he certainly would have seen the advantage in being in the good books with Greeley's

Tribune, not to mention Greeley's reputation for taking the plunge on risky investments.

Dodge emptied the sack of its happy charge, and the men leaned over the glittering pile. Rubies, sapphires, emeralds, and diamonds sparkled in the afternoon light, throwing colorful fractals onto surfaces and the men's covetous faces. Tiffany quickly went to work sorting and examining the stones, holding them to the light, and being altogether cooperative in his role as lapidary-for-hire. He declared the stones all genuine but would need time to assess their true worth.

Tiffany took two days following the meeting to come back with an assessment of $150,000 for the pile of stones, which was one-tenth of the bag Arnold and Slack had presented Harpending in San Francisco. Harpending offered an impressive $1,500,000 on the spot.

In his defense, Tiffany would not have had much experience in South African diamonds so likely didn't know what he was looking at. He would have known, however, that uncut and rough stones were not his bread and butter but did not readily broadcast the fact in Barlow's study, surrounded by hungry investors. Still, the assessment was made, and the first provision had been satisfied.[14]

THE FIELD

The closest Union Pacific station to the site he deemed most likely to be a diamond field was Black Buttes Station, Wyoming, seventy-five miles to the north of Arnold's chosen spot. In the northwest corner of Colorado Territory, adjacent to the border with Wyoming and Utah, was a 3,000-acre mesa that seemed to sing with possibilities. At the foot of what would later be named Diamond Peak, at the junction of Vermillion Creek and Ruby Gulch, was Arnold's field. The natural landscape seemed to most closely resemble what Arnold had in mind for the ideal circumstances for diamond formation. The access road was tricky and weather-dependent, guaranteeing the site would only be accessible certain times of the year, meaning his investors—dupes, really—wouldn't be able to pop in or check up whenever they pleased. Its inaccessibility, coupled with the underlying threat from neighboring territories, also meant Arnold could feel relatively safe in leaving his chosen, planted paradise unsupervised.

Keeping the location secret was paramount; the scam would not pay out if revealed too soon. The care Arnold took to keep his secret might have registered as mania to an unknowing observer. Though Black Buttes Station was closest, Arnold would debark at a different station on each trip so as to not be associated with just the one location. Once he was well and truly on his way to the field, he wore moccasins to hide his tracks and wrapped his horse's hooves in canvas for the same reason. He did all he could to hide the location and mask his intentions to curious onlookers. The care he took, however, was not inappropriate nor unprecedented in the golden age of rushes and claims. But he intentionally sowed confusion, as well, and the sum total of his various methods would have stunk of subterfuge to anyone who knew to do the math.

Pfeiffer and Miller, jewelers in Laramie, Wyoming, saw Arnold a number of times. After a trip to his field, Arnold would, each time, come in with a hard-luck sob story particularly customized for the jewelers. He would blame known enemies of lapidaries: harsh weather conditions and unsympathetic pawnbrokers. Having been ostensibly unable to raise money from his horse, Arnold would offer to pawn a diamond in exchange for some on-the-barrelhead cash to get him wherever it was he was supposedly going. But, each time, he was dodgy about the provenance of the pawned jewel but showy in plucking said jewel from his hefty buckskin sack. That he readily admitted to knowing he wouldn't receive the full worth of the jewel simply made his hard luck, will-take-whatever-I-can-get attitude more believable when he would settle for a few hundred dollars and an exorbitant interest rate. This encouraged the jewelers' credulity. Arnold would, of course, know the actual value of the diamond (given he had purchased it in London), but the downtrodden, take-what-I-can-get attitude was more valuable for Arnold re: the setup than any jewel's on-the-books valuation at that point.

Arnold continued this ruse throughout his planting missions, though he would leave a larger, more valuable stone each time. He hoped the jewelers would surmise that the stones were local given Arnold's repeat appearances and apparent bad luck—prospectors weren't rich until their claim was invested in, after all—and the apparent good luck that had befallen the jewelers did not go unnoticed for long. Word of mouth turned into local news items, which turned into broadcast rumors; the country was abuzz with the potential finds in the Wyoming and Utah territories.[15]

—

The Golconda Mining Company was officially established on October 31, 1871, with an initial capital offering of $10,000,000. That was a lot of money. Especially for a diamond field that only Arnold and Slack had seen. Slack had taken his $100,000 and hightailed it with the promise he would return for the field expedition, but Arnold hadn't been paid. He huffed and puffed and threatened to walk without some cash and assurance his secret was safe. Ralston coughed up $100,000, and Arnold promised to return to the site with a company expert once the site was no longer snowbound. Now, the eager investors just had to wait.

Coincidentally (or *was* it?) a "Mr. Lock" visited London jeweler Keller & Company twice in December and once at the Paris branch, each time buying thousands of dollars' worth of uncut stones. "Burchem," "Aundle," and "Mr. Lock" spent a total of nearly $28,000 on rough jewels in 1871. A pretty penny for salt.[16]

—

Provisions 2 and 3 of the investors' initial incorporation of the mine were satisfied on almost the same day. "An Act to Promote the Development of Mining Resources in the United States," or "Sargent's Mining Bill," was passed by the US Congress on May 10, 1872, thanks in large part to General Butler's persuasion. Yes, that same Butler who'd ogled a pile of riches in Barlow's home not nine months earlier. This bill allowed the fortune seekers to incorporate in states beyond that of their claim; this was the bridge to the New York market.

Two days later, the Company found their expert in Henry Janin, whose reputation was ironclad in mining and geological circles. Clarence King's Fortieth Parallel crewmember said of Janin, "He was a keen observer, with critical mind and decided business sense and ability, not carried away by his feelings, and too sagacious to be caught in the traps that the mine-sellers usually prepared for the inspecting engineer."[17] Janin was reserved and smart and careful. For $2,500, expenses, as well as one thousand shares in the Company at $10, he was on board.

The provisions had been met, and Harpending, Lent, Dodge, an Englishman named Rubery, and Janin boarded a train for St. Louis that same day to meet Arnold and Slack. The diamond field was calling.

———

June 1, 1872: Arnold, Slack, Janin, Harpending, Rubery, and Dodge departed Rawlins, Wyoming, for The Field. Intentionally starting out twice as far from The Field as Black Buttes Station, the journey was made to be tiring, and Arnold was appropriately and actually prickly when the group finally began the expedition in earnest. Arnold had met the team in St. Louis a week prior and raised hell as Dodge had shown up with four additional men to act as representatives for the San Francisco set, none of whom Arnold had vetted, and therefore refused to include in the mission. He sent them packing, leaving the mantle of verification to rest solely on Janin's shoulders.[18]

The horses were packed with picks, shovels, canvas, provisions, and empty buckskin sacks, waiting to be filled with their sparkling charge. The men kept their eyes on the prize during a decidedly challenging trip wherein Arnold led them around in circles, seemingly lost. Even Harpending lost patience by the third day: "We seemed to follow no definite course, but appeared to be riding at random. . . . Arnold said he would ride on ahead and see if he could tell where we were . . . by going a few miles, he might be able to observe some landmark which would set us right." Luckily, kismet smiled on the group, and Arnold returned to confirm they were on the right track. "We started and in four hours and fifteen minutes, arrived at the diamond fields" around 4 p.m. on the fourth day of their journey, about June 5, 1872.[19]

The group was tired, dirty, and worn out with each other's company. But upon reaching the field, they did not waste a single moment and immediately fell to their knees, their noses practically in the dirt to make a close inspection of the ground, like a pack of hunting dogs hot on a scent's trail. Their eager search was almost immediately rewarded. Rubery recalled, "I found the first diamond. Arnold told me where to scratch for them and I dug the diamond out with a Bowie knife. All the rest of the party were close by and every one of them discovered diamonds."[20] Harpending was equally excited: "I had not been on the ground three minutes before I found a large diamond. That day we got over 500 diamonds, rubies, sapphires, and emeralds. Arnold would generally tell me where the best places were to dig for the gems. . . . We had only the gold pans, so two men were washing and two more were sorting the dirt."[21] And Dodge, representing his own and other San Francisco interests, was also firmly in The Field's sway and readily accepted Arnold's helpful geological hints: "It was then proposed to wash some gravel at the suggestion of Arnold, who said it was impossible to find diamonds without doing so, and some was placed in a bag and washed, and yielded twenty to forty diamonds, and a large number of other stones. . . . The washing was continued the next day. . . . The result of the washing was another find of about eighty diamonds and a large number of stones supposed to be rubies. Arnold, assisted by Rubery, generally got the gravel."[22] It had taken them four long days to reach their destination, but Arnold made sure the journey had been worthwhile.

Whatever exhaustion the party had experienced in trying to reach The Field was quickly replaced by surging adrenaline at standing in what must have seemed like God's own jewel box. A mania had seized them all, and they worked feverishly for two days. Janin's reputation for reticence preceded him but was completely undermined by his roiling excitement at The Field. Alas that all his geological sense and training should be obscured by the glinting jewels; science dictated that he should have been highly suspect of such a varied collection of stones occurring in the same spot—a geological anomaly heretofore unheard of. The group benefitted from Arnold's particularly helpful identification of "likely spots" for scratching and digging. In between washing and hauling and discovering, Janin quickly enlisted the party to survey and stake claims along the field, posting signs and notices along nearly three thousand acres to legitimize their claim. Arnold and Slack did not help with the staking.

There was much to be done, and Janin and Dodge were champing at the bit to move forward with legitimizing and assaying the claim. Signs and stakes notwithstanding, Rubery and Slack were conscripted to stay behind and guard the site as the rest of the party made haste to report their findings to their eager investors waiting on both American coasts. Their distaste for one another made Rubery and Slack strange and irksome bedfellows, and their watch summarily ended after only two days. They would have gladly abandoned each other sooner had their horses not gotten loose; even two days together was two too many.[23]

Janin, with his reputably staid hand and careful eye, soon reported to lawyer Barlow, "While I did not have enough time to make the investigations which would have answered very important questions, I do not doubt that further prospecting will result in finding diamonds over a greater area than is as yet proved to be diamond-bearing; and finally, I consider any investment at $40 per share, or at the rate of $4 million for the whole property, a safe and attractive one."[24]

The parts were all in play. The marks had taken the bait. The wheels were beginning to turn.

Slack, for his part, was through with it all. When he and Rubery quit each other's company, Slack slouched eastward and was never seen by the cabal again.

By August 1, the San Francisco and New York Mining Company was incorporated to the tune of $10 million divided into 100,000 shares at $100 apiece. Twenty-five men were invited to invest, and their initial infusion of $2 million was held in escrow in Ralston's Bank of California. As was later noted, "When the stock of the diamond company was ready to be issued, what did Ralston do? . . . He took the stock of that company and locked it up. Not one solitary share was ever issued; not one attempt was made to float it to the public; but he locked it up and swore he would keep it locked up until its truth was proved beyond peradventure [speculating], and so it was, through him and him alone, that those who believed in that thing were not made the innocent causes of suffering, and misery and want and destruction."[25] Ralston's apparent greed was, ultimately, insurance; he was not hoarding the jewels but the promise that they existed.

Holding the stocks back, of course, did nothing to dampen the public's enthusiasm and even less to shed light on the mystery and drama surrounding The Field. America was buzzing with guesses at the probable location of the storied diamond lot and all the possibilities that might come with it. States and territories vied for bragging rights to the seemingly holy site, and Harpending's flair for drama only bolstered the hysteria; when asked where the fields were, he gleefully pronounced that "his" diamonds were safely situated "1,000 miles to the east of Ralston's office."[26]

Arnold's oft-demonstrated anxiety over his site being revealed earned him an additional $450,000 in assurances from his investors. They paid him readily, and they paid him well for access to the score of the century. Even when the stones they grabbed on the confirmation expedition were valued at just 25 percent of what Janin and Harpending had self-assessed ($8,000 versus $30,000); even when Arnold swanned around with a Cheshire cat grin and gleefully gave intentionally conflicting reports to local newspapers to confuse the trail; even when Arizona's legislative body warned of tricksters and frauds, the diamond lust could not be derailed.

Multiple return trips to The Field had been planned over the summer, but each time, something came up. Arnold's big mouth blew their cover at least once. Janin's cold feet following the increasing public interest and chatter sidelined them not long after. General McClellan and his private Pullman car were even called in to talk some sense into Arnold in mid-August. To keep their location their own, multiple diversion parties set out from various points to provide any potential spies with as many goose chases as they could handle. Fake diamond missions were used to cover the tracks to the (fake) diamond field; all bases were covered.

By August 21, Ralston and the board wouldn't wait any longer for full confirmation of The Field's value. Though their claims were staked, the law was such that a company could only own a 160-acre tract. Chopped up like this, the company was going to need at least eighteen subsidiary companies to own the entire field, which also meant they were looking at a valuation twenty times larger than the already inflated $10 million. But the moneybags wanted thorough vetting of The Field before they went public with the absurdly assessed valuation of $250 million for the whole kit and caboodle.

A small band, headed by Roberts, made for The Field—a decoy party headed in the opposite direction—but their journey was disorganized and arduous. When they finally reached The Field, they "scratched and dug with [their] knives, among the sand and gravel down to the bedrock, which varies in depth from six inches to ten feet. The diamonds . . . varying in size from a drop of water to a white bean . . . are found almost close to bedrock."[27] They ferreted out nearly four hundred diamonds and quickly made their way back, eager to make headway with the investors.

Clarence King [seated, left] in the Fortieth Parallel Survey camp near Salt Lake City, nearly two years before Arnold and Slack came through.
US GEOLOGICAL SURVEY, DEPARTMENT OF THE INTERIOR/USGS, US GEOLOGICAL SURVEY/PHOTO BY TIMOTHY H. O'SULLIVAN.

The Green River Station was busy the day they made their way back to San Francisco. Emmons and Gardner, of the Fortieth Parallel Survey team, were also heading to San Francisco to brief their team on their recently completed fieldwork. They, like the rest of America, were intrigued by the prospective diamond field, not the least of which because their reputations as geological surveyors would be on the line if they'd missed something as important as The Field. Their ears were already to the ground when the Roberts party boarded their train. The diamond party was eager to return to the West Coast offices to confirm Janin's report that The Field was glittering with diamonds. Their enthusiasm did not escape notice by Gardner and Emmons, who, as naturally and unobtrusively as possible, probed the Roberts party for information about the site; trees, gullies, hills, rocks, and rivers were valuable markers to the master surveyors. The helpful details were few and far between, but Gardner and Emmons had some of the most extensive and intimate knowledge of the land, so they kept their ears pricked and their notes handy—Clarence King would want to know.[28] In a letter he would write later that year, King made clear his interest:

"I had been so absorbed with the legitimate works of the Exploration during the summer, that it was quite impossible for me to devote any attention whatsoever to the consideration of the expected diamond discovery. During all this time, however, I said to the members of the corps, that after the regular campaign was done, I would probably give the subject careful study.

I was certain there was only one place in that country which answered the description and, as that place lay within the limits of the Fortieth Parallel Survey, I determined to go there. The main reason why I went was that if it was good or bad, it would be a blight on any geological survey not to have known of the existence within its area, and I had to do it as a matter of self-defense.

Gardner and I had, without formerly mentioning the subject, *reached an identical conclusion as to where the spot was. He by adroitly putting together topographical hints let drop by the diamond parties, and I, by an occasional geological item they told, and by the*

almost certainty that no other place met the geological conditions."
—Clarence King, to Brigadier General A. A. Humphreys, November
27, 1872.[29]

When their train arrived in San Francisco the parties went their separate ways: Roberts and company to the Bank of California and Ralston's waiting vault, and Emmons and Gardner to King's office. As quickly as Arnold's marks had been willing to believe in The Field, King, Emmons, and Gardner began a methodical interrogation of its legitimacy.

"Where do you think the diamond fields are?" Emmons asked of King, his boss and compatriot.

"They are not in Arizona, I am convinced of that, or the knowing ones would not so readily admit they are." Clarence King was smart and clever.

"Well, supposing they are within the boundaries of my last summer's work, what would you consider the most probable location from a geological point of view?" Emmons already had an idea and was probing the geological expert for his notions.

"I should judge the tertiary beds."[30]

King and Emmons were no fools; they were ready to set the record straight. This would have been impossible with all of the diamond/hunter/trackers, so they took great care to advertise their mission as a search for "carboniferous fossils" to throw potential busybodies off their trail.

Meanwhile, Arnold had hightailed it back to Kentucky.

King and his trusted men left Wyoming and made for The Field. After four days of late-in-the-season riding through snow and wind and bitter cold, they made camp in a concealed gulch. The geologists immediately set to scoping things out when, as King later reported, "We had ridden scarce 500 yards, when a small fresh [scar] on one of the little cottonwoods attracted our attention. Dismounting, we found at the foot of the tree a slip of paper on which was written a claim to the water privileges of the (now dry) gulch, dated . . . June 15, and signed, Henry Janin . . . we knew we were now 'very warm' and began to circle around for tracks which we soon found and followed out to the gulch onto the mesa."

They had found it. They found The Field. They immediately began their inspection.

Emmons recalled:

The diamond fever had now attacked us all with vigor, and while daylight lasted, we continued in this position picking up precious stones. We were, perhaps, a little disappointed at finding but one diamond each, but attributed our slight success to want of training . . . our eyes, since the stones we found were all about of the same size and shape as the quartz grains of which the rock was composed, and could only be distinguished from them by the difference of lustre, which, in the rough diamond is of a steely tinge. The work was rendered slow also by the intense cold, for there was no protection from the fierce wind which swept, scarcely broken, for hundreds of miles over these barren mesas, and when a diamond was found, it was quite a time before our benumbed fingers would succeed in grasping the tiny stones. That night we were full-believers in the verity of Janin's reports, and dreamed of the untold wealth that might be gathered.[31]

Clarence King's right-hand man, Samuel Emmons, was more at home in the dirt than in a photographer's studio.
"SAMUEL FRANKLIN EMMONS, GEOLOGIST, THREE-QUARTER LENGTH PORTRAIT, FACING RIGHT," LIBRARY OF CONGRESS, PRINTS & PHOTOGRAPHS DIVISION, LC-USZ62-66584 (BLACK AND WHITE FILM COPY NEGATIVE), http://loc.gov/pictures/resource/cph.3b14077/.

The party continued their work as best as they were able in the weather conditions over several days. They methodically went over every bit of ground they could. The vicious weather notwithstanding, they were able to track Arnold and Janin's footsteps, and not a single precious stone was found in undisturbed dirt. They found a ruby on top of an anthill. They found a diamond wedged into a crevice. They found stones lying on naked rock. None of this bade well for Arnold and the San Francisco set because, while perhaps one of these anomalies could be written off, when considered together, the geological likelihood that these stones would be thus scattered and arranged was exactly zero.

The appearance of city-slicker Berry was their worst nightmare made worse. The oversized swindle had made Berry's mouth water, and the danger of damage was doubled. Secrecy was even more paramount now than on the first leg of their exploratory mission, and King could smell that Berry was ready to make trouble.

Once he arrived at the Green River station—having taken the shorter, far more dangerous route to beat Berry to the station—King elected *not* to telegraph his supervisor; "I would have telegraphed . . . a full statement but the operators all along the line are on a *qui vive*, and no dispatch is safe in their hands. Secrecy and dispatch were necessary to the honorable and judicious exposé of this."[32] "Mum" remained the word of the day.

———

King arrived in San Francisco on November 10, 1872, weathered and travel-worn. He did not stop to rest or relax, though, but found Henry Janin at once. He stayed up the night with Janin, coolly explaining his logic and methodology in determining The Field had been salted. Janin must have gone through the full spectrum of grieving in his sleepless night with King: denial, anger, bargaining, depression, and, finally, resigned acceptance. The cat was out of the bag, and the bag had been full of empty promises.

Janin called a meeting of the Company Board of Directors the very next morning. He delivered the bad news with King solemnly standing proxy, the ghost at the feast. Imagine the furor that must have erupted from the collection of the most powerful men in America who had, until that very moment, embraced the power and fortune that the good earth seemed ready to bless them with. They railed against King and accused him of subterfuge—a double, reverse hoax?—but he stood firm. They wanted confirmation of King's confirmation, and he agreed to accompany a Company representative to prove his theory. They wanted secrecy in the meantime—their reputations and diamondiferous fortunes were on the line, after all—but King replied, "There is not enough money in the Bank of California to make me delay publication a single hour! If you do not, I will, but it will come with much better grace from you. Stop all the transfers of stock; appoint competent men to represent you, and I will give you my camp outfit to take them to the spot, where they may convince themselves."[33] King was not happy with the men, their claims to the sullied earth, or their less-than-honorable secrecy; they'd wanted The Field for themselves and then wanted absolution for wanting it.

A confirmation party—the last in a long line—departed two days later with King at the helm, a sullen Janin, and three Company representatives in tow.

King was right to worry about the unscrupulous Berry, who had been planting the road to Salt Lake City with salted diamonds from Arnold's Field. What nerve! His ethics, it seemed, were not as shiny as the baubles he was peddling, and once he had created a stir, much of the damage had already been done. As Emmons wrote, "It was like talking to stones to try to convince men in this state of excitement."[34]

General David Douty Colton had been appointed the general manager of the New York and San Francisco Mining Company on November 1, 1872. Less than three weeks later, on November 18, he arrived at The Field, full of hope that Clarence King, America's preeminent geologist, was full of hooey.

Colton's report to the Company was colorful, thorough, and definitive:

> *After making fifty-six different tests of the most thorough and careful nature, from surface to bedrock, the day closed on us without our having found a diamond or ruby outside the limits of the bare rock first described. . . . Among other places I examined, was a point of rocks nearby and overlooking the place where Mr. Janin and others did the washing of the dirt that produced the precious stones brought to California in August last. . . . I found some rubies scattered on the bare rock where . . . it would have been impossible for nature to have deposited them as for a person standing in San Francisco to toss a marble in the air and have it fall on Bunker Hill Monument.*
>
> *All these investigations forced upon my mind the irresistible conclusion that the general assortment of precious stones found on the ground were strewn by the designing hand of one whose supply was sufficient to place a limited number in the most conspicuous places where the eye of a coming expert would most reliably discover them . . . Believe me, gentlemen, I was not unmindful of the great responsibility of carrying out the expedition and of making this report, which today pronounces absolutely valueless a property having, when I left home, a cash value of millions of dollars. . . . [S]pare neither time, money, nor skill in finding the guilty parties of this unparalleled fraud and bring them speedy justice. The good name of the State and the credit of our mining interest demand it.*[35]

The Company had its answer.

From *Engineering and Mining Journal*, December 10, 1872:

> *We have warned the profession, again and again, that the devices of swindlers are innumerable and profoundly ingenious. The more eminent an expert is, and the more widely known for cautious and even cynical judgments, the more anxious are speculators to secure, by*

fair means or foul, his favorable opinion. We have known of plots, concocted for the express purpose of "getting even" with an engineer, who had previously defeated some scheme of the conspirators. Yet the innocent conceit with which chemists, mineralogists, paleontologists, new-fledged mining engineers, experts with foreign experience only, take up, without hesitation, the delicate business of reporting on mining property, is a phenomenon only equaled by the coolness, audacity and dexterity of the operators who make easy victims among these classes and now and then outwit even the practiced expert. Henry Janin's mistake may well teach us all humility and caution.

Ouch.

That same day, the Company concluded its investigation after collecting extensive testimony from, among others, Harpending, Rubery, and James B. Cooper, who had resurfaced to make sure Arnold and Slack got their just desserts for cutting him out of the scheme. The Company did not file any charges. The grand jury, however, quickly slapped Arnold and Slack with misdemeanors. These indictments were quickly quashed, perhaps by the Company itself, as the members' reputations were still on the line. But at the very mention of legal action, Arnold grew defensive and addressed the Company by way of his local paper: "As you are all going into the newspapers, I'll take a fling at it myself some of these days. I'm going to the fields on my own book in the Spring with fifty men and will hold my hand against all the experts you can send along. If I catch any of your kid glove gentry about there, I'll blow the stuffing out of 'em."[36]

Arnold's vitriol, his Kentucky brotherhood, and the Company's reluctance for bad press made legal action challenging. Arnold's house, safe, and all its contents were seized and tied up in the courts for weeks because one investor, William Lent, *had* pressed charges. Arnold was under threat of extradition to California, so he was on the lam.

The seized assets, it should be noted, only accounted for about half of Arnold's total take of nearly $450,000. The following twelve months saw a game of legal cat and mouse play out in the Kentucky courts. Though Arnold eventually paid out $150,000 in a settlement to Lent, he protested every step of the way and lamely explained, "I did not owe [Lent, Ralston, Dodge, Harpending, and Roberts] one cent, but I paid the money to purchase my peace and get loose from this most powerful and world-renowned ring, and besides, I could not afford to lose the time I would necessarily have had to lose in attending to the suit for four times the money I paid." Arnold used the money they'd paid him to pay them back in order to get them off his back about the money they'd paid him. Harpending had again inserted himself as an oh-so-helpful intermediary and was instrumental in getting Arnold's money to Lent.[37]

That the swindle was revealed on the eve of its public offering had ultimately spared almost everyone from too much financial ruin. The Panic of 1873 undid poor Ralston, who was dead less than two years later. Harpending and Rubery continued punching above their weight in the London courts. George Roberts would not only recover but flourish with his hand in the Death Valley borax mining of the 1880s. Arnold was living larger-than-life in Kentucky, and Slack finally had his wish: to be left alone.

⸻

The years 1873 and 1874 were rife with litigation by and against Arnold. He was taken into custody, under constant threat of extradition, and spun tales of bribery, escape, false imprisonment, and libel. He demanded legal satisfaction left and right and threatened practically everyone in his path, and yet he flourished in Kentucky. Truly, his notoriety seemed only to help his local standing and he was seen, unequivocally, as a proud and pompous son of Elizabethtown.

When not simultaneously running from and encouraging his reputation as a sharper, Arnold fancied himself a business magnate. And a farmer. And a horse breeder. There was little he wouldn't try to master. Of his venture raising pigs, the local papers wrote, "Philip Arnold's one-thousand-pound hog is a cross of the Berkshire and Poland China, *just as his thousand dollar mine was a cross of salt and fiction*."[38] He was able to lead a life in Elizabethtown high-on-the-hog (indeed!) and embraced a wide range of ventures. His associations with the local bank, Thomas, Polk & Company, gave him a chance to try his hand at banking, even. This foray, no matter his level intentions, would be his undoing. But helming the Diamond Hoax of 1872 had only further emboldened his already defiant nature; Philip Arnold would do whatever he darned well pleased, and to hell with anyone who said otherwise!

After a disagreement over a loan, its due date, and the associated interest, Arnold filed suit against a Louisville bank, setting off a chain of legal tit for tat that saw suits and countersuits filed at rapid-fire pace over a three-month period.

But on August 15, 1878, it all bubbled over when Arnold met his legal opponent, Holdsworth, the agent of the competing bank, in the local saloon. At 5:30 p.m., Arnold was drinking a beer when in strode Holdsworth and a friend, who promptly tried to defuse the discomfort by inviting Arnold to join. Arnold looked to Holdsworth, ire and fury in his eyes, and said, "You have done me a mortal injury, and you are following me up."

Arnold pounced on Holdsworth and laid in. Though others tried to intervene, Arnold spat, "If you touch me, I will kill you." Arnold pinned and punched Holdsworth for five painful minutes, rendering his face a bloody pulp. Holdsworth cried and begged, but Arnold was unrelenting. A marshal was summoned and pulled Arnold off Holdsworth as he delivered a final, contemptuous kick in the ribs.

Holdsworth was quickly delivered to his bank to clean himself up. An otherwise decorative sawed-off shotgun was in the bank, handy as you like, so Holdsworth took hold and strode out, his face still bleeding.[39]

William C. McCague was a young boy on the scene who later recounted, "I helped lead Holdsworth to the bank and kind o' hung around, expecting. Holdsworth washed the blood off and staunched the bleeding. Then he got a sawed-off, single-barreled shotgun that was part of the bank furniture—relic of the Jesse James days—drew the charge, oiled the gun thoroughly and reloaded it with thirty-two buckshot. All this was done with deliberate care. Holding the gun in the crook of his left arm, he started back to the saloon. I tagged along, but off on one side of him."[40]

"There he comes!" shouted a bystander as Arnold stood in the street, livid and gesturing toward the courthouse. Holdsworth strode toward

Arnold, gun under his arm, his intentions clear. Before he could fire a shot, Holdsworth ducked behind a tree as Arnold pulled a revolver and fired twice, missing Holdsworth but shattering the shop window across the street. Holdsworth returned fire twice, hitting two bystanders. Arnold charged ever forward, and Holdsworth flailed but got Arnold square in the right shoulder from point-blank range on his final charge, the buck-shot taking bits of flesh with it. Holdsworth dropped his weapon and dodged bullets as he ran away. Arnold's return fire missed Holdsworth completely but took down another bystander. Holdsworth was arrested almost immediately at his bank, as Arnold was taken to *his* bank for medical attention; the physician feared the wound would cost Arnold his arm, if not his life.[41]

He survived but was not well. For six months, Arnold was in and out of the courtroom filing and fighting lawsuits. How bittersweet for the courts to have one man be the source of so much business! Come February of 1879, though, Arnold went to the hospital with pneumonia and, after being admitted, died. His take from the diamond swindle was nowhere to be found, and his legacy seemed to consist of little but lawsuits. Still, his funeral "was the largest ever seen in Elizabethtown" and brought thousands of mourners to the streets to pay their respects, wonder, and gawp.

The cellar in Arnold's house in Elizabethtown fueled a hundred-year rumor that it was salted with diamonds.

—◆—

John Slack lived up to his name insofar as he was a lackluster participant in The Great Diamond Hoax of 1872. His distaste for the limelight and madding crowds landed him in New Mexico Territory by 1875, where he lived out his remaining twenty years as the local undertaker. The memorial upon his death in 1896 veritably glowed and, perhaps, spoke more to his character than his association with Arnold's scheme: "[Mr. Slack] was always honest and just in his intercourse and dealings with his fellow men and generous to those who gained his ready sympathy and confidence."[42]

Or, perhaps, he had simply learned his lesson. The dead were safer than diamonds. And a good deal more honest.

CHAPTER THREE

Bad Blood

THE TIME: 1865–1891
THE PLACE: New York, NY
               Boston, MA
               Providence, RI
THE TAKE: $0, heartache, consumption, jail time, decapitation
THE PLAYERS: Dr. E. F. Townsend
               The Sawtelle Brothers
               C. Ernst Weber
               Miss Jeanette Nickerson
               Edelberto Giro
               Mrs. Christiancy
               Dr. C. L. Blood

SWINDLERS MAKE OPPORTUNITIES WHERE THEY FIND AN "IN." IN THE 1860s, American medical science was progressing at a rapid pace and generated a host of new industries, almost all of which were unregulated. Also booming were new opportunities to spin innovation and newness into getting something for nothing.

Gardner Quincy Colton first used nitrous oxide—laughing gas—as an anesthetic in the 1840s. It was revolutionary to pair a medical procedure with the exhilarating effects of the gas, thereby granting relief to the patient (and administrator) during the operation. By the end of the decade, medical professionals were sold on the effects of nitrous oxide while dentists clamored to stock it in their offices.

In 1836, in little Ayer, Massachusetts, the first and only son of Louis Blood was born: Charles. Charles often claimed his father was a respected doctor, which was half true; he was respected but not a doctor. Charles named Pepperell, Massachusetts, as his seat of learning, which was also half true; when about seventeen, he left home to attend school in Pepperell but left after two weeks.[1]

New England in the 1850s would have been hard and exciting for a young white man of a certain age. "Teenaged," as a developmental stage, was not really a concept yet so citizens were either children or adults, and Charles Blood became an "adult" as soon as he ran away from school. How he spent his time from the 1850s through the end of the Civil War is a mystery, save for an arrest in 1856 for selling a nontransferrable train pass from Boston to Worcester and spending thirty days in jail for it.[2]

Come 1865, though, Charles's days of anonymity were over. That year, his name became a regular sight in New England newspapers. "Dr. C. L. BLOOD" was featured in big, bold print in the advertisements he placed in papers from Maine to Massachusetts. For Blood had not been

BLOOD, DOCTOR BLOOD.
DR. BLOOD'S CALLING CARD, FROM FERBUARY 19, 1890. *CHICAGO INTER OCEAN*, CHICAGO, IL.

idle those ten years under the radar. Whatever the circumstances that led him to Boston in 1865 they propelled Blood, equipping him with the nimbleness, resourcefulness, and vanity needed to make it in the golden age of swindlers and quacks.

There was a blurry line between quack and con man; much like a square is a rectangle but a rectangle is not a square, so, too, is a quack a con man, but a con man not a quack. There is a distinction in preying upon the fear of one's own body—parading magic as science to relieve fear of what lies unseen within the mortal coil—that paints quacks eviler than their counterparts. Money is man's invention, and the con man is an inevitable by-product, whereas innate physical and mental health are beyond control and, therefore, outside the realm of conceivably excusable crimes. A con man pulls a trick to make money and maybe that money helps him reform his wicked ways. A quack mistreats his patients because he is sick and inherently twisted. C. L. Blood was a con man at heart and a quack in practice.

Starting in September of 1866, huge newspaper ads, entire columns long, started running in Connecticut and Massachusetts papers.

INHALATION of the OXYGENIZED AIR, All Diseases of the Nose, Throat and Lungs, PARALYSIS, EPILEPSY, NEURALGIA, RHEUMATISM, AND SCROFULA . . . Dr. C.L. BLOOD, The Inventor of This Remedy, has given it in OVER 20,000 EXTREME CASES personally. A majority of these patients had been suffering for years with the diseases enumerated above, and had been hopelessly abandoned by physicians, and were considered far beyond the reach of any medicine—yet a few applications of Oxygen were only required to impart new life to their wasted systems and to restore them to per-fect health.[3]

Blood knew there was money to be had in "healthcare," not the least because the end of the Civil War flooded America with veterans whose wounds would dog them for the rest of their lives, and there was only still-developing infrastructure to support them. Tuberculosis was the leading cause of death in America and it would be another twenty-plus years before sanatoriums appeared in the United States, so Blood would never want for patients. And if the bottom fell out of the consumption market, there were always hemorrhoids, sciatica, headache, arthritis—if you had it, Blood would find a way to sell you a treatment.

These ads were clever in their construction, for the Oxygenized Air was not just being advertised but hawked by local physicians; no need for blind faith that Blood's discovery/invention/potion had merits all its own, take Dr. Davis's word for it. Or Dr. Cottell's. Or Dr. Piper's. Blood used these heretofore respectable doctors as shills to spread the word about his miraculous cure, and relied on their reputations to provide him stable piggybacks.

To be very clear, Charles Louis Blood had not invented anything and was not in the business of actually curing people. Physicians and dentists were elated by the laughing gas–induced euphoria in their patients because it gave them the time and space to perform procedures without as much struggle with/from the patient. Blood was selling the anesthetic as a cure; patients would leave his practice feeling revitalized and renewed, but nothing had actually changed. It was as if Blood latched onto the troublesome illness/horrible treatment/celebratory lollipop progression and decided to cut out the middleman of actual medical attention. His scheme kept him one step removed from spokesman, one step short of treatment, and that much closer to plausible deniability should things go south.

Shortly before the newspaper advertisements started appearing in late 1865, Blood visited a Boston manufacturer of the apparatus used to mix and make the nitrous oxide. He announced his intention to purchase a machine and wanted to know all the ins and outs before the transaction. Demonstrations and exhibitions followed. Upon reaching the point of sale, however, Blood offered a half-hearted apology while admitting he had neither the credit nor cash to make the purchase but found the manufacturing process fascinating. The manufacturer was out a sale, but Blood was now in business.[4]

Unfortunately for readers in Boston and Philadelphia—Blood's chosen haunts—their papers did not run the notice that appeared in the Bangor, Maine, *Daily Whig and Courier* on October 20, 1865.

An exchange warns the public against Dr. C.L. Blood, who, according to the statement, fails to pay printers' bills. Let them adopt our custom

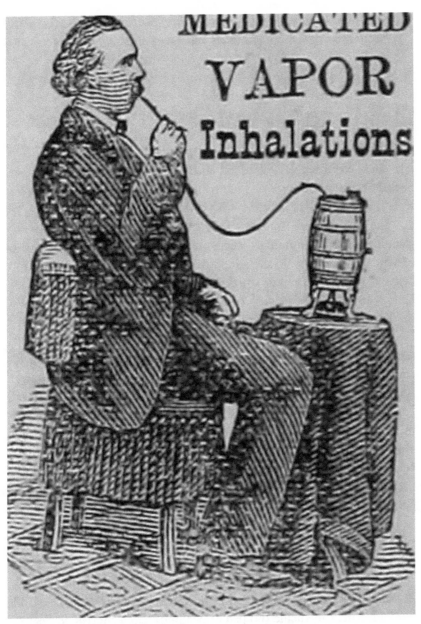

A man seeks relief from a barrel of air.

IMAGE FROM PAGE 267 OF *THE PHYSICIAN AND PHARMACEUTIST* (1868), PUBLIC DOMAIN, ACCESSED VIA INTERNET ARCHIVE'S FLICKR "MEDICATED VAPOR INHALATION, 1868."

of making all transient and traveling concerns pay in advance, and it will save a good deal of trouble and heavy losses. All weak shows, without money enough to pay their bills, have withdrawn from us since we adopted that plan, and transferred their patronage to other offices. We haven't had any difficulty with responsible shows, where there is merit in the performance. They always have money enough to pay their bills.[5]

Alas and alack for everyone Blood encountered from 1865 on as a brief, buried notice would have told them all they needed to know for dealing with Blood: DON'T.

The Oxygenized Air advertising campaign—unpaid bills notwithstanding—was quantitatively successful. With a steady influx of new patients and new physicians, Blood began running multiple offices. His original place on Chauncy Street, Boston, was no longer adequate, so he also rented larger, fancier rooms on Harrison Avenue. The setup was impressive: patients entered a well-furnished waiting room, were greeted by one of Blood's lackeys before said lackey would tug on a bell pull that sent a cheerful sign to Blood that someone desired to see him in his consultation room at the back. Blood, again, was one step removed from sight. The rooms alone were imposing enough for investors to approach Blood in hopes of co-partnership. Early investor/dupe Humphrey Cummings poured nearly his entire fortune—$4,500—into Blood's operation after just one visit. He demanded his money be returned once he saw the true nature of the operation. Cummings never received his investment back, let alone a return, and died soon after demanding Blood to make good—a harbinger of Blood's capacity for destruction and callousness.[6]

The newspaper ads ran continuously. They stretched from the top to the bottom of the paper and sometimes spread across four columns, filling the entire page with "DR. C.L. BLOOD" and "CATARRH" and "CONSUMPTION." To all outward appearances, Blood's business was not only on the level but booming. So much so that Dr. Blood and his bunkum patent medicine (no patent pending) had a copycat competitor within a year.

Boston's Chauncy Street was thick with Oxygenized Air in 1866. Blood found a competitor in Dr. Jerome Harris, who was peddling a treatment of "Superoxygenized Air," from offices right down the hall—literally in the same building. Blood had maintained an arm's distance in his scheme—other doctors sold his remedy, and attendants dealt with patients—but kept an iron grip on his "proprietary" formula for Oxygenized Air. Harris's gall at peddling his own iteration of laughing gas a stone's throw from Blood's setup was both opportunistic and taunting, neither of which Blood appreciated.

One day a man called Carvill sought treatment from Dr. Harris and his superoxygenized formula. He was handed the treatment, took a big breath in and immediately fell to the floor in a fit, his mouth frothing and his limbs convulsing. He thrashed around Harris's offices for nearly an hour. Once his humors settled, Dr. Harris saw Carvill home and promptly summoned his usual physician . . . Dr. Blood. Once Dr. Blood had seen to him and Carvill was satisfactorily revived, accusations of poisoning and blackmail flew left and right. Carvill brought suit against Dr. Harris, and Dr. Blood was good enough to give newspapers up-to-the-minute reports on his patient's well-being. An attendant was stationed outside Harris's offices to ensure no others could be tragically maltreated like Carvill, and to make sure the public was reminded of *which* of the two doctors was the *really* bad one.

Harris never took the blackmail bait and never answered the suit, though Carvill tried to settle many times. They were both broken by the incident. Blood had no need for them anymore, so he promptly lost interest. Harris's nerves were shot; he abandoned the practice and fled Boston. No skin off Blood's nose.[7]

Blood was flying high and opened countless offices in the next decade. "Countless" because half of them were under other physicians' names, in keeping with his advertising strategy; "Physicians wanted to adopt this system of practice," just as the ads said.[8] The other half of the businesses was simply Blood using aliases or a lackey as front man. To open a business, one merely needed to hang a sign on a door; Blood marked doors across America in the 1870s.

In 1872, he transformed from "Dr. C.L. Blood," to "C.L. Blood, M.D." He traveled to Europe and South America. He got married, for the second time. There was a pesky $13,000 fine for lost sales tax awaiting him in Boston, so Blood steered clear as he pushed on.[9] To Philadelphia. To New York. To Buffalo. To Chicago.

Newspapers continued to run Blood's ads and testimonials. "Fact-checking" was not yet a guiding principle, and Blood must have been paying his printer's bills promptly. His vanity led him to include small pictures of himself on tranches of his self-styled circulars. His pamphlets served double duty in getting his name on the streets and in acting as "stock" that Blood could sell to the many doctors in his syndicate, alongside their bottles of Oxygenized Air. A small cry amid Blood's advertising furor came from the *Vermont Farmer* in 1874:

Sometimes the literature of quackery is simply disgusting, and one feels ashamed, when he reads the transparent lies which are told about the discovery of these wonderful nostrums, and the absurd claims made for them, to think there can be found persons so simple and gullible as to place any confidence in such trash. But there is a still worse feature very common in the quack pamphlets and circulars, their IMPIETY AND NEAR APPROACH TO BLASPHEMY . . . This Blood sends out a large, four-page sheet [in/around Providence], with the cheerful title in large black letters of "Life or Death;" beneath this are two American flags, which he has had the impudence to besmirch by printing his sanguineous name upon them. At one corner is a picture of what is apparent the Virgin, as Mater Dolorosa, with over it the legend "Why will you die?"—and at the opposite corner the head of Christ, crowned with thorns, with a face expressive of great agony. Now we claim that it is absolutely impious to use sacred emblems to advertise one's business of any kind. It would be just as proper for an apple-woman to put up a cross to call attention to her stall as it is for this Blood to use the image of the Saviour in his suffering to embellish his quack-sheet. With such gross impropriety at the heading, we are not surprised to read beneath, that "where oxygenized air has failed to relieve a patient, nothing but the interposition of Heaven could save him" It is the duty of every parent to see that such wickedly repulsive literature as this is kept out of the family—not only upon sanitary grounds, but upon moral ones.[10]

This polemic was in response to a street circular in Providence, Rhode Island. But while Blood was making waves in the streets, he also made the reacquaintance of Providence's Dr. E. F. Townsend, the two having crossed paths some ten years before. They fell in like old friends.

In the early days of January in 1876, Townsend set up shop in Boston and ran ads for his "Oxygenated Air" to cure diphtheria. Blood's name was conspicuously absent from the ad; perhaps "Oxygenated" and "Oxygenized" really were two different processes? It seems reasonable that this fine distinction escaped readers' notice, and a safe, humdrum, uncontested product would hardly gain attention.

By the end of the month, readers would have little trouble finding an oxygenized hoopla given a competing ad had appeared next to Townsend's, this one under a bold heading of "OXYGENATED AIR," with text that read, "The undersigned, having the SOLE RIGHT to manufacture and sell the celebrated Medical Remedy called, 'Oxygenized Air,' . . . offers for sale on liberal terms the SOLE AND EXCLUSIVE RIGHT to use the same in one or all of the New England States. This is a good chance for the right man to make money. Call or address THOMAS LEWIS, 63 Court Street, Boston."[11] What cunning! Without the benefit of context, readers would have assumed they were witnessing the start of a feud.

By the following week, Townsend had upped the ante and called out his competition by name. "Mr. Lewis has no knowledge of medicine, cannot tell one drug from another, and has no right or claim whatever upon 'Oxygenated Air.'"[12] Two items of note: First, Blood was still persona non grata in Boston thanks to his long-overdue $13,000 fine; and second, Blood's middle name was Louis, which he pronounced, "Lewis." Townsend, Blood's compatriot, had opened a shop selling a propriety version of Blood's proprietary snake oil and had cried foul at any linkage to Blood in a city where he was unwelcome. When considered a pair, Blood and Townsend were having a field day in Boston and making money hand over fist by making lemonade out of Blood's lemon reputation.

The so-called competition: Thomas Lewis's tiny ad [right] is dwarfed by the Townsend broadside [left], though profits from both flowed into one man's pocket—Blood's.

COMPETING "AIR" ADS, JANUARY 26, 1876, *THE BOSTON GLOBE*, BOSTON, MA.

Just after he'd spun "Lewis" into a payday in Boston, Blood sold his Philadelphia operation—he'd been doing business as Dr. J. A. Goldenberg peddling "Goldenberg new life remedies"—for $140,000.[13] With his wealthy (second) wife in tow, Blood *must* have been satisfied enough with this windfall to play it straight, retire from the game, and live out his days a wealthy eccentric, right?

No. Instead, he increased the frequency and volume of his plays. Blood had offices in at least eight cities, with at least as many trusted agents on the ground to oversee the operations. He made sure all his agents were diploma-wielding physicians. Townsend managed the Boston racket; a couple, Joseph and Theresa Barnum, did work in New York and Chicago, respectively; James Veniere was a floating supporting player. So, as the lady Barnum was answering petty forgery charges in Chicago, Blood and Veniere were working up a scheme in New York City—his house of cards had satellite offices.

Even so, Blood found time to dabble. In 1878, he made a cameo in a body-snatching case in Brooklyn wherein Blood played the role of "helpful witness" who came to the defense of the man accused of impersonating a doctor when he was, in fact, George Christian, who had only two years prior been implicated in the attempted theft of President Abraham Lincoln's body in Washington, D. C. It was perhaps fitting for a man who peddled in false hope for the living to join ranks with one who abused the security of burial for the dead. Blood's circle of compatriots was a diverse band of baddies, grave-robbers included.[14, 15]

Though he was dabbling in more sensational villainy, Blood maintained his commitment to his first love, Oxygenized Air. With Townsend capably handling the Boston shop, Blood would have felt little incentive to pay the pesky $13,000 fine that dogged his name but not his business—an important distinction. Buoyed with confidence having outfoxed the Revenue Service in Boston, he did nothing to amend his business practices. Therefore, when the New York City police came for him on a charge of failure to affix revenue stamps to his bottles of overpriced air, at 50 cents a bottle, Blood had racked up a $50,000 fine.

For the first time—as far as is known—Dr. C. L. Blood was hauled into jail. He wallowed in self-pity and ire for his partner, Joseph Barnum, who had been taken in with the doctor but had since gotten cozy with the cops. Blood stewed and seethed for several months in New York City's Ludlow Street Jail in lieu of the $50,000 for the fine or $50,000 bail. Reports had it that his father, who would have been in his seventies at that point, made a deal with the government that facilitated Blood the younger's release.[16]

With his newfound liberty Blood had a chance to remake himself. He could have gone anywhere—except Boston or New York—and made a go of it. The year before his $50,000 arrest, in 1877, he'd been laying groundwork for a deal in Brooklyn with Veniere playing the supporting role. They had worked on a pair of New England locals—Orville Harmon and Henry Walker—and given them a strong-armed sales pitch that leaned on Blood's and Veniere's credentials (i.e., their diplomas) and the supposed annual take from an NYC Oxygenized Air store ($16,000 to $60,000). Veniere had posed as a fresh-faced business interest, and when things quickly unraveled for Harmon and Walker, they invited Veniere to be a plaintiff in their suit against Blood. When he refused, they (aptly) assumed he was in cahoots with Blood. Money had been transferred to Blood from each of them, and sometimes through Veniere, and the men had an empty store full of bogus products to show for it. Blood's credentials and his reported sales record had no relationship to Walker and Harmon's reality on the ground, which was immediately revealed to be a dud of an impressive order. Walker and Harmon bought and abandoned the store in early 1877 and promptly filed suit against Blood.

As there were no immediate actions taken—he knew the wheel of justice to grind slowly—Blood furthered his cause while filling out the ranks of Blood products. In 1880 he published his book, *A Century of Life, Health and Happiness, or A Gold Mine of Information, For One Dollar: A Cyclopedia of Medical Information for Home Life, Health, and Domestic Economy*, by C. L. Blood, M. D., Physician for Disease of the Head, Throat, Lungs, and the Liver and Kidneys. Published by the Author, 38 West Thirtieth Street, New York—A FIVE DOLLAR BOOK FOR ONE DOLLAR. Before the introduction, before the title page even, Blood made clear to his readers the type of relationship they should expect; Blood held the secrets and was eager to share them, for the right price. "In consequence of the many paralytics and physical and mental wrecks through the use of vile adulterations called 'Baking Powder;' and in consideration of the good health of the living, I have prepared a *chemically pure Baking Powder*, which is superior to any known preparation for baking purposes. . . . Ask your grocer to furnish you with DR. BLOOD'S BAKING POWDER ONLY . . . to overcome any obstacles *I will send my preparation, postage paid, upon receipt of the price.*"[17] This was all before the introduction, which Blood used to speak out of the other side of his mouth: "The vast medium of ideas between man and man—the newspaper press—has hitherto been insulted by our *learned* profession—handed over bodily to the most disgusting and mischievous form of advertising, and made the medium of the lowest and most degrading forms of quackery. The people, uninformed as to the nature, causes, and cure of disease, have been easily caught by vulgar assertion and names without explanation, and quackery flourishes apace, till the professional name has become almost a byword and a reproach."[18] Whether Blood was a quack, or a doctor, or a regular physician, was probably unclear to his readers, but his book laid bare the transactional terms of the patients' relationship with the so-called doctor.

Before he let loose his book upon the world, Blood did a bit of traveling. He went south. On his return journey from Peru, he made acquaintance with a Cuban gentleman, Edelberto Giro, and the future ex-Mrs. Christiancy, as then still married to Senator Isaac Christiancy, who would serve as America's Envoy Extraordinary and Minister Plenipotentiary to Peru from 1879 to 1881. The three became chummy on the journey home, and Giro and Blood did a little business on the side. Giro was interested in the book and Blood's latest leaflet, "Man's Invisible Enemies, or Death in the Air," and bought distribution rights for half of New York City as he believed Blood to be a fully qualified physician with honest aims. Blood was interested in the Cuban gentleman as simply another mark, so he had no qualms accepting from Giro $2,000 cash and $1,070 worth of diamonds for the worthless distribution rights. With his cash already in Blood's hands, Giro's increasingly close friendship with Mrs. Christiancy was a bonus for Blood; whatever Giro couldn't provide him in their business dealings, Blood would at least have ample material for blackmail.[19]

The three jetsetters returned to the States; Mrs. Christiancy immediately began divorce proceedings against Senator Christiancy, and he against her. This was in the early summer of 1880. By that winter, whatever hope all parties had for anonymity or privacy was out the window, and their names were featured in the papers almost daily.

On September 10, Blood was arrested and taken to the Ludlow Street jail on a warrant granted in the Harmon/Walker case. He was quickly released after providing sureties for his $5,000 bail in Joseph and Theresa Barnum. When called to testify on behalf of their securities (i.e., funds), the Barnums refused. Had Blood not immediately scarpered after his release from jail he would have been rearrested.[20]

His flight from Harmon/Walker justice kept Blood out of jail only for as long as he was able to avoid and appease Giro, which was about five weeks. On October 14, Blood was again arrested, this time on a charge brought by Giro for the $3,070 in cash and diamonds, and he was taken to the Tombs Police Court (as opposed to the Ludlow Street jail, which was for civil suits). Blood claimed Giro was being vindictive because Blood claimed to have compromising letters between Giro and the soon-to-be-ex-Mrs. Christiancy. Giro said the letters were a lie—though he admitted to being a party in the divorce suits—and simply wanted his money back after Blood had spent months promising to show Giro a legitimate medical diploma upon request but never did.[21] As Blood had made very clear to Giro in his patent spiel—the one Blood gave to all his potential partners—the diploma was the key to credibility.

By December, it looked like all Blood's chickens were coming home to roost. On December 18, his lawyer in the Harmon/Walker case had the unpleasant job of finding Blood and making him answer for the as-yet-unpaid $5,000 Barnum bail. To his surprise, the attorney found Blood already in the Tombs on Giro's charge. The judge in the Giro suit dismissed the case on December 23, saying the evidence was technically defective. Blood was released from the Tombs directly into the waiting arms of the deputy sheriff, who immediately arrested him on Giro's charges, this time levied in a civil suit. Blood was moved back to Ludlow Street on the spot. Having failed to meet the $7,500 bail—he did not use the Barnums again—Blood was left to think about what he'd done.[22]

Within the week, Blood had brought a countersuit against Giro claiming that he'd been imprisoned on false charges and that Giro had been intimidating and offering bribes to witnesses. In fact, Blood knew of an altogether helpful witness who would testify that Giro had offered him $25 to say that Blood had never made a claim about his diploma—enter: James Veniere. On December 28, while he was still cooling his heels in Ludlow Street, Blood had Giro arrested just as he was on his way to be deposed in the Christiancy case. This obvious ploy was to keep Giro from testifying, but Giro had secured bail within hours and his deposition went as planned, just a few hours later.[23]

February and March of 1881 saw Blood in court on competing, though similar, charges. Harmon/Walker claimed he'd defrauded them through dishonest methods, including his claim to a legitimate diploma. Giro claimed the same. Blood did everything he could to prevaricate and quantify his claims: he'd never said he was a doctor, per se; he'd never claimed to hold a diploma *before* June 1880; and the plaintiffs were less-than-honest, so why believe their charges at all? He thrashed and squirmed to get out of the competing clutches.

Just *how* he managed to escape the legal talons closing in on him from all sides is unknown. Senator and Mrs. Christiancy's divorce was granted; Harmon and Walker gratefully fell out of the limelight; the Barnums were no longer in Blood's inner sanctum. But while the paper trail of Blood's legal proceedings from this period went cold, his name was still appearing in the press. In March 1881, one of his "copartners" was brought up on fraud charges in Wilmington, Delaware. But the coup de grâce came at the end of the month when Dr. John Buchanan sang long and loudly about the extensive output from his diploma mill. For as Blood was peddling cures with no science behind them, Buchanan was peddling diplomas with no learning. The Eclectic Medical College of Philadelphia had its charter repealed for diploma selling in 1872, but Dean Buchanan's well-oiled diploma mill was humming along and, in a sense, too big to fail. He'd sold upwards of $100,000 worth of diplomas before being caught trying to fake his own death. But Buchanan had no qualms about bringing Blood down with him and confirmed that not only had he sold Blood a diploma but also that Blood had in turn sold over one thousand diplomas for Buchanan. Schemes within schemes![24]

Though his credentials were busted, Blood had somehow slipped the court's grasp and quickly fell into his tried-and-true methods for raising cash and quickly. By November of that year, he was in and out of Boston setting up an office and advertising for a silent partner to own a third of the business. Woe betided the men who had just arrived in town, looking to start afresh, who answered Blood's call: Francis M. Andrews and Francis A. Waterman.

The following three years were likely the busiest in Blood's life. He was in and out of court in New York, Philadelphia, Washington, D.C., and, finally, Boston. In 1883, the $50,000 revenue stamp penalty in New York caught up with him, though the case fell apart after Joseph Barnum—onetime rat for C. L. Blood and flip-flopping stool pigeon for the US government—claimed complete ignorance of the contents of his own affidavit. Giro appeared for the prosecution, and Barnum was committed for perjury in lieu of $5,000 bail.[25] Perhaps he should have listed Blood as a security?

Blood was working overtime to shore up his house of cards with more and newer cards, no matter their flimsy nature. In early 1884, Blood's Boston operation was his home base. Given his legal troubles, it would stand to reason that he would lay low and stay out of sight, but instead, he diversified. Perhaps with his diploma unmasked, Blood simply leaned into his true nature and embraced the life of a haughty swindler? Maybe he was lonely? Whatever his reasons, Blood's actions saw him back in court by May 1884, his old chum and compatriot Dr. Townsend at his side as a codefendant.

They were charged with attempting to blackmail German musician C. Ernst Weber out of $25,000 for alleged crimes against Miss Jeanette Nickerson. The whole affair was sordid and absurd, with Blood claiming platonic relations with Miss Nickerson at one moment, romantic inclinations the next. Townsend—at one time a practicing regular physician—was revealed as the inelegant liaison between Blood, Nickerson, and Weber. Throughout his badgering and threatening Weber to leave Nickerson alone—Blood and Townsend acting out of chivalry on

DIED YESTERDAY.

DIED OF
CONSUMPTION
CAUSED BY
CATARRH.

INHALE
OXYGENIZED AIR.
IT CURES ALL
CHRONIC DISEASES.
DR. E. F. TOWNSEND,
331 Westminster Street, Providence, R. I.

CONSULTATION FREE.

Townsend's less-than-subtle approach to advertising.

the lady's behalf, apparently—Townsend served Weber with a writ for $25,000 in damages but said he would take $500 cash just to make the matter go away. Upon hearing this cash discount, Weber immediately left Townsend to ostensibly fetch a note for the amount but instead went straight to the police.

Peppered throughout the testimony were references to Blood's Oxygenized Air and other products. District Attorney Adams seized on this and, in cross-examination, drew from Blood the following:

Question: At what institution did you graduate, doctor?

Answer: I am not a graduate in medicine.

Q: Haven't you published a book in which you attach "M.D." to your name?

A: No, sir.

Q: Do you mean to say that the words, "Charles L. Blood, M.D.," do not appear in your book?

A: They appear there, but WITHOUT MY AUTHORITY. My partner, Mr. Barnum, attended to that part of the work.

Q: Where did you ever study medicine?

A: With a Dr. Collett in New York, in whose employment I spent a considerable period.

Three things of note: First, Buchanan's diplomas were fraudulent, and everyone knew it at this point, so Blood had no reason to even claim he was a regular physician. In fact, later that morning, the district attorney drew from Townsend the confession that his was also a Buchanan diploma. Second, with Barnum already out of the picture, Blood had no reason *not* to make him the fall guy. Finally, in his early days, 1866, one of Blood's first shills for his Air was a "Dr. Cottell" of Connecticut. Given his fondness for playing games with names, it's safe to assume Blood conjured a plausible name in a plausible place using a real person who'd had a glancing brush with Blood's orbit and that there was no "Dr. Collett."[26]

For all their nimbleness and wry ways of speech, Blood and Townsend's reputations did not fare well on the stand in the Nickerson trial. They were shown to be greedy and bankrupt of morals and ethics. The jury found them guilty on all four (joint) counts of attempted extortion, while Townsend was found guilty on four counts of acting as the principal and Blood was guilty on all four counts as Townsend's accessory. From June to December, as they waited on sentencing, the disgraced doctors mounted an aggressive appeal on the grounds that the verdict had been against the evidence, not the men, and that members of the jury were compromised by outside influences, including the newspapers. In December, they were granted a new trial and released as the court date was set.[27]

As was his custom, Blood immediately began turning his wheels within wheels when released in December 1884. He managed to have a circular printed before he was yet again arrested on January 23, 1885. This circular, a warning screed titled, "BORROWERS AND SPONGERS," made its way to the streets of New York with the following in its opening paragraph: "These adventurers are as numerous as office seekers; too lazy to work, too cowardly and dishonest to steal, they play the confidence role and borrow, or ask credit 'until tomorrow' for any amount they think your kindly feeling will prompt you to place at their disposal. Having no conscience, manhood or decency, but possessing volubility and plausibility of speech, brass, cunning, hypocrisy and falsehoods, they have the elements that make dupes of the kind-hearted and credulous."[28] What wicked gall to warn readers not to trust those who displayed the very qualities and practices on which Blood relied! Gaslighting in a pure, stunning form.

However trusting the public might or might not have been on the heels of his SPONGERS alarm, they were given the opportunity to reassess when Blood was hauled into Boston court on January 23, 1885, to answer fraud charges from the two Francises (Andrews and Waterman) from 1881. And whatever hope Blood might have held out for the public to forgive and forget was dashed utterly when the court clerk began reading the charges at 10 a.m. and didn't finish until nearly 11. An entire hour's worth of charges put the jury and gallery practically to sleep. The trial did not improve for Blood from there.

More intel on Blood's ridiculous diploma dance came to light, as did a larger repertoire of hokum medicine products, including an electric coil that supposedly improved blood flow when used in conjunction with prescribed exercises. The plaintiffs, when delivered what little stock Blood made good on, quickly realized the impracticality of a medical business run by men without medical training; Blood was rarely around, and his partner, Evans, refused to treat anyone. The Francises were strung along long enough for Blood to extract at least $2,000 from each of them.

The song and dance in the courtroom were familiar to Blood. Some familiar names and faces made appearances (e.g., James H. Veniere, aka "Voldo" in this scheme, provided a deposition for Blood's defense), but the prosecution had over a decade's worth of Blood's victims to supply the witness stand. A particularly damning letter written by Blood to Evans, his confederate, was read aloud: "Fasten your hand on the pocket of some sucker with $2,000."[29]

On January 31, 1885, the Boston jury found both Blood and Evans guilty on all charges. Blood's attorney appealed and filed every motion available, and Blood hissed and spat all the while. But on June 1 of the following year, the judge agreed with the district attorney that Blood was indeed the "Prince of Swindlers" and handed down a four-year sentence to be served in the Charlestown State Prison. He was processed in the following day.[30]

How ironic that Blood, who had spent his life ingratiating himself to others only to then fleece and flee them, was welcomed with open arms and willing hearts by the inmates of the Charlestown prison. These men were ready converts to Blood's ministry, but with nothing to give, they were the opposite of what Blood looked for in his sheep. Without money to transact, Blood dealt in information instead. He was readily admired by the most exclusive prison cliques and became fast friends with the shrewdest convicts.[31]

Of his four-year sentence, Blood served just over three. He was released early, on Thanksgiving Day, 1889, for good behavior. How fitting, for prison was probably the only construct that would ever allow Blood to model anything close to "good behavior." He lost no time in placing an ad in the Boston papers, but instead of wanting silent partners in a medical office, he sought "a young lady, under 35, with good form, fair skin, for artistic business; only those having no family complications and

The afflicted were encouraged to put their faith in self-described healers and their proprietary contraptions: "Blow into my tube, young lady, and I will cure what ails you . . ."

IMAGE FROM PAGE 274 OF *THE PHYSICIAN AND PHARMACEUTIST* (1868), PUBLIC DOMAIN, ACCESSED VIA INTERNET ARCHIVE'S FLICKR, "WOMAN BLOWING INTO CONTRAPTION, 1868."

are willing to travel need apply."[32] Luckily for them, the few women who answered the ad could not get a clear idea of the business and so moved along. One shudders to think what Blood had in mind with an explicitly unattached young woman. Though his crimes had been chiefly financial in nature, Blood had been exposed to new (i.e., bad) people and their broad (i.e., bad) ideas when in Charlestown.

Indeed, by Valentine's Day the following year in 1890—just over two months since his release—Blood was implicated in his final crime, the murder of Hiram Sawtelle. He was never concretely tied to the case, but the convicted murderer, Hiram's brother, Isaac Sawtelle, had been a bosom friend to Blood when they were both in Charlestown. Isaac was cagey in his remarks about Blood after the arrest, then tried to pin it all on Blood six months later, then recanted all and fully confessed shortly before dying in his cell six days before his execution. When processed out of prison, convicts are supposed to have experienced a personal reformation so they can become contributing members of society: Blood had indeed reformed, but to all appearances, into something worse.

Isaac Sawtelle had poisoned his niece to draw Hiram—his brother/ her father—away from the family farm, which Isaac wanted control over. When Isaac drove Hiram into the snowy New Hampshire woods to demand the controlling interest, Isaac shot Hiram three times in the back and then dismembered and decapitated the body in an attempt to hide it. Isaac had been released from Charlestown on Christmas Day of 1889, and he had murdered his brother by February 6, 1890. This is the kind of man with whom Blood had spent the past three years dealing. Blood was implicated but never pursued nor charged in the Sawtelle murder case.

Dr. C. L. Blood, M.D., did not make waves in the papers, the courts, or the prison records again for the rest of his life. A train porter had spotted him in December 1889, and he remembered Blood specifically because Blood had tried to stiff the lad on payment, even after he'd lugged Blood's zinc-lined box, labeled "TOWNSEND, M.D.," across the station.[33] A "Mr. Blood" was listed as a passenger aboard the Gate City out of Boston headed "for the sunny climate of the South" in October 1890.[34] Perhaps he had experienced a personal reformation and seen the error of his wicked ways. Perhaps he had seen the error of Isaac Sawtelle's wicked ways and reformed then. When he died in his home in New York in 1908, his obituary said little other than "he was in a manufacturing business."[35] And, indeed, he had been. What he failed to manufacture, though, was a legacy as anything other than Dr. Blood, Prince of Swindlers.

PART OF BLOOD'S RECORD.

Dr. Charles L. Blood, alias Dr. C. H. Lewis, alias half a dozen other names, and for whom the police are now anxiously looking as an al-

For all his vanity, and despite his guilt, Dr. Blood likely had little compunction with the glamourous headshots the papers so readily supplied.

SKETCH OF DR. BLOOD, FROM FEBRUARY 19, 1890, *CHICAGO INTER OCEAN*, CHICAGO, IL.

CHAPTER FOUR

The Magicians and the Princess

THE TIME: 1870–1888
THE PLACE: New York, NY
THE TAKE: $6,000–$1,000,000, a 5th Avenue Mansion, all expenses, paint supplies
THE PLAYERS: Luther R. Marsh, Esq.
                Victoria Woodhull
                Carl Hertz
                Herrmann the Great
                Justice Kilbreth
                "General" Diss Debar
                William F. Howe, Esq.
                James O'Sullivan
                Albert Bierstadt
                David Carvalho
                The Spirits
                Princess Editha Ann O'Delia Diss Debar Montez

"CARL HERTZ!" RANG OUT THE CLERK'S VOICE IN THE STIFLING COURT-room. One of the worst snowstorms New York had ever seen dumped over fifty inches of snow on the city just six weeks prior in early March, but the air in the court was thick and humid the morning of April 19, 1888. That morning, the Tombs was crowded with the most spectators heretofore seen at the court's special sessions. And this particular examination by the court was indeed special.

Slim, dapper, and fastidiously put together, Carl Hertz veritably glided to the witness stand. His thin mustache sat above pursed lips, and dark eyes betrayed nothing. He was following ribald testimony from New York Police Chief Inspector Byrnes, which had the standing-room-only crowd practically rolling in the aisles. But when Hertz was called to the stand, there was an audible gasp and his staid walk to the front of the room was met with bated breath. Composed and prim, he took the stand.

"What's your business, Mr. Hertz?" asked the prosecutor.

"I am an illusionist, magician, and conjurer. I have been in the profession eleven years."

Though "magic" was still broadly perceived as dark arts, nineteenth-century technological advances had come at such a rapid pace that science and faith were no longer strictly at odds with one another. The courtroom was thrilled to have in their presence someone who could delight both the zealous and the scientific; Hertz was a man whose deftness was so precise that it confounded the empiric and awed the faithful.

"Are you a Spiritualist?" continued the prosecutor.

"No, sir."

"Do you know anything about what is alleged to be Spiritualism?"

"I know a little about it," answer Hertz.

"Do you know anything of the trick of a communication alleged to come from the spiritual world to this?"

"I perform these tricks myself—that is, the communications are supposed to come from the spirit world."

"Is it or is it not a trick?"

"The one that I perform is."

In this response, Hertz's deftness was on full display in that he'd preemptively appealed to the secular crowd by confirming his sleights were done with a man's hand, which put the sacred set at ease by tacitly reassuring them that the divine was not giving testimony.

"Can you perform that trick now?"

"Yes."

Hertz descended from the stand to prepare and stood briefly behind a screen as the audience murmured excitedly. When he appeared from behind the screen, he was in full-on showman mode. He called out for a volunteer from the denizen to be his willing "subject," but the crowd sat on their hands. Like any professional live performer, though, Hertz had a plant. He whispered to the prosecutor, who then yelled into the room, "Is Mrs. Hertz in court?!" To this, the audience had a marked response, and their whispers reached a thrum as they gawped at the beautiful, tiny blonde woman who made her way to the stand.

With a practiced flourish, Hertz handed his lovely assistant a blank piece of paper. Mrs. Hertz confirmed the page was blank, then presiding Justice Kilbreth verbally confirmed it for the court.

"Now, fold it—once, twice, thrice. Place it upon your forehead." Hertz's commands were dutifully followed by the fetching Mrs. Hertz. With the sheet of paper pressed to her brow, Hertz announced, "Ha! I see a light, as we say amongst the Spiritualists." If Hertz had been a different kind of showman he would have cheekily winked at the defense.

Mrs. Hertz carefully unfolded the sheet once, twice, thrice, then reported the paper was no longer blank. There was writing on it.

"What is it?"

"Luther R. Marsh—Editha."

This sent a ripple of murmurs and titters through the crowd.

The prosecutor stood to ask Hertz, "Did that come from the spirit world?"

And Hertz, in Cheshire cat fashion, responded, "If I were to tell the truth, I would say no."[1,2]

In 1860, John Fallon's Stereopticon—an upgrade on the Langenheim brothers' invention at the 1851 Crystal City Exhibition—further broke ground toward moving pictures. In 1878, the legend goes that Leland Stanford famously hired Eadweard Muybridge to settle a bet, which he did in June of that year with his "Animal Locomotion" series. And by the late 1880s, New Yorkers were regularly attending glass lantern shows to be entertained, fascinated, and horrified. There were an increasing number of ways to "see" things.

Central New York State in the mid-nineteenth century was the unlikely crucible in which Mormonism, Christian Adventism, and

Spiritualism were all forged. The origins of each of these schools were wrapped up in prophecy and divine sight; Joseph Smith saw two holy figures in a grove who inspired him to devote himself to Latter-day Saints, Seventh-day Adventist forerunner Ellen White's prophecies were central to the still-forming doctrine, and the Fox Sisters began hearing bumps in the night that were credited to disembodied spirits.

Americans were spoiled for choice among gifts of sight, and each was a marvel in its own right. The irony was that with technological advances, spectators were tacitly asked to suspend disbelief while seeing more and new things; trick photos and projected images would rumble their worldview so completely as to unseat them from reality otherwise. Inversely, the sacred brands of "seeing" asked those *without* sight to double down in their belief; what they couldn't see, but were told was there, was gospel. It was "See, but Don't Believe," versus "Don't See, but Believe." This made for highly interesting and sometimes combustible configurations.

Enter: Princess Editha.

Born in Mercer County, Kentucky, about 1849, a year after Kate and Maggie Fox first heard mysterious rapping and tapping in their Hydesville, New York, farmhouse, the Princess was obstinate and crafty from an early age. She refused to let her family's humble circumstances define her; she saw herself above and apart from her genetic lineage. How she saw herself and how others saw her were at odds, so she made short work in bombastic fashion of reconciling the two.[3]

By the time she arrived in New York City in 1870, she'd brought the public up to speed. She was Princess Editha Montez, a once-secret illegitimate daughter of famed Irish dancer Lola Montez and the King of Bavaria, Ludwig I. She'd been placed with the family in Kentucky to hide her identity before she was shuttled from school to school and finally shipped off to complete a novitiate but was subjected to severe mistreatment at the hands of villainous Catholic nuns, from whom she only narrowly escaped.[4] She was the source of wonderful narratives about her time in Bavaria, Florence, and among the royal courts of Europe. She was literally larger than the average woman, and her eccentric dress was bemusing but explained away with the eccentricities that come with royal blood. She spoke a host of languages and was well-educated, but her mortal form was poor, and she suffered from violent fits.

One of the more flattering representations of the Princess.
"LITHO OF MME. DIS DEBAR," https://order-of-the-jackalope.com/wp-content/uploads/2020/03/spirit-princess.jpg.

Unfortunately—and of course—none of this was true. Her real name was Blanche, or Annie, or Claudia Solomon, and her insistence that the world see her as she saw herself had been a source of constant frustration for her family. It seems likely that she was in a convent during her youth, but with the sudden death of Mr. Solomon, she'd quit the nunnery and forsaken all attempts at the day's prescribed brand of respectability. After a spot of trouble in Dayton, Ohio, her family had been sent for, but the reply that came was that "she had given the family a great deal of trouble, and they were unable to control her," and that she was, in a word, a lunatic.[5]

Surrounding that last point was unending discussion and agita; was she crazy or clever? Were her claims delusions or designs? Just as she readily swapped her supposed pater King Ludwig of Bavaria with King Leopold of Belgium, the assessment of her mental faculties changed each day. The Ohio Commissioners of Charities did not think the Princess was at all insane, but by the following June, all of New York was debating the question.[6]

The interrogation of her sanity came when people took her out-sized claims and actions at face value. Specifically, the Princess had gotten serious mileage out of others' sympathies for her supposedly compromised constitution, as she was prone to violent fits and bleeding from her mouth. More than once she'd made a memorable first impression by arriving at a place and immediately falling to the floor and thrashing while blood poured from her lips—an act which never failed to impel ministrations, sympathy, and generosity from horrified onlookers.

Physicians were called in, and the Princess typically requested a priest, as well, should last rites be needed quickly. Being in the throes of a violent fit gave the Princess some leeway in her behavior in that her melodramatic nonsense could be ascribed to her "illness." The Princess's handy trick of sucking blood from a tooth cavity was a highly effective special effect for most observers. But as she lay in her sickbed, blood dripping from her mouth and groans, wails, and gurgles filling the air, physicians were quick to diagnose the gruesome scene as "voluntary" and "self-produced."

During the Dayton incident, the summoned priest grew so tired of her histrionics that he left and would not come back "until there was a reasonable prospect of death."[7] Legend had it that when the priest did finally return to her "death" bed, she was so agitated at being found out that she leaped to her feet, knocking over the priest and a couple of nuns for good measure, before she ran out of town with the law literally steps behind her. The truth of this can be legitimately questioned because, if for no other reason, the Princess was physically too large to run. Though this trait, too, depending on the day, could be seen as an asset—she was rotund, commanding, profound—or an indictment—corpulent, massive, fat.

Though Ohio had branded her compos mentis and undesirable the year prior, New York was debating the question in June of 1870 when the Princess gave an infamously terrible lecture at Steinway Hall on the "Equality of Women" and "The Wrongs of Her Distinguished Mother, Lola Montez." The lecture had been organized by Victoria Woodhull, Tennie C. Claflin, and Elizabeth Cady Stanton, all leaders in the woman's suffrage movement and happy to have the Princess's voice in the growing chorus for equal rights between the genders. What they got, however, was an uncomfortable improvisation that "created a decided sensation even among the stronger of the strongest-minded women present. . . . During her rambling and incoherent remarks she strutted heavily up and down the platform, her feet falling on the boards with elephantine pressure." That she chose to wear a dramatically gilded robe "designed to ape an Eastern Princess" while holding in her hand a man's broad-brimmed hat, which she dangled and swung by its chinstrap, did little to inspire confidence in the Princess's lecture. Or sanity.[8]

Before the evening in Steinway Hall, the Princess had gone to Woodhull and Claflin's newly formed, first-of-its-kind, woman-owned brokerage firm in New York to beg for a job. She marched into their offices and grabbed an accountant's ledger to demonstrate how quickly and ably she could perform sums. She was desperate and broke and said that her next stop would be a house of prostitution. Her story did not fall on deaf ears but, rather, pitying ones. Though they did not grant her employment, Woodhull had given her $5 to keep her off the streets and helped arrange the Princess's lecture, and in return, the Princess charged Woodhull with stealing $3,000 to $5,000 worth of diamonds. In rapid succession, the Princess had achieved an "in" with some of America's most powerful women, received from them charity and a platform, then flouted every one of their good graces.

The brief court proceedings were colored by embarrassment and pity; Woodhull testified, "[The Princess] was entirely lost to truth and likely to involve me and my friends; I think the girl never had a diamond or knew what a diamond was." Princess testified that her "intention was to join the firm of female brokers, and to see if Mrs. Woodhull was the woman she represented herself to be . . . she urged me to do something by which

I could make money; I told her she had begun as a clairvoyant, but that I had no such gift, no such foresight." The Princess's own attorney, William F. Howe, didn't even show up but instead sent a letter to the presiding justice that he was declining to represent the Princess and her mental condition, and appealed to the justice's chivalry and pity instead. The case was dismissed that day, and the Princess was given over for assessment.[9]

By the end of that same week, though, she'd been declared "perfectly sane" and released.[10]

And by the end of 1870, she had given at least one more disastrous lecture, this time in an oversized muslin frock with a wreath of flowers on the front and an unidentifiable foreign medal hanging from one shoulder. She pontificated on "The Proper Sphere of Woman," which she forcefully announced was "home." Victoria Woodhull was not in attendance this time.[11]

On the heels of her latest wave-making appearance, the Princess's mouth started bleeding (again). In early December, she was admitted to the hospital for treatment. Her rerelease back into the unwelcome jaws of New York society loomed, so she did everything she could to prolong her stay. When her physicians caught wise to her bleeding-cavity trick, she set fire to her mattress and assaulted the physicians, stabbing a medical student in the process. By the end of the month, she was declared "hopelessly insane" and committed to the insane asylum on Blackwell's Island, just as she'd planned.[12]

———

At 166 Madison Avenue stood a stately mansion, over three stories high. Inside was a cavernous library, numerous studies, apartments, and a seemingly endless string of well-appointed rooms lined with books, papers, and oversized paintings. It had been the home of Luther R. Marsh, venerated New York lawyer, onetime partner to Daniel Webster, and current chairman of the New Parks Commission that was overseeing the creation of the Bronx, Van Cortlandt, and Pelham Bay Parks. It was Marsh's books and paintings and mahogany furniture that filled those Madison Avenue rooms in 1888 and Marsh's servants who stalked the halls, and Marsh himself was a resident. But the house was not his. It wasn't even really still a house; it was the "Temple of Spirits," and the doors had locks.

Lawyer Marsh was a fast-aging man of seventy years in 1888, but he was spry. He was a lifelong antiquarian and classicist and revered ancient minds, deceased for thousands of years. Aristotle, Socrates, Appius, Plato, and Cicero had been his steadfast companions as he deftly maneuvered the law and clumsily managed emotion. For Marsh's world had been rocked by the death of his beloved wife of over forty years in August of 1887, and only his truest friends could offer him solace. Fortunately, he'd been found in his hour of need by someone who could find him comfort.

Marsh was immensely wealthy, an abolitionist, and a Swedenborgian. He was not a Spiritualist but rather someone who saw the divine through interpreting what lay around him and the observable world's potential for being made sacred when seen with the correct vision. He believed people were spirits wrapped in a mortal coil, and their choices would

The honorable Luther R. Marsh, pre-Princess.
LUTHER R. MARSH, FROM *SPIRIT-ISM, HYPNOTISM AND TELEPATH AS INVOLVED IN THE CASE OF MRS. LEONORA E. PIPER AND THE SOCIETY OF PSYCHICAL RESEARCH* (1902), RETRIEVED FROM THE INTERNET ARCHIVE'S FLICKR.

make manifest a tailor-made heaven or hell once they were through with this plane of existence. Marsh believed in God and in what he could see with his own eyes. With Ann O'Delia Diss Debar, he got both; it was a two-for-one.[13]

In 1880, shortly after Ann had given birth to her second child, she and her babies and a servant girl moved into furnished rooms in an apartment on Leroy Street. Mr. Diss Debar was away on business, more often than not. After a few months of domestic peace when Ann was confined to these rooms as she recovered from giving birth, she sought a diversion in the form of a séance—a wildly popular entertainment curiosity at the moment. After attending the clasped-hands meeting, she returned home, and disturbances began just a few hours later.

There was the sound of violent banging as if someone were repeatedly knocking against the bedstead with a heavy stick. A cup whizzed across the room. A small porcelain bell levitated to the ceiling, ringing on its own. A ball was thrown so forcefully that it tore the carpet where it landed. A disembodied hand moved and shook pictures on the wall. The Leroy Street apartment was beset by a highlight reel of some of the most notorious signifiers of a classic "unseen presence."

Poor Ann was made quite ill by the whole affair. The family physician, macabrely referred to as "Coroner Knox," was sent for and held a consultation with another doctor. While there, they heard the knockings and rapping and banging that had so frayed Ann's delicate nerves. The physicians determined that Mrs. Diss Debar was suffering from hysteria, but they were flummoxed by her repeated fits and the blood that poured freely from her mouth. Everyone was much concerned for Mrs. Diss Debar.

But the occurrences continued: "The noise was like as if a person had struck heavy blows on the floor with a stout stick. A teacup was thrown across the room and narrowly escaped striking [a witness] in the face!" said the shocked proprietor of a neighboring liquor store to a *New York Herald* reporter. And a priest from a local parish gave his earnest account: "As I was going into the room I heard the bell tingling, and as I was crossing the threshold it was dashed at my feet. It is also true that I saw white wings floating in the air, near the ceiling. I have witnessed these things myself, with my own eyes. . . . I am simply telling the truth—just what I saw with my own eyes."[14]

The disturbances and their persistence made quite the news item. Ann's mysterious circumstances were broadcast across the country. Oh, to be beset with notoriety when already afflicted! Poor Ann could barely keep up with the interview requests, let alone in an evidently haunted apartment. Additionally, Ann was feeling much better now; her massive mortal form recovered almost as quickly and miraculously as the spirits had arrived at her sad apartment. So, she moved herself and her family to nicer lodgings. Through moving, perhaps, it could be better determined whether the occurrences were surrounding the apartment or Ann herself.

The family left the Leroy Street apartment with their belongings. Only one item was left behind: "a pasteboard tube with a wooden slat attached, which [Ann] utilized during her illness for summoning her nurse, served also as a prestidigitorial wand in the manufacture of 'spirit rappings.' Last Sunday evening, Mrs. Debar attended a spiritualistic séance, and the ghostly performances began immediately upon her return home. Comment is unnecessary." Though the Debars had left in haste in apparent distress over the disturbances, not everyone agreed on the nature of their motives.[15]

Over the following years, the disembodied noises, levitations, and mysteries dogged Ann O'Delia Diss Debar and manifested at practically every place she stayed. The sudden onset of spiritual sensitivity was permanent, it seemed. The family moved constantly, but the aggressive spirits invariably presented manifestations within days of arrival. Their lives were so consumed by the manifestations that they could not stay in one place for any significant length of time, nor make any money, apparently, since they were constantly broke and sponging off their hosts.

Sometimes, the spirits were so moved by Ann's circumstances on the corporeal plane that they would intercede on her behalf in tricky situations. When Ann complained that her (then) landlady, Mrs. Florence Mayo of the Imperial Hotel, was insane and a danger, the spirits let loose their frustration on Mrs. Mayo in the form of her belongings being stolen, the gas pipes in her rooms mysteriously breaking and leaking, and a chair being violently hurled down a flight of stairs. The two women had come to blows and were soon in court. The presiding justice heard their stories, and then asked of the complainant, "Do you believe in spiritualism, Mrs. Debar?"

"I believe in spiritual manifestations. My beliefs are that—"

The justice had heard enough. He interrupted Ann mid-statement with, "One moment . . . The case is dismissed." The justice, it seemed, was not in the mood to split hairs over seeing and believing.

A week later, Ann's litigious attempt to forestall eviction from Mrs. Mayo being unsuccessful, the Debars were facing homelessness again. Ann made one final plea to Mrs. Mayo on the eve of her eviction, which Mrs. Mayo recounted as: "I told her I had had enough of her. Then the old tricks began again. The burner was wrenched off a gas pipe, and the room rapidly filled with gas. I thought we would all be killed by an explosion. Mrs. Diss Debar and her children went out just about this time. Again, when I went into a dark room one night, I saw an unearthly light in a corner, and something struck me and I fainted. I have felt a strange sensation in my face and side since, and I have been told that I was probably stuck with a sandbag."[16] Ann's spirits sometimes moved in violent and not altogether mysterious ways.

When they weren't assaulting her mortal enemies, Ann's spirits began exhibiting their artistic flair. It is unclear whether the spirits' artistry revealed itself before or after Ann began holding sittings with some of New York's painters, but the spirits' paintings started appearing regularly after Ann's marriage to Joseph Diss Debar, who, at one time, was known as a decidedly sub-par painter of landscapes. But in 1881, the pictures were coming apace with the three daily séances the corpulent Mrs. Debar was hosting. "[Albert] Bierstadt has one of these [paintings], one of the more ambitious ones, of which the artistic merit is small but the creation a marvel, for which he would not accept a thousand dollars." Beauty—and cash value—were in the eye of the beholder, and Ann seemed to know her market. This was not the last meeting between Ann and Bierstadt, but it was certainly the most lucrative.[17]

And to this end, when among more elite members of New York's society, Ann would drop her guard and trust them with a secret she knew would make the hair on the back of their necks stand straight up: she was not a fat, lowly family woman but instead a royal-of-unusual-size, and they should call her "Princess Editha."

Yes—*shocking* as it might be—Ann O'Delia Diss Debar was actually Princess Editha Montez, who was actually Annie, or Blanche, or Claudia Solomon. She fed them this delicious secret but kept the meat of the matter to herself. She never mentioned her stint in the asylum on Blackwell's Island, nor the calculated assault on the physicians there, nor the fact that by the time she was released, the attendant—the one she'd stabbed—was so in her thrall that he married her. In reality, Mr. Diss Debar was her third husband, at the very least. But whatever facts and figures she kept to herself were in service of the larger narrative of how she wanted to be seen. And by whom.

By coloring herself the "Artists' Medium," Princess helped shape the makeup of her most ardent sitters. As one reporter aptly wrote,

Among practical business men such impalpable truths or untruths as this weird philosophy presents make slow headway or none at all; but in this crowd of speculative thinkers, who are always ready to see a shade of probability and plausibility in the totally impossible, the occult sciences . . . have cast their spell without a doubt. For this reason Mrs. Debar found an audience and a support the moment she showed herself possessed of supernatural powers.[17]

Princess made herself the sole means by which people could get a glimpse of something that might reinforce their belief in the unseen. She was the "thin" veil between this vale of tears and beyond.

Her audiences were artists, spiritualists, members of high society, and skeptics, and with only a few persons overlapping in all categories, her act was at less risk of being universally debunked.[18] For it was bunk. There was panache and style and creativity, but hers was a show, make no mistake. Whether she tended to have genuine insight into the human spirit ultimately does not matter because that is not what she was selling. The Princess was there to reaffirm beliefs in the unseen by providing evidence through objective methods that were actually rooted in subjectivity. Whatever a person needed from the spirit world, the Princess would help him find.

Lawyer Luther R. Marsh needed soothing and stimulation. His heart was heavy with loss, and his mind ached for the inimitable solemn profundity of his beloved ancients. A close friend of his, John O'Sullivan, onetime Minister to Portugal and coiner of "Manifest Destiny," became an ardent Spiritualist after the death of his mother. He'd found solace through mediums and was one of Princess's most vocal champions. He published a flowery letter of introduction and praise for her gifts in *The Banner of Light* in 1885, wherein he classed her a set apart from other mediums of the day thanks to her artistic bent. He saw the divine in the paintings and slate etchings that materialized from her sittings. He introduced his friend, Marsh, to Princess out of pity for the former and awe for the latter.

What was it that was so impressive about these paintings? Just why had New York City lost its grip on logic in the face of this oversized charlatan? Her method, though imperfect, was indeed impressive when well in hand. As was related in the *Narragansett Times*, a curious party sought out Mrs. Debar by way of Mr. O'Sullivan, who was only too happy to bring Princess another disciple to testify to her gifts. When the men arrived at Princess's current place, she was just finishing up with another sitter who was on his way out the door, a freshly got spirit picture clutched to his breast and amazed wonder in his eye.

Princess, apparently, had not been expecting O'Sullivan and his uninitiated companion and was far too busy to make another appointment.

"For two or three days my time is fully taken up and I cannot say when I could give you a sitting," said Mrs. Debar/Princess Editha/Annie Solomon.

"Could you not now?" asked the caller in a lilting brogue, dulled by over two decades in America. He had sought her out because he was genuinely receptive but did all he could to retain an air of objectivity.

Princess looked him straight in the eyes for a moment before saying, "I don't know." In her moment's pause, perhaps she was doing a mental cost/benefit analysis on holding an unanticipated reading for someone on the arm of her unofficial spokesman, Mr. O'Sullivan. Perhaps she was mentally assessing the strength of the spirit vibrations at that moment.

An inspirational poster for crusading spiritualists with a prescient sign-off: "It is but a step, from the Sublime Natural, or Spiritual state, to the ridiculous, or Dog eat Dog state of Society."

Perhaps she was running low on oil paints. Whatever her reason, the implication of her "I don't know" was that she was the pipe through which the spirits flowed, not the pump, and further tacit confirmation to the sitters that the unseen, the immaterial, was the real power at work. The men's credulity was suitably coddled, and the three repaired to Princess's séance room.

The room was well-lit, with sunshine pouring through the curtains. The men sat in chairs with well-worn grooves, and Princess walked across the room to a table where lay a blank mounted canvas. The frame was maybe six by nine inches, and the canvas was stretched taut. Walking back to her patron and his uninvited guest, she placed the frame, canvas facing up, on the latter's head and directed, "Let that rest there." The man used one hand to steady the frame and keep it perched in place while Princess walked backward to the other side of the room, ten or twelve feet. She stood by the wall with her gaze fixed on the man, ostensibly looking for spirits. Her intense stare might have been for those who'd passed on, but the living in the room were drawn in like moths to an ethereal flame. "I see a light over the frame," she said in a clear, even voice after half a minute or so.

Princess returned to the man and placed the frame so that it was resting on his right knee, canvas side up, and instructed him to keep his hand over it, as if feeling the heat from a cooking pot that'd been warming on the stove. His hand above the canvas, Princess began pacing the room on the wall opposite the man, her steps even and measured.

"I hear the name of Mary called; that is for you." She stared intently at the man as he mentally leafed through his memory bank's address book. Mary . . . Mary . . . there'd been no "Marys" since he'd left Scotland, bidding his last farewell to Cousin Mary on her deathbed, who wanted nothing but good things to come to the man in America. "I once had a cousin named Mary who died years ago," the man offered.

"That is she," confirmed the Princess, "and your guardian spirit is with her." The man was breathless.

"K----, and B----" she called out, maintaining eye contact with the man. He returned her gaze but did not know the names. Helpfully, tragically, Mr. O'Sullivan chimed in that those were the names of dearly departed friends of his, to which the man disappointedly remarked that "matters are getting mixed up." Crossed wires, as it were. Princess encouraged her champion to move his chair from his companion, but Mr. O'Sullivan was not willing to risk interfering with Princess's ability to manifest her gift, so he left the room, the hall, the house to wait in a park across the street. Hopefully, the spirits would positively respond with a little more breathing room.

The man and Princess were alone. She began pacing again, the man still seated and looking at her expectantly.

"Elizabeth," she called out.

The man thought for a moment before saying, "No."

"No?" asked Princess, a little surprised.

"No."

She furrowed her broad brow in thought a brief moment before eagerly shouting, "Bess ... Bessie! Bessie was related to Mary."

A brief flash of recognition was in the man's face as he asked, "Bettie?"

"Yes, Bettie!" she confirmed.

"Aunt Bettie was Mary's mother," he informed Princess, who grinned.

"Annie ..." she called out. And with the man's nod of approval, continued, "Willie. . . . Annie and Willie?"

"These were my parents' names," confirmed the man.

"Is it possible?" The Princess, apparently very impressed with her abilities that day.

In a flurry of movement, she came directly to the man and grabbed from him the canvas resting on his knee. "We can get nothing this way," she said in exasperation, then wiped the face of the canvas hard with her open hand, as if to brush off any unseen residual gossamer. "Rest this on your head with the frame to your forehead and the canvas facing out," she commanded. She handed the frame back to the man who, before putting the frame to his head, wiped the canvas with his hand, as Princess had done.

She placed a small hand mirror on the man's chair, just beside him. "What's that for?"

"I will tell you by and by." Princess's eagerness had melted into showmanship. She returned to pacing the room with her measured, even steps, all the while staring at the man sitting before her with a blank canvas on his head and a mirror beside him. Perhaps the showmanship was the only way to suppress her giggles at what surely was a ridiculous sight.

After a few minutes, she told the man to hold the mirror up so that he could see the reflection of the canvas.

"Do you see anything on the canvas?"

A brief moment passed, but then the man breathlessly said, "Yes." There was something cloudy appearing in the center of the canvas.

"What color?" she asked.

"It seems light brown."

"They are working," said the Princess contentedly. She let another minute pass, staring at the man, before she instructed him to raise the mirror again, which he did. "What do you see?!" she asked with barely contained excitement.

"Why, I see the picture of a female form, seemingly painted in oil, but incomplete." From the muddy brown blotches was revealed the torso and head of a young woman.

"Good! Keep it still on your head," Princess exclaimed.

Another minute passed with the man in the chair holding a blurry brown picture to his skull. For the final time, she asked him to use the trusty mirror. In the reflected image, he could see the arms and hands had appeared and the female form was unmistakable. "It is completed," announced the Princess in satisfied tones.

The man took the frame from his head and beheld it in wonder. The clouds of brown had arranged themselves into a picture of a woman. He touched the surface, and it was tacky, and the smell from the oil paints was strong and fresh. He gaped in amazement.

After a moment of staring at the miracle painting, the man remarked in a distinctly disappointed tone, "That is not Mary's picture."

"No," cut in the Princess oh-so-helpfully, "that is your guardian spirit; Mary was with her."

"You have not given me Mary's family name," the man said flatly.

"No, I have not got it yet." The Princess considered a moment, as if listening to the air, then pronounced, "Mary was laid in the kirk yard far across the sea three decades . . . three decades and a half ago. She is high up in spirit life. She suffered much and was purified by it."

The man did some mental math. "Yes, it is thirty-five years and more since Mary died."

"Yes, more than that," agreed Princess. After one more meaningful pause, she called out, "Mary Drysdale."

"Yes. Mary Drysdale was her name." The man slumped a little as he said it, exhausted from the excitement of having his past reach out to him. The still-fresh painting on his lap, he then thought of Mr. O'Sullivan waiting patiently though breathlessly in the park. He was fetched.

When he returned, the man went to unlock the door to the room to let Mr. O'Sullivan into the sanctum studio. The two met at the door and pored over the painting. The man wondered aloud how he would protect the painting when taking it home. In a moment, a large slate was brought to which the frame could be strapped, thereby protecting the sacred painting. The man turned the slate over to inspect it, and seeing it was unmarked, he laid it against the canvas. As he was handling the picture of the woman, he dejectedly confided in Mr. O'Sullivan, "I wish it had been Mary's."

Princess appeared with some brown paper in which to wrap the precious cargo and helped the man secure it. With the package safely wrapped and placed on the table, the men returned to their chairs. The Princess was standing apart from them, looking over the room when she said in clear, even tones, "I see a light over the package." She joined the men at the table.

The Princess took hold of one end of the package and clamped it between her fingers and thumbs. She asked the man to do the same with the remaining corners, and Mr. O'Sullivan placed his fingers along one side of the brown paper package, tied up with string. The three sat motionless with their fingers on the package, planchette-style. After a minute a faint scratching was heard, as if someone were using a tool to cut into the slate that had been so carefully wrapped. Short scratches, and then long, and then faint taps. For nearly two minutes the trio sat without moving, the slate scratches echoing through the room. The men were transfixed and only roused when three raps came from the package, as if to indicate "I'm all done."

"It is finished," announced the satisfied Princess. "Open it, but examine the package and see if there is any break in the paper." The man complied. He inspected the unbroken paper before removing it to look upon the slate.

"There is nothing there," he said sadly.

"No, it must be on the inside."

The man took the slate and turned it over, and over, and over again. Not a single mark.

"What meant the cutting we heard?" he asked, logically.

"Put them together again!" said Princess, almost manic with eagerness.

The man replaced the slate on the painting, and the three took hold with their fingers, as before. Almost as soon as they touched the painting/slate, three raps were again heard. Princess withdrew her fingers and Mr. O'Sullivan his.

"Finished," the Princess announced as she leaned back in her chair, most satisfied.

The man raised the slate from the canvas and turned it over, and there, on the slate face that had been touching the painting, was an etching of a female form in long, flowing robes. She held a torch aloft in one hand and pointed to the side of the frame with the other. Underneath the figure was a simple engraving, "Mary D."

The man was astonished. Speechless. In awe and abject wonderment. He stared at Princess as if he were staring into the face of an angel just stepped down from Heaven to walk amongst mortals.[19]

Such was the power of Princess Editha Montez Ann O'Delia Diss Debar Claudia Solomon when her method was perfected; she brought men to their knees in gratitude for her gifts and for giving them the proof they so desperately sought that what they believed, though unseen, was as real and tangible as the spirit-hewn art they now held in their hands.

When Mr. O'Sullivan brought the man to the Princess's sanctum, it was likely Luther R. Marsh they met in her hall, gripping his just-received painting as a sacred treasure. He would have been on his way to his office downtown, having made the trip to see his preferred seeress first thing. For all Princess's artistic-cum-spiritual prowess, it was the inexplicable thrall into which men were drawn that was her true power. Luther Marsh was thus transfixed.

He believed in the Princess completely, whole-heartedly. His legal reputation was nigh unassailable, but his devotion to the Princess was questioned; from the outside looking in, all signs pointed to Marsh being taken advantage of. Whatever Marsh saw in the Princess was not outwardly visible to everyone else. Their concern was evident, though.

A year after he crossed O'Sullivan's path in Princess's foyer, Marsh was at his home—now called the Temple of Spirits—talking to a *New York Times* reporter who was there to better understand the household's unconventional operations. Just two days prior, on March 29, 1888, an item was telegraphed to *Dispatches* around the country: "The Mrs. Debar, who as a spiritualist medium has obtained such influence over the prominent lawyer Luther R. Marsh, as to lead him to think that Phidias and Raphael, are producing masterpieces in his house, claims to be a daughter of [Lola] Montez. It was learned yesterday that she has procured from Mr. Marsh, a deed to her of some valuable city property."[20] The property in question was his house at 166 Madison Avenue, which had lately been dubbed Temple of Spirits, and was now home to Marsh, Princess, Mr. Diss Debar, and the two children. His eccentricities notwithstanding, this was an unusual home life for the aged lawyer. That the property had been deeded to the Princess was revealed by Marsh himself in a letter he'd written to the press to extol the rare and wonderful gifts of his Princess, who had been readily supplying Marsh with paintings "done" by Raphael, Michelangelo, Rubens, and Rembrandt. She'd also communed with lettered spirits and had gotten Marsh reams of correspondence from Queen Elizabeth, President Abraham Lincoln, and seventeenth-century religious liberal Anne Hutchinson. Marsh announced his plan to hold an illustrated lecture at Chickering Hall on April 1, wherein he would show projected images of the marvelous paintings before inviting the woman of the hour to the lectern.

There were questions, both furtive and point-blank, surrounding Marsh's sanity and reporters were clamoring for insight. When Marsh greeted the *Times* reporter the day before his lecture, he clapped him on the shoulder and brayed, "Do I look like an insane man?! I know that I am not insane, and that I have been enabled to see the great and holy truth through the mediumship of that divine woman, Mme. Diss

Debar. . . . What do I care for the talk of a rabble of reporters! They are unbelievers, and for that reason should never have been sent here to deal with these holy truths. They are materialists, and cannot understand spiritual manifestations." In one breath, Marsh had tacitly asked, "Do You See What I See?," and answered, "You Can't!" How, then, could the reporter—let alone the world!—convince Marsh that what he was being shown was not the whole picture?

Over the course of the rest of the interview, Marsh held forth on his collection of spirit paintings and spirit writings. When handed a black-and-white portrait of his deceased father-in-law, recently completed by "the Spirits," the reporter asked for a photograph to compare the likeness. Marsh had no photo but, instead, an engraving that had once appeared in a magazine and was now prominently displayed in the house. Except for the flowing robes the figure now donned—the prescribed dress for the spirit plane, apparently—the painted image was an exact copy of the engraving, though very poorly executed.

"Could this engraving have been obtained at any time by anyone in the house?" asked the reporter.

"Certainly!" declared Marsh. "Ah, yes, I see; you are trying to find out if Mme. Diss Debar could have been practicing fraud upon me. You are like all the rest—skeptical. That holy woman does not need to use subterfuge, for her gift is divine, and these works from heaven, the product of an art that is now all holy." *Credo igitur sunt*: I believe, therefore they are. Marsh's bulwark of credulity could not be breached, it seemed. The reporter continued to press Marsh on Princess's methods, but this only expedited the conclusion of the interview.

As the reporter was leaving Marsh in his study, brimming with spirit pictures, the doorbell jangled. "Don't let in another reporter!" he shouted down the stairs. But the man at the door was identified as one of Marsh's colleagues from the New Parks Commission, so Marsh quickly shouted, "Oh, let him in by all means!" The distinguished gentleman entered and stood just inside the front door.

Marsh, from the landing near his study, shouted, "Hello, George, old man! I'm mighty glad to see you. Come to see if I'm crazy, eh? Hah! Do I look like it?!" With this, Marsh mounted the banister like an impish boy and slid halfway down the stairs, the wood groaning and creaking with the friction from his pants. He alit halfway down and rushed to shake his visitor's hand with aggressive cordiality.

The reporter made to exit the madhouse—er, mad Temple—but was met by Princess in the door. She was curt and brusque and gave him a metonymic dressing-down for the entire Fourth Estate. How dare he print such unkindnesses about her! She was the proud daughter of King Ludwig, as sure as the sun was shining!

That very moment a cloud passed in front of the sun and cloaked the Princess in shadow. The Princess and the reporter regarded each other in the darkness. She tittered nervously before saying, "It's still shining behind the cloud, you know." She returned to the Temple to work on the evening's lecture.[21]

From their first appearance in 1880 on Leroy Street, through her time at the Temple of Spirits on Madison Avenue in 1888, the Princess's spirits would reliably manifest for her at séances and against her enemies. For nearly a decade, she fascinated and bemused New York society with her marvels, making her a polarizing figure, to say the least. She demanded to be taken seriously and would erupt at those who dared question her motives or credentials.

An early supporter, Bierstadt, had since recanted his support. He'd attended her séances willingly and readily. But at one sitting, when the lights were low and the room waited expectantly for the spirits to reveal their talents on a blank canvas, Bierstadt was seated across from a mirror. Not a small one provided by the Princess, as she'd done for O'Sullivan's guest, but a mirror hung on the wall. Bierstadt saw in the mirror's reflection Princess quickly swap the blank canvas with a painted one from hidden panels in the wall. He smiled to himself and said to the other sitters, "It was rather hard on us rising artists to compel us to compete with Raphael and Michael Angelo."[22] To this, Princess had rejoined, "If Albert Bierstadt does not stop talking about me I'll tell something about him that will hurt him. . . . He never amounted to anything until I had his pictures finished for him by the great masters now in the spirit land."[23]

The spirits' ostensible posterity was no match for Princess's bitterness, and poor Bierstadt that he should need such divine help to make his paintings good! One skeptic had made a lasting impression indeed when, as Princess refused to pay her wages, the young servant girl left her mark by driving the point of an umbrella through one of Princess's paintings and sneering, "Just let the spooks mind that, now."[24]

With doubters, naysayers, and skeptics out in full force, the night of the lecture arrived. And just like her infamous lecture on "Woman's Sphere" back in 1870, this one was a spectacular failure and did little to assuage fears that lawyer Marsh had lost his sense. On April 1, 1888, Chickering Hall was thick with looky-loos.

Marsh took the stage once the hall was filled (and it was filled) to make his presentation on "Spirit Paintings." He was flanked by some of his most prized portraits: Shakespeare, Rembrandt, Adelaide Neilson, and Lola Montez. They were there as proof to the audience and as silent pillars of support for the much-bedraggled Marsh. Images of his other portraits were to be projected onto a white screen. The Princess and her entourage were just off stage.

The lecture went smoothly on the whole. The audience was a queer combination of devout spiritualists, esteemed businessmen, rabble-rousers, and policemen. There developed a kind of call-and-response in that whatever Marsh asserted was given vociferous support from his friends shouting "True!" or "Downright fact!" Then the hecklers would cackle and bray. One man laughed so hard and so long that a reporter wondered if he'd taken laughing gas (Oxygenized Air, perhaps?), but whatever the cause, the man's course cachinnations were contagious, and the hoi polloi followed suit. Marsh continued: "If we here tonight are men and women of this world, in this house, if this is a world, if this is a house, if we are not all myths, impalpable, intangible, if I am not a shadow addressing shadows merely, if anything is anything and anybody anybody, then are these phenomena actually, real, genuine, bona fide, true and proved by the same evidence." Whatever weight his tautological ontology might have commanded was quickly diminished when the images were projected.

The projected images, though imperfect, were accurate enough to capture the poorly rendered likenesses which, when accompanied by

Marsh's earnest narration, rendered the scene perfectly absurd. "Rembrandt by Raphael: Raphael by Rembrandt, gentlemen—one painted by the other and the other painted by the one! . . . This is St. Augustine dictating to a reporter or stenographer a thirty-page communication which he sent me! . . . Artists tell me that this head of David cannot be equaled, but they are not accomplished like my friends the reporters! . . . Apelles, my own friend, the artist of Philip of Macedonia, for whom Alexander the Great would pose, and to nobody else, gave me these five medallion pictures. . . . Another painter of the ancients, Polygnotus." Whether this list of impressive names registered with the audience was impossible to determine over the roars of laughter.

The coup de grâce came with a projected image of a thirty-year-old woman who Marsh described as his deceased wife's elder sister who had died over seventy-five years ago. At the age of six. Cue the laugh track.

"What age was she?" screamed the audience.

"Six. She's grown up since she died."

"What age, sir, did you say?" The audience was getting their money's worth.

"SIX. What's the matter?" asked Marsh, weary of japery.

"Oh, nothing. You're all right."

"Oh! I thought I had said or done something to make myself ridiculous. Well . . ."

Just as Marsh's argument that the paintings were real because he saw them and he was real, the evening was absurd because the audience behaved as such, and they, too, were absurd.

The lady of the evening was called for—"Diss Debar! Let's see Madame!"—and Marsh gestured to Princess, calling her to the lectern. When she stepped on the stage she cast a dramatically withering eye over the wags in the crowd. She puffed out her chest and steeled herself as Marsh introduced her. "Madame Diss Debar. If she's a fraud, she's a big one." There was raucous laughter. Poor Marsh, apparently too sane to know a joke when he made one.

If the crowd had been expecting a demonstration or an explanation or any information whatsoever from the Princess, they were sorely disappointed. She did put on a good show, though, by berating every reporter in the room, some by name. She excoriated their attempts to undermine her gifts and balked at insistent cries for a demonstration. Had the crowd not been buoyed with cheer from Marsh's comical opening act, the Madame might have withered, but their gleeful scorn only made her mad.

She was on stage for mere minutes to deliver her screed and summarily wrapped things up by offering sittings to any and all skeptics, but that it would cost them from $250 to $5,000.[25]

Marsh and the Princess left that lecture with bruised egos and inflamed ire. The world was refusing to understand the rare access to divinity they'd been granted through Princess's gifts. What philistines! There were a few clarion calls among the doubters' din, though, and they came from a logical though wholly unexpected quarter: magicians.

The gall and bile from the Temple of Spirits were palpably roiling and did little to silence the doubters' chorus. "Just show us so that we may see," was asked of the medium a thousand times in a thousand different ways, but she had little incentive to give them what they wanted. "You cannot see because you do not believe," was essentially her cheeky response. This logical fallacy would not work on magicians, though, for their art was predicated on the audience *not* wanting to see because they already knew the truth that what they were shown was fiction.

The two weeks following their disastrous appearance at Chickering Hall in April of 1888, were an absolute furor for the Princess, her accomplices, and old Marsh. By April 4, New York's leading wizard, Professor Herrmann, issued a challenge for the Princess to appear on the same stage as he, whereupon he would perform her spirit painting trick as well as, if not better than, she could. If he failed in this he would donate $1,000 to charity. If she was deceiving the provenance of the portraits and Herrmann could detect her method, she would have to hand him $1,000 on the spot. "I will do all the woman does, and will show her to be a humbug. I can produce all the phenomens of spiritualism. . . . I can make pictures appear and disappear and bring up celebrities on call. . . . If madame shows me her method I will repeat it."[26]

Professional rivalries were baked into the professional magician's livelihood—arguably a central tenet as it was unrivaled in generating

One of Herrmann the Great's greater advertising posters.
"HERRMANN THE GREAT CO. 3RD ANNUAL TOUR OF THE HERRMANN THE GREAT . . ." ADVERTISING POSTER, 1898, LIBRARY OF CONGRESS, PRINTS & PHOTOGRAPHS DIVISION, LC-USZC4-13441 (COLOR FILM COPY TRANSPARENCY OF TOP) LC-USZC4-13442 (COLOR FILM COPY TRANSPARENCY OF BOTTOM), http://loc.gov/pictures/resource/var.1972/.

ticket sales—and in the spring of 1888, both Professor Herrmann and Carl Hertz were presenting the latest illusion out of Paris. "Le Cocon" began with an empty wire frame suspended above the stage, and the illusionist then drew a leaf on a papered side of the frame. The illusionist would utter his magic words while standing apart from the frame as the paper leaf burst open to reveal an outsized chrysalis. The chrysalis, two feet in diameter, then elegantly opened and a grown woman would emerge garbed in shiny silks with a set of fully metamorphosed wings on her back.[27] Hertz and Herrmann were already battling over who had a better version of the woman who was not-as-she-seemed but paused their public vendetta to expose the pretending Princess. A gauntlet had been publicly thrown such that the Princess, barring legitimate spirit powers and physical manifestations, was guaranteed an ignominious exposure by at least one magician. Still, the Princess haughtily accepted Herrmann's challenge—his astute marketing had piqued her interest, so she called an agent.

Not just any agent but one of the foremost theatrical booking men in America, James W. Randolph. She called him to the Temple to arrange terms for the gangbuster tour she envisioned. Their one meeting covered an impressive amount of ground, but the gist was that, on April 4, Princess and Randolph signed a contract for a three-month engagement of exhibitions at Randolph's discretion, all proceeds to be divided equally after costs.[28] Standard stuff. To keep the marketing machine well ginned up, a response to Herrmann's challenge, now set for April 8, was drafted and signed and Randolph immediately began to make arrangements for his newfound cash cow.

By April 6, Princess had pulled out. She was mercurial and her temper was volcanic, but this was breakneck vacillating. Herrmann was unruffled and vowed to perform Princess's tricks anyway, at some future date. Randolph was less understanding. So incensed was he that the following day, April 7, his repudiation of the Princess made headlines and only further bolstered her doubters' suspicions that she was not what she said but exactly as she seemed.

Randolph's one tour of the Temple was enlightening, to say the least. Princess led him through the massive brownstone, pointing out Marsh's extensive collection of pictures and baubles, many of which had since been claimed for the Temple. Over the course of their tour, they discussed business.

"Now you are my manager and confidential man," Princess said imperiously to Randolph, who was no slouch but was also susceptible to wiles. "How do you like the looks of my house?" she asked while broadly gesturing to the Marsh mansion.

"It is a fine establishment. You are a fly mug to work a man as smart as Marsh for such a big prize." Randolph—her confidential man—quickly slipped into the street vernacular common among showbiz types and crooks.

His hushed tones and smart slang let Princess know she was okay to let her tongue wag: "I can give you fellows with sawdust on your feet pointers on working soft snaps. Before the end of April I will have $150,000 more, and you are in with it."

"Do you mean to say that I am in with all your work out of Marsh?" Randolph asked, trying to wrap his head around the scope of the scheme he was undertaking with the massive medium.

"If you will work with me, and as I want you to, I will divide every dollar. Do you understand me?" Princess was clear in her terms as the tour continued upstairs. It came out in court that Princess made "a little love" to Randolph that afternoon. Confidential man, indeed![29]

"There are too many in this picture business. It will all go up in a balloon before long. But we have got a new scheme I am working on, and it is this marble business. Did you ever hear of it? I have got $3,000 out of Kidd for restoration of a finger [which she'd broken]. I do not intend to let even my husband know anything about how it is done. You are the only man that can ever know how to do it."

Randolph pressed her, his client, to answer Herrmann's challenge and showed her a draft response that he characterized as a "bluff" and added, "We'll give New York a 'rip up the back' and skip." He was all in.

"That's it; you are a daisy [a compliment]. Make any bluffs you choose, only get me out of it. I am in your hands. Do as you please with me, but look out for Marsh. He believes it is all genuine and must be worked gently. He is pretty fly, and we can't afford to make any mistakes where he is concerned; besides, he is our star." This statement alone, in the wrong hands, would have done her in. She must have been very confident in the many skills she showed Randolph that afternoon.

To make money on the venture once Marsh was bled dry, or dead, they considered an exhibition of the spirit paintings that would require a great deal more paintings than the seventy-five currently stashed around the Temple. This concerned Randolph.

"Oh, I can have as many as you want."

At this, Princess led Randolph back to the upstairs hall, and then to a second, smaller hall that had a partially obscured, barely noticeable door. Without knocking, she turned the knob and opened the door so Randolph could see inside.

Seated at an easel in a tiny room filled from floor to ceiling with canvas, paints, paper, unmarked bottles of various chemicals, brushes, notebooks, slates, and pencils, was Mr. Diss Debar. He was dwarfed by the ridiculous portraits of the dead in flowing robes whose poorly painted eyes followed Mr. Debar around the room as if to say, "Let us rest."

Debar hissed when the door opened and launched a string of epithets at Princess for disturbing his work, let alone opening the door for a stranger. Randolph, faced with Princess's husband and his denizen dead, retreated to the front room. Princess followed close behind.

"He don't trust nobody," she said, referring to her hidden husband. "There will be a grand split-up here before long. . . . I am going to shake him [Mr. Debar]. I wish it was only you and I, but we have got to take Marsh, as he will be useful and easy to handle."

"Can we produce pictures on the road?" asked Randolph, still processing everything he'd seen in the Temple of Spirits.

"We might be caught, and it would kill the goose with the golden egg. A promiscuous public are not so easily handled as Marsh." Princess's wisdom was buried deeply and misplaced.

Finally, Randolph posed the question of the day: "How do you do it?"

"Well, I don't do it for everybody. You know you could take a picture out of some people's hands and replace it with a red hot stove." Princess knew how to read the credulous, no doubt, and went on to describe how she'd managed the largest of Marsh's beloved spirit paintings, a portrait supposedly of Marsh himself garbed in a flowing toga. "I sat in his room one time, and he fell asleep in his chair while talking to me. I got the picture that was just finished, and had it set in the place of the blank frame; then I sat down and pretended to be asleep. [Mr.] Diss Debar came and knocked at the door, which awoke Mr. Marsh. I also started up, but fell back in a trance, and pointed toward where the picture stood. Mr. Marsh looked, and being half asleep declared he saw the picture coming. It was a very complete job."

"Ain't you afraid he will tumble himself and have you pulled?" Randolph thought it risky to make Marsh the lynchpin as his devotion was constant, but his enthusiasm was unpredictable.

"I don't fear God or the devil. I have had hard knocks enough, and the balance of my life will be one of luxury." Ladies and gentlemen—the Princess, in a nutshell.[30]

On April 11, 1888, the Temple of Spirits was breached by a pair of officers with a pocketful of warrants for larceny and conspiracy to defraud, for both the Princess and her rarely-seen husband. The charges were brought by Luther Marsh's law partners and members of the Bar Association who feared for the safety of his property, his sanity, and his health while in the Princess's thrall. The sad pair were taken immediately to the Tombs where Princess railed and raved and showed her teeth to any in her path. Marsh heard the news as he was presiding over a meeting of the New Parks Commission and spent much of the night trying to give bail to free his sorry houseguests but to no avail. Princess was in jail—the only setting in which most of New York wanted to see her.

Her miscalculation was to involve, and then quickly stiff Randolph. He was the brawny brains behind magicians and circus folk and was no fan of being on the wrong end of a con, but Princess was brash and blinded by misplaced confidence in herself. Additionally, as much as she leaned on Marsh to be her credulous mouthpiece, she underestimated New Yorkers' appetite for comeuppance; fool me once, shame on you. End of aphorism.

Before the trial was the special sessions held in Justice Kilbreth's court, assembled to handle Princess's case specifically, presided over by him and without a jury. There was a cast of thousands: Princess, Mr. Debar, Princess's real brother, George Solomon, Randolph, O'Sullivan, Marsh, artists, spiritualists, photographers, and magicians. And unprecedented crowds thronging to get a look.

The day Carl Hertz performed Princess's trick on the witness stand was a busy one, and Hertz returned to the afternoon session to perform a "test" with Marsh, whose property, credulity, and sanity were the fulcrum on which the case rested.

Marsh was on the stand, lecturing on the provenance of his spirit paintings and waxing rhapsodic about the ancients, when Hertz was recalled. He was there to show Marsh just how easy it was to trick someone, specifically through legerdemain. Hertz produced a blank notepad similar to the scores

Marsh and Princess—a sketch of the dispirited pair.
MARSH AND PRINCESS ILLUSTRATION, AS APPEARED IN APRIL 11, 1888, *HARRISBURG TELE-GRAPH*, HARRISBURG, PA.

of pads supposedly filled with correspondences from Queen Elizabeth and King Solomon Marsh had at home . . . er, the Temple.

"Mark your pad, Mr. Marsh!" shouted the seething Princess from the defendants' table in an effort to use Hertz's own tools against him. Marsh sat up straight at attention, catching Princess's drift, and quickly ruffled all the papers in front of him to throw Hertz off his guard.

"You must let him do it his way, Mr. Marsh," sighed Prosecutor Howe.

"No. I want to see him do it my way." Marsh's obstinacy was befitting a child, or a Princess, in a state of arrested development but hardly a leading member of New York's legal circles. His tantrum was met with a round of excessively boisterous applause led by the Princess. But Marsh's legal mind was not entirely dormant, for his curiosity won the day: "Well, I would like to see what this man can do, anyway."

With this, Hertz took a seat at one end of Justice Kilbreth's table and Marsh the other. The stage was set. It was a wise decision to have the test performed at the justice's table not only because it gave him the best access to the test, its subject, and its subject's reaction, but also because there was a veritable mob rush to get a glimpse. The over-filled courtroom was already excited, but when Marsh and Hertz met on the tabletop battlefield all hell broke loose. People rushed to see, climbing over tables, chairs, and each other. The cacophony was deafening.

In spite of the bedlam, Hertz performed his test on Marsh. While guards were trying to secure peace and order in the room, Hertz had secured Marsh's attention and held it while ever-so deftly exchanging the blank notepad with one already filled with writing. When Marsh took hold of the pad, he marked it, as Princess had demanded, not realizing he'd already failed the test in not noticing that Hertz had made the switch. Princess whispered furtively to her counsel, who approached Marsh to quietly warn him that Hertz intended to switch the pads.

"I don't see why [counsel] should be near Mr. Marsh now at all," shouted the justice over the din.

At the same moment, Marsh shouted indignantly, "You could have cheated me! You would have changed the pads without me knowing it!" Alas, poor Marsh; his logic and devotion were no match for good magic.[31]

There was a great deal more testimony over the course of many days. Princess's stay in Blackwell's Island in 1870 was mentioned. Also mentioned was testimony she gave on the stand when accusing Victoria Woodhull of petty theft when she said, "[Woodhull] urged me to do something by which I could make money: I told her she had begun as a clairvoyant, but that I had no such gift, no such foresight."[32] The justice system's memory was longer than Princess's, apparently.

Artist Augustus Maurice Friedlander took the stand to testify to the quality of the paintings: "This is a very poor drawing on canvas. The drawing and execution are very poor." He continued with words like "vile," "abominably executed," "very vile," "absolutely worthless," and "beneath criticism."[33] Except for the fact they were supposedly done through spiritual manifestations, the paintings were, as Friedlander put it, "the worst daubs ever used to impose upon an ignorant mind."[34]

One of the final and most damning pieces of testimony came from handwriting and ink expert David N. Carvalho who would, a few years later, be instrumental in exonerating Dreyfus in his namesake Affair. His presence indicated the prosecution was wrapping up its case as Carvalho's word on paper, parchment, handwriting, and inks was final. He was there to draw a line under the sum total of Princess's spirits' catalog.

Prosecutor Howe set him up with, "Mr. Carvalho, have you a piece of paper in your hand?"

"Yes," he answered as he produced a large sheet of blank paper, perhaps twenty-five by thirty inches.

"Now, Mrs. Ann O'Delia," said Howe, turning his attention to the fuming Princess, "will you kindly tear a piece off this paper for the purpose of identification?"

"No, I will not mark it as I have not supplied it," was her curt reply. Her face flushed a deep red.

"Very well, then, the public will judge you. You refuse to mark the paper because you have not furnished it." Point: Mr. Howe. The officer of the court held up the paper for the whole room to see. Howe continued: "That paper is the same which you have handed to . . . the female defendant—it is perfectly blank to all appearances. Now . . . in what way can a picture be instantaneously produced on that paper?"

Expert Carvalho's ready response was, "By one touch with a wet sponge. It is merely a chemical change. It is no trick." His dry delivery underscored his seriousness; science, not magic. With the word "sponge," Howe began dramatically casting about for some water. Justice Kilbreth offered his glass.

"The water that the Judge drinks is good enough for us. We do not question his purity." Mr. Howe was leaning in for the kill. "Now, Mr. Carvalho, what picture do you intend to produce on that paper?"

"The picture of Adelaide Neilson." Marsh, had he been in court that day, would have taken special notice of this "dig" as his admiration for the late actress was well known.

"Is she dead?" asked Mr. Howe.

"Yes, she died some five years ago."

"Well, then, go ahead and produce the spirit portrait of Adelaide Neilson."

Carvalho moved to the white-as-snow piece of paper still stretched between the officer's hands. He lightly dipped a small sponge in the judge's drinking glass and ran it lightly over the surface of the page. Almost immediately a clearly defined portrait of the actress appeared and became more clear with each moment. The thin layer of gouache he likely used to obscure the portrait melted as soon as water touched it, which would make the portrait's appearance seem miraculous.

The courtroom, which had already seen more excitement in the past ten days than ever before, erupted into cheers and wild applause. Shouts of "Bravo! Excellent! Wonderful! Admirable!" rang out loud and clear. It took the officers some minutes to quell the crowd's enthusiasm, during which time Howe and Justice Kilbreth both did little to hide their satisfied smiles. If the Princess had any pull in the spirit world, surely she would have used it to strike down Howe with lightning bolts in that moment.[35]

The prosecution rested. The defense's case was comparatively brief and far less exciting. Princess's counsel called in sympathetic spiritualists, artists to denigrate the expert testimony, and the defendants themselves. There was little for them to add to the sordid affair that might change the justice's mind. Poor Mr. Debar was unmasked as being akin to a bigamist, his having left a wife and seven children to swan around with the Princess, and he spent the remainder of the hearings covering his face with his hands. Princess also took the stand but was more furious and feisty than helpful. She said Marsh had gifted her his home to use as a temple and that, one night in the Tombs, she had received a clairvoyant message to "Get up and write!" And with that letter, written at the spirits' behest, she'd returned the house to Marsh. But, it was too little, too late.[36]

On May 1, Justice Kilbreth sent the Princess and Mr. Debar to appear before the grand jury. By June 18, they'd been found guilty by a jury of their peers and sentenced to six months apiece on Blackwell's Island. Calls over injustice came from both sides; the spiritualists thought this too harsh and resented their beliefs being ostensibly on trial (they weren't), and everyone else thought the sentence absurdly lenient. Certainly, Blackwell's Island was no walk in the park, but Princess could do a six-month term standing on her head. Or, someone's head, anyway.

THE PRIESTESS RECEIVING THE ADULATIONS OF HER ADHERENTS.

Princess provided ample fodder for the day's cartoonists.
"THE PRIESTESS RECEIVING THE ADULATIONS OF HER ADHERENTS" CARTOON, AS APPEARED IN AUGUST 2, 1891, *THE BOSTON GLOBE*, BOSTON, MA.

The Academy of Music was standing room only on the night of May 27, 1888. There was excited chatter from all sides, and some familiar faces dotted the crowd. Luther Marsh was seated in the orchestra section. When the curtain rose, Herrmann the Great appeared in his signature black velvet tuxedo, black top hat, and brilliant white gloves. His handlebar mustache was curled up at the ends, slightly obscuring his impish smile. The audience was expectant and enthralled.

His first trick sent ripples of laughter through the house. An audience member wrote something on a sheet of paper, which Herrmann then tore in two, pocketing one half and placing the other in a slot and apparently burned. A messenger rushed the stage with an oversized envelope that, when Herrmann opened it, contained a smaller envelope addressed to a known audience member. The addressee opened the envelope only to find a smaller one within addressed to Justice Kilbreth, who was watching from a box. Kilbreth opened his envelope and inside was—wait for it—another envelope! This final letter in the matryoshka envelope was for Herrmann himself and contained the missing half of the paper. The crowd was delighted.

Herrmann followed this up with slate-writing, card-throwing, table-tipping, and a cabinet scene. The main course, though, was served when Herrmann the Great manifested a spirit painting. With flourish and panache he moved his hands over a mounted canvas, apparently blank. His white gloves gleamed under the stage lights. When the smoke and mirrors had cleared, there it was: an accurate (if not flattering) portrait of Princess Editha Montez Ann O'Delia Diss Debar. The crowd leaped to their feet and cheered the house down. Herrmann then took the time to explain this method—the people deserved to see the truth—which was, like all illusions, ultimately disappointing. Herrmann's expert legerdemain had made it imperceptible when he palmed the very thin sheet of paper that had been fixed to the face of Princess's portrait. With a wave of his hand, he could make Princess appear, just as with a wave of her hand, she'd made Lawyer Marsh's homeownership disappear.

The portrait was passed around for inspection and landed in Marsh's lap. He turned it over and over before dismissing it as a trick because the paint was not fresh enough. Tough crowd.

To close the evening, Herrmann conducted a spooky, séance on stage with accompaniment provided by disembodied musicians and gyrating skeletons.[37]

Less than six months later, on October 21, the Academy of Music was again packed with spiritualists and spiritualism skeptics. And again, the

The sly Fox sisters.
THE FOX SISTERS, FROM *ABRAHAM LINCOLN AND RELIGION, GENERAL*, BY
LINCOLN FINANCIAL FOUNDATION COLLECTION, 1857, RETRIEVED FROM THE
INTERNET ARCHIVE, FLICKR.

former would be chapped and the latter vindicated, for on this evening the poster children for the movement—the Fox sisters, now in their fifties—had experienced epiphanies and doubts that prompted them to come forward. Maggie Fox-Kane and her sister Kate took the stage to read a statement. Maggie's voice was so quiet and timid that most of the audience thought she'd been struck dumb. "But if her tongue had lost its power, her preternatural toe joint had not."[38] A small wooden stool was placed in front of Maggie, and she solemnly removed her shoe and then her sock from her right foot. Everyone in the building collectively held their breath and strained their ears as Maggie Fox placed her bare foot on the stool. *Tap, click, tap.* The collective response was half gasp and half groan. Three physicians—volunteers from the audience—climbed the stage to more closely inspect the "Toe Heard 'Round the World." They decreed, unequivocally, that Mrs. Fox-Kane's marvelous gift was less akin to communing with spirits than it was to arthritis. For thirty years, the Fox sisters had created and then shouldered the Spiritualism mantle based on their ability to communicate with things unseen. But six months after Princess's paintings had been on trial, Maggie Fox's big toe was ready to testify.

By January of 1889, the Debars were out of Blackwell's. Mr. Debar quickly quit his companion's company, likely grateful to have survived the affair. Princess, however, was still in Marsh's good graces somehow and was reportedly pursuing the purchase of a $65,000 house on Broadway immediately following her release.

Her time in New York would be brief, though, as her many names and prodigious likeness were spurned by everyone in the city. She sent a pitiful "suicide note" to the papers and jumped off a ferry in April of 1891. She bobbed in the water a moment before swimming to the shore, where she put on a nun's habit and a blonde wig and walked away from her once-charmed life as a terrible medium.

Unfortunately, Princess went on to have a terrifically full career as a cult leader and serial impostor all over the world. Her increasingly serious crimes—conspiracy, fraud, rape—necessitated reinvention, so her list of aliases grew to mammoth proportions.

Princess—pictured later in life as "Swami Laura"—would continue to break fashion molds.

MME. DISS DEBAR, LATER IN LIFE AS "SWAMI LAURA," WEARING STRANGE ROBE AND OVERSIZED RING THAT SHE'D STOLEN FROM THE KORESHAN UNITY CULT IN CHICAGO IN THE LATE 1890S, LIBRARY OF CONGRESS, PRINTS & PHOTOGRAPHS DIVISION, LC-DIG-GGBAIN-01274 (DIGITAL FILE FROM ORIGINAL NEG.), https://www.loc.gov/pictures/resource/ggbain.01274/.

In 1901, Princess was on trial with her (then) husband in London. She was then known as Swami Laura Horos and had claimed to be the inventor of a new religion, which she'd actually simply plagiarized from an American sect she'd stolen sacred texts and jewels from five years earlier. The case was sensational, and lurid details were splashed across every London newspaper.

Upon opening up his paper one morning, the Princess's old friend, magician Carl Hertz, recognized old Mrs. Debar and her old, wicked ways. He immediately notified Scotland Yard just who it had in custody, which helped secure her conviction and seven-year sentence in Aylesbury Prison. In the end, the magician's power of sight recognized her as a shade of something formerly human, bloated and stripped bare from avarice. She'd demonstrated to the magician the kind of person she really was, and when he truly looked at her to *see*, he'd believed her.[39]

CHAPTER FIVE

The Three Trials of Betty Bigley

THE TIME:	1879–1907
THE PLACE:	Woodstock, Canada
	Cleveland, OH
	New York, NY
THE TAKE:	$1,400,000, Cleveland mansion, endless string of gaudy jewelry, chintzy furnishings, excessive generosity, a toy for every orphan at Christmas
THE PLAYERS:	Mrs. DeVere
	Betty Bigley
	Cassie Chadwick
	Dr. Leroy Chadwick
	James Dillon
	Herbert Newton
	Detective Belford
	Andrew Carnegie

IN THE LATE 1890S, CLEVELAND, OHIO, WAS A HOT SPOT FOR MILLION-aires, both old and new. The moneyed set was either the latest in a long line of wealthy white families, many of whom could trace their lines back to founding members of the city, or was of a newer variety of rich, John D. Rockefeller–style. Rockefeller made a nearly inestimable sum in Standard Oil during the Civil War and Reconstruction and became an unwilling poster boy for the Gilded Age. Cleveland was geographically situated such that railroads passed through on their way to all points west. Western Union was formed and based in Cleveland. There was a well established political link between Washington, D.C., and Cleveland, for, by the late 1890s, Ohio had supplied the former with four presidents: Grant, Hayes, Garfield, and McKinley. Being a central hub of overland transport and burgeoning industry made Cleveland a perfect environment for fostering wealth, its trappings, and those who sought them.[1]

Anyone who was anyone among the well-to-do set of Euclid Avenue in Cleveland bought diamonds at Cowell & Hubbard's. The city's premier jewelry store had rows of glass display cases that ringed the cavernous showroom, each holding regimented trays of sparkling baubles. The shop would have been positively bursting with fur-clad ladies and spit-spot salesmen. And the occasional detective.

In 1901, former detective Irving Belford, later clerk of the United States Circuit court at Toledo, was in Cowell & Hubbard's. Whether he was shopping for his wife, his mother, or himself no longer mattered to him once he bumped into an imperious woman mid-spending spree. She was casually waving in the general direction of trays of shining jewelry, announcing, "I'll take that one, and that one, and that one, too" in a way that demonstrated money was no object. She was holding forth on her spending power to any within earshot—jewels included, it seemed. The sophisticated lady amassed a $6,000 collection of rows of trays of mounted jewels and unset stones.

Belford watched from the periphery as the lady chose her jewels. He kept his eyes trained on her, observing her carriage, her features, her selections. She was tall, but the way she carried herself made her seem giant. Her hair was gray, her lips pursed, and her eyes glinted when she narrowed them in her intense gaze. Her clothes were demonstrably expensive. She spoke clearly and slowly with a barely perceptible lisp.

That lisp . . . Why did it seem so familiar, wondered Belford.

"I'll take that one, too," said the lady, apparently finally finished choosing her treasures.

DING. Belford snapped to attention. The lisp was familiar because he had heard it before. Ten years before in Toledo, Ohio. Her hair was different, and she was shorter—not to mention those clothes!—but that lisp was the same. He approached the shop clerk.

Belford leaned close to the clerk and furtively intimated that the lady might not be what she appeared and that he should ask for payment for her purchases in full and on the spot. The clerk was alarmed but attentive. Belford stood by as the lady approached the counter.

The clerk was in the unfortunate position of having to weigh Belford's words against a $6,000 sale to an obviously wealthy woman and likely repeat customer. After all, Cleveland was home to some of the world's wealthiest but also the neediest who had little else than aspirations. The clerk was in a pickle, so he proceeded gingerly.

The clerk, Belford behind him, cleared his throat when the lady approached the counter. He begged a thousand—nay! A million!—pardons but wondered if the lady had evidence she could pay for all the items she'd selected? A matter of policy, you see. She pursed her lips, her scowl turning to a frown, and narrowed her eyes on the clerk. Did the clerk even know who she was, she demanded. Who was he to question her?! She peered at the clerk contemptuously, and then she saw Belford. They locked eyes, and she stared him down while reaching into her mesh purse to pull out a slim stack of neatly folded papers. Slamming the notes down forcefully on the glass counter, she suggested the clerk examine them carefully; each was from a different prominent Cleveland personality, each name sure to hold weight with anyone in the city, and each note indicating it bore significant spending power. Promissory notes were common and widely accepted among, by, and from the upper crust whose resources were considered nigh unassailable.

With an obsequious bow, the clerk backed away from the counter and slunk to collect the lady's jewels. Her notes were impressive, and he needed to keep his job. He hoped she would forget the insult.

The lady turned on Belford and let him have it. She was rich! And respectable! And who was he to so callously dredge up a painful past that she had worked so hard to forget! For the lady had recognized Belford, as well. She knew him as the arresting officer and key witness for the prosecution in a forgery case some ten years prior. She was not interested in reliving the past and upbraided him for his poor judgment.

He stood still while stoically receiving her screed. He let her have her say while the clerks wrapped and boxed her $6,000 worth of jewels.

When she sputtered to an end, huffing and eyes blazing, he tipped his hat and turned to leave. The bell over the entrance tinkled as he opened and shut the door behind him before she could correct or chastise his parting words:

"I bid you good day, Madame De Vere."[2]

<hr />

Woodstock, Ontario, Canada, in the 1850s was a rough place. The first half of the century saw an exponential expansion of population, townships, and infrastructure. But it was hard-fought, and even the well established towns were surrounded by dense wilderness. The lines between tamed and untamed were physically stark on the maps but blurry among people; populations were a diverse mishmash of homesteaders, explorers, moneyed white men, and laborers. The Bigleys were the latter.

Daniel Bigley worked as a railroad section hand and lived beyond the city limits with his wife, Mary Ann, to support their eight children, six of whom were daughters. The fifth daughter born was christened Elizabeth, but she was usually called Betsy, or Lyndie, or Betty. Their life on the outskirts of town was hard and simple and plain. Betty Bigley was ill-suited for small town life. From very early on, she was dubbed "peculiar" and presented an absolute mania for clothes—particularly those far finer than what her family could afford.

Shortly after Daniel Bigley's death, Mary Ann moved her passel of children to the heart of downtown Woodstock and opened a rooming house. This would have been in the late 1860s. Mary Ann did not care to scrape by on the outskirts of town, and Woodstock offered a fresh start for the family after toiling for so long. Woodstock also offered more entertainment, distractions, and diversions.[3]

As relatively exciting as Woodstock might have been to the rest of the family, Betty made her own entertainment. Before she was twenty, she'd had multiple run-ins with the constabulary. When she was thirteen, she wrote a letter, to herself, informing herself that a beloved (fictitious) uncle had passed and left her a small (nonexistent) inheritance. Though she was barely able to see over the bank teller's stand, young Betty presented the letter to the bank and received blank checks in return—the letter seemed real enough, and she was just a young girl, after all. The checks were authentic and drew authentic funds from an established bank but from imaginary accounts. It was only after a few months of spending that she was caught and arrested, but being a young, impetuous girl, they chided her and let her go.[4] Not five years later, shortly before the death of her father, was the Brantford barbershop incident, which confirmed for the townspeople just how "peculiar" Betty was.

Betty walked into the Brantford barbershop with thick, curly hair that fell around her shoulders and down her back, all of which she wanted chopped off. This being a full fifty years before bobs were all the rage, this took the barber aback. She said the doctor had ordered her hair cut off to relieve her headaches. With her hair cropped to her ears, she then asked the barber for a false mustache. For her brother, she said. And once he had done that, would the barber be interested in purchasing a gold watch she happened to have in her pocket? She'd been needing some new clothes, after all. This was one request too many for the barber; he summoned her father to fetch her home.[5] This was not long after she'd already been caught in Brantford in a well-fitting suit of boy's clothes, having fled there after trying to pass a promissory note bearing a neighboring farmer's name.[6]

The town tolerated (barely) her escapades as a caveat of her peculiar nature. Her eccentricities were certainly challenging, but her gall became unnerving. By 1879, she had saved enough money to purchase high-quality paper and pens. With these, she carefully created letterhead for a supposed London, Ontario, attorney, and then wrote an official letter to herself notifying she was heiress to an inheritance from a recently deceased philanthropist. With this ostensibly official letter in hand, she had a printer fashion a calling card with her picture elegantly captioned, "Miss Bigley, Heiress to $15,000." These cards were regular currency among the upper crust and respectfully honored by all others. While the seed money for this gambit was reportedly honestly come by—though who's to say—she was able to spin her small investment in papers and pens into a $15,000-plus sum.[7]

Armed with her official "Heiress" card, Betty went on a small spending spree: $250-worth of dry goods and a reed organ from a local vendor.

For these, she gave her own promissory note as payment, her self-styled card acting as collateral—a clever move, really. She had manufactured legitimacy and sold it with boldness. When the merchants came for the full remittances, they were handed another promissory note, this one signed by local farmer Reuben Kipp. Except, unfortunately for the vendors Betty—and, indeed, Reuben—the farmer Kipp had been dead for longer than the note was good for. Betty was accused of forgery in the Woodstock Assize Court.[8]

Whether Betty was scheming or insane was a question the jury apparently had no difficulty answering. "So well did she play her part, that even Crown witnesses in giving testimony could not affirm her sanity. She played her part during the whole trial with wonderful ability, behaving, apparently, in the most insane manner," said Howard Duncan, who had known her case while he was a law student.[9] She had been caught red-handed, but her reputation preceded her; her peculiarity both explained and excused her actions, it seemed. Woodstock's old-timers talked for many years about her hypnotism of the jury.[10] Peculiar, indeed.

Betty was released and quickly moved on, leaving her hometown, its residents, and their pesky rules behind her. She was destined for bigger things.

—✦—

Everyone in America and Scotland knew who Andrew Carnegie was. As the Laird of Skibo and American Master of Vertical Integration, Carnegie's largesse supported his native Scotland, and his steel supported America's infrastructure. When he sold his controlling shares of Carnegie Steel to J. P. Morgan in 1901 for an unprecedented $480 million (Carnegie's share being about $225 million), he retired from money-making to focus on philanthropy as one of the world's richest men. From the overworked, underpaid immigrant workers to the fat-cat, graft-laden bankers, everyone knew, feared, and respected Carnegie's name and his associated spending power.

The spring following the historic transaction, in 1902, Mrs. Cassie Chadwick took a train to New York. She was accustomed to the journey from Cleveland and always traveled in comfortable style. Mrs. Chadwick

Cassie in her prime.
JANUARY 4, 1905, *THE BARBER COUNTY INDEX*, MEDICINE LODGE, KS, https://chroniclingamerica.
loc.gov/lccn/sn82015080/1905-01-04/ed-1/seq-7/.

was very social and a terrific spender, so a jaunt to New York City and its diversions as her husband traveled in Europe was hardly noteworthy. And luckily, she met one of her hometown acquaintances almost as soon as she arrived.

The rarefied set of Euclid Avenue—"Millionaire's Row"—in Cleveland socialized chiefly among itself, ever confirming it kept to its own kind. Cassie had worked on counting herself among these elites since marrying the venerable Dr. Leroy Shippen Chadwick in 1897. Her acceptance by Cleveland's uppermost echelon—"The 400"—was hard-won but assured after a few years' worth of her extravagant parties and legendary generosity.

So when Mrs. Chadwick bumped into a good friend of her husband's, Cleveland lawyer James Dillon, in the lobby of New York City's Holland House, their interaction was cheerful and informal. So much so that Dillon thought little of it when Mrs. Chadwick asked him to escort her on a quick visit to her father's place in the city. Why *wouldn't* he accompany one of Cleveland's upstanding citizens? They chatted easily as the hansom cab drove down Fifth Avenue toward the address Mrs. Chadwick had given the driver; 2 East 91st at Fifth.

When they arrived, Mrs. Chadwick begged Mr. Dillon's pardon as she would need to enter the house alone. Dillon assented out of grace, and astonishment. The cab had stopped at a stately four-story mansion whose wrought-iron gate, deep red bricks, and seemingly countless windows were iconic . . . imposing . . . and undeniable markers of the Carnegie mansion. As Mrs. Chadwick climbed the few front steps to greet the butler before going through the front door, Dillon focused on not appearing inappropriately curious about the woman's visit.

For Mrs. Chadwick had told Dillon in hushed tones that she was the niece of Frederick Mason, a long-time associate and close confidante of Carnegie's. When he had died, she was heiress to the $7,500,000 Mason estate, which Mr. Carnegie had charitably managed for her as he pyramided the sum into an $11 million fortune. She said she was there at Carnegie's behest as "he wanted to shift this trusteeship to a reputable Cleveland bank."[11]

When Mrs. Chadwick reappeared from the impressive house, she shifted her coat such that Dillon could plainly see she was carrying a carefully bundled package. She was beaming. Lawyer Dillon did all he could to keep calm and hide his wanton curiosity, but Mrs. Chadwick had a remarkably keen sense about people and could tell that her fellow passenger was itching for information.

Could he keep a secret, she asked. She was still all smiles as her eyes darted furtively, as giddy over telling her delicious secret as Dillon was to hear it. She leaned closer and lowered her voice. Her usual slow, measured tones—she was partially deaf and had a slight speech impediment—felt weighted with importance.

As she spoke, she carefully showed Dillon the contents of the package: securities (e.g., stocks and bond certificates, deeds of trust, etc.) aggregating over $15 million, all signed with the name "Andrew Carnegie." Dillon's eyes boggled when he saw the notes. Mrs. Chadwick whispered, her words thick with implication, that she'd been so brief at the Carnegie mansion because her presence was not altogether welcome, that she was a sore reminder of youthful impropriety, and that Mason's name was actually a blind to shield the identity of her true relative who wanted her to be taken care of but did not want their genetic connection to be public knowledge. After hinting at the inevitable conclusion, she couldn't help herself and connected the dots for Dillon: famously chaste Andrew Carnegie had an illegitimate daughter, and it was her. Mrs. Chadwick. In the flesh.

"And now, don't tell a soul," she urged Dillon, knowing full well that he would.[12, 13]

～⌒～

Betty Bigley returned to Woodstock in 1889 using the name Mrs. Lydia Hoover, with an infant son, Emil, in tow. In addition to her new name and new son, she brought with her a claim of a $50,000 inheritance from the recently deceased Mr. Hoover. She looked quite different—her clothes were very fine, as were her manners, and she was practically encrusted in diamonds—but it was definitely Betty Bigley, the peculiar girl who had left ten years prior.

She and little Emil stayed in Mrs. Bigley's rooming house in downtown Woodstock. Mrs. Hoover caused minor furors everywhere she went as her spending habits upended Woodstock's little economy. She insisted on paying her mother's store bill and always in cash. But she did so in denominations so large that no till in town could make change, which sparked a specie war among local vendors. Merchants would run in search of change while she waited, smiling at the uproar. She clearly didn't mind causing a big-spender fuss because she continued to pay all the bills that way. She spent lavishly on her friends and relations, "fitting her mother's house with a piano and burdening the old lady with the costliest of silks and fine garments of every kind."[14] Her generosity was legendary and perhaps more than a little self-serving.

Mrs. Hoover seemed very content to be the talk of the little town. She bought a vacant lot next to her mother's and announced plans to build for her a well-appointed home. Excavation was completed and the cellar wall underway when Mrs. Hoover was called away. Little Emil was equally popular in Woodstock and stayed with his grandmother when Mrs. Hoover—Betty—was summoned to Toledo, Ohio, in January of 1890.

The inverse relationship between town size and rumor-mill output did little to help Mrs. Hoover when she was suddenly called to Toledo. Some said she was a clairvoyant. Some said she was the madam of a brothel. Emil's parentage was questioned. As was Mrs. Hoover's sanity.

Upon arrival in Toledo, she immediately went to the shop of a local hypnotist and catchall occult seer, Madame De Vere. Mrs. Hoover—Betty—was right at home with the several young women, including an attractive lady with one leg, and their elaborate house/shop.[15] She kept herself busy through tending to the never-ending procession of upper-crust gentlemen on whose patronage the outfit seemed to rely. And though she was invigorated and cheerful in Woodstock's refreshing air, she claimed to be poorly once in Toledo. She switched her trousseau from the flashy, eye-catching dresses she'd paraded through the Canadian street to somber and dowdy outfits. She took to an invalid's chair.[16]

When Detective John Manley, chief of Toledo City detectives, arrived at the home brimming with feminine seers, he went straight to

Betty—Mrs. Hoover—wrapped tightly in her invalid's chair and arrested her on forgery charges committed by local express clerk Joseph Lamb at the behest of Madame De Vere. For Lamb had given the Madame $1,000 for an operation she said she needed, but her financial needs were unending, and she and Lamb had then forged promissory notes from multiple local personalities. Lamb made a false claim against a broker out of Youngstown re: his niece's reputation to back up the false paper. And Madame De Vere had been writing notes as "Florida G. Blythe," who, strangely, was a real person in Toledo but never appeared to press charges, or even defend her name. De Vere tried to pose as Lamb's niece on the stand, and then she refused to testify on her own behalf. In the end, they got between $13,000 and $40,000, most of which was already

MME. DEVERE.

A sketch of Madame De Vere in her prime.
JANUARY 4, 1905, *THE BARBER COUNTY INDEX*, MEDICINE LODGE, KS, https://chroniclingamerica.loc.gov/lccn/sn82015080/1905-01-04/ed-1/seq-7/.

spent—Madame De Vere bought an especially fine sealskin coat—or remained unaccounted for. Lamb was labeled a "Class-A Dupe" and acquitted. Madame De Vere—Mrs. Hoover, Betty Bigley—maintained her silence and, "Like Mother Eve, the madame bore the burden and was convicted."[17] She said it was to spare dear friends the embarrassment of a public trial and that she would rather serve a long time in prison than break confidence. Strong words from the recently convicted con-woman.

On January 23, 1891, "Lydia De Vere" was incarcerated in the Ohio State Penitentiary on a nine-and-a-half-year sentence. And just as Betty Bigley had transformed into Mrs. Hoover, who then transformed into Madame De Vere, the incarcerated Madame De Vere transformed into a new Mrs. Hoover upon her early parole by (then) Governor William McKinley in late 1893. She emerged from prison with her body broken but spirit renewed. By the following year, this new/updated/reformed Mrs. Hoover had taken little Emil from Woodstock and set up shop in Cleveland.

Dr. Leroy Shippen Chadwick suffered from a persistent malady that affected his limbs. He worried it was incurable. He also suffered from loneliness; his wife had died a few years before. Mary, his daughter, was away at school, and Dr. Chadwick felt the emptiness of his Euclid Avenue home weigh heavily upon him. One day, for the first and only time, he found his way to a house of ill repute.

Dr. Chadwick had inherited substantial wealth from his father, who had struck oil in Pennsylvania before moving his family to Cleveland, John D. Rockefeller–style. He was a fine doctor, and Cleveland considered him a perceptive judge of character. His small features and well-trimmed black mustache lent him an approachable look and helped put his patients at ease. But the doctor was anything but at ease waiting in the dim parlor of that Cleveland bagnio in 1894.

When Betty heard who was pacing downstairs, she acted quickly. Dr. Chadwick was not famous or flashy but was of the Euclid Avenue set and precisely the kind of contact Betty needed to set herself amongst them. With much drama, Betty introduced herself—as "Cassie"—to the doctor as a boarder who had only just arrived and, out of desperation, had taken the cheapest room she could find. She teed up the doctor to have to explain to her the true nature of her lodgings and, upon hearing him say she was in a brothel, she fainted in an impressively melodramatic fashion. The good doctor was aghast that such a lady would be so distressed and insisted that she move out that very moment. After he offered, cajoled, and then pleaded with her, she assented. They left the "rooming house" together, and neither ever returned.

"Cassie" was quickly installed in the charitable doctor's large, if sad, house. His ailing mother and delicate sister lived upstairs, but the rooms were dusted in mourning for the late Mrs. Chadwick. Though the finery was not to her taste, Cassie made herself at home in the Euclid Avenue house and ingratiated herself to the doctor. When he mentioned his aching back and legs, Cassie was charitable with her extensive massage skills. The doctor felt *much* better.

In 1896, they were married in the lobby of a Pittsburgh hotel. They'd traveled east at Cassie's request to be married "near her father." Cassie had been guarded about much of her past but had solemnly confided in Dr. Chadwick that her upbringing was unconventional out of a need for secrecy for her father's sake. For she was the product of a youthful indiscretion, and "Papa Andy" wanted to keep reputations intact. Dr. Chadwick was moved by her story, which seemed to explain a great many of his new bride's eccentricities.[18]

Cassie worked quickly to impress Millionaire's Row in hopes that they would accept her as one of their own. She threw sumptuous parties. She made gifts of touring cars. She lavished gifts upon everyone she met. In 1898, she took a coterie of young girls on a European tour, all expenses paid. In December 1901, she treated Dr. Chadwick to dinner, shopping, the theater—a grand night on the town! While they were out scores of laborers completely redecorated their house; the wallpaper, the furniture, the fixtures, and the paintings were removed to make way for Cassie's chintz and velvet and gilt and crystal. Dr. Chadwick nearly fell over when he opened his own front door, to which Cassie squealed, "This is my Christmas present to you, dear!"[19] Her obvious and garish spending did little to impress the old money set, but she kept at it. Perhaps the upper echelon disapproved of Cassie's indiscriminate generosity. One Christmas, she strode into a toy store with a list two yards long for presents and baubles totaling $800, which she paid for in cash and on the spot. The toys were then distributed among the orphan asylums and children's wards throughout Cleveland. She was a notoriously generous tipper.[20]

Cassie and Dr. Chadwick settled into their own marital routine, which saw them apart much of the time. He had his medical practice, and she had her increasingly complicated schemes. For as strongly as she sought acceptance from Euclid Avenue's exclusive population, they were merely players in her high drama and stepping-stones to the real windfall. A few well-placed mentions of "Papa Andy" peppered throughout conversations with bankers' wives or audibly whispered around corners from investor neighbors, did more to further her plot than any debutante's ball. Now when people murmured to each other as she passed, it was not about her garish clothing or blanket of jewelry but, instead, about the power of her absent parent.

Dear Cassie,

I am glad our mutual money plans are moving along so well. I took that first five million we discussed and bought you stock in the Caledonia Railway. The shares are being registered in your name and you can pick them up from me the next time you are in New York. By then I will also have worked out where best to invest for you the next five. I am glad you agree that the money should be turned over to you now and in small lots like this. That way, we will avoid the glare of publicity falling on you when I go. Take care of yourself, my daughter, and come to see me soon.

As ever, your affectionate father,
Andrew Carnegie[21]

A certain Cleveland banker's wife was shown this letter in Cassie's parlor and told to keep it a secret. She did not keep the secret. When Cassie approached the banker for a financial consultation he was practically salivating over the depth of the potential moneybags she brought in tow. He encouraged Cassie to share the secret of her lineage with investors as security for their loans; Andrew Carnegie would no sooner walk out on a loan than across the Atlantic. Surely, the same could be said of his daughter. Right?

An Oberlin, Ohio, bank manager, C. T. Beckwith, believed Cassie wholeheartedly and enjoined the bank's cashier, A. B. Spear, to write her a check for $240,000 from the Citizens' National Bank, and $102,000 from his personal account. Beckwith was also promised to be made manager of her affairs once she had sorted it out with Papa Andy. Meanwhile, she still had the neatly wrapped bundle of papers she'd received on her day trip to New York.

When Beckwith's loans came due and she claimed confusion—the money business was so tedious and dizzying for a woman, after all—he helpfully reminded her of the package. Mrs. Cassie Chadwick took her parcel to the Wade Park Banking Co. in Cleveland in hopes of raising some cash, using the notes as collateral. There were notes for $250,000, $500,000, and bonds aggregating $5 million, all signed by Andrew Carnegie, neatly packaged in fine white paper. The bank's treasurer, Iri Reynolds, knew Dr. Chadwick and had certainly heard of the heady Mrs. Chadwick so was more or less amenable when she strong-armed him into writing her a receipt for the notes, sight unseen. This receipt was as good as gold; she had a banker's signed note that she was good for $5 million based on the securities in the Wade Park vault, and allowed her to take loans from a dizzying number of banks between Cleveland and New York for upwards of $1.6 million.

She worked overtime to secure loans from banks to fund her breakneck pace of spending, but also to pyramid into more loans. What she secured from one bank she would use to settle with another. The scheme was complex and tightly knit. But as long as the banks were happy, she was in the clear. She rightly figured that whatever personal loans she might have forgotten or failed to honor would be too embarrassing for those less powerful than Carnegie—which was everyone in America—to call in. For all the financial shrewdness she possessed, the woman was a crackerjack judge of a person's social limits; she transacted in money but dealt in humiliation.

She had lenders across the east, both private and institutional. Banknotes were traded at a dizzying speed such that even they got confused about who exactly owned how much, and when. She kept it straight, though, and retained all their receipts, which, when taken together, became an investment portfolio with its own spending power. She had a paper trail that led to legitimacy. One lender, Herbert Newton, was not so bumbling, however, and came knocking when his note for $190,800 was due.

The woman was elusive and ducked Newton's calls, meetings, and inquiries. He and his attorneys tracked her down to a New York hotel and pressed her for an explanation or, better still, Mr. Newton's money. She didn't have either. On November 22, 1904, he filed suit against her, which did not go unnoticed by the press. A week later, the Citizens' National Bank collapsed, its capital drained by Beckwith's loan. There were runs on multiple Ohio banks known to have dealt with her, several of them shutting their doors as clients ran to drain their accounts to keep their money safe from her outstretched hands. The bank in Willoughby, Ohio, was bailed out with literal sackfuls of cash, hand-delivered by wealthy men, including Henry Frick of Pittsburgh; the bank was infused with funds while the press was having a field day. The following day, a "confidant" of the woman's stated—unprompted!—"Mrs. Chadwick states that Mr. Carnegie never had any connection with her affair."[22] This sent the press into a frenzy.

Less than a week after their bank collapsed, banker Beckwith and cashier Spear were arrested. Beckwith had kept the woman's paternity secret and was facing ruin for it. "I am either an awful dupe or a terrible fool!" he cried. The woman's attorney traveled to Oberlin, Ohio, to make good while forcefully stating that his client was either an honest woman, "or I am the worst duped man in America!"[23] However difficult it was for the dupes to identify themselves, the woman could smell them a mile off.

Her preternatural sense for ill-gotten funds had carried her for over a decade in Cleveland. But on December 7, 1904, Cassie Chadwick was arrested at the Holland House in New York City and remanded to the Tombs.

Early March of 1905 was when Cassie Chadwick's trial was scheduled. Her health was poor, but her spirits were aflame. She had spent four months in jail awaiting trial—first in New York, then in Cleveland—and spent half her time lecturing reporters, the other half chastising them. Her moods were erratic and her attitudes unpredictable. Dr. Chadwick had been traveling during the whole arrest nonsense but had since returned, but not to Cassie. He was bewildered and fell ill and out of sight.

A week before she was arrested in late 1904, the *New York Herald* printed pictures of Cassie Chadwick and Madame De Vere, side by side. Ontario wired that a young woman, Betty Bigley, had posed as an heiress but was acquitted on a forgery charge before moving to Cleveland to marry a doctor. As the world learned more about Cassie Chadwick/Madame De Vere/Lydia Hoover/Betty Bigley, her chances of vindication dwindled.[24]

Beckwith, Spear, and Reynolds protested loudly and often that the woman was all she claimed. There were documents, after all. The competing suits filed against Cassie Chadwick made for a legal tussle over who would open the bundle of securities in the Wade Park vault. On December 31, 1904, as others strode gaily to New Year's Eve parties, awash in the glow of revelry and excitement for the tabula rasa granted at midnight, Iri Reynolds opened the package on a judge's orders. He was careful and measured with his movements in a manner befitting a $5 million package. Inside, he found the following: a $1,800 mortgage against Daniel Pine of Pennsylvania; a promissory note for $5 million signed with the name "Andrew Carnegie"; a copy of this same note; and a trust deed for $10,240,000 printed with the following:

Know all men by these presents that I, Andrew Carnegie, New York City, do hereby acknowledge that I hold in trust for Mrs. Cassie L. Chadwick, wife of Dr. Leroy S. Chadwick of 1824 Euclid avenue, city of Cleveland, county of Cuyahoga, and state of Ohio, property assigned and delivered to me for said Cassie L. Chadwick by her uncle Frederick B. Mason, which property is of the appraised value of 10 million two hundred and forty-six thousand dollars ($10,246,000).

A political cartoon showing Andrew Carnegie [bottom left corner, kilted] amongst his scion brethren; the men of power and politics who each shaped the nation according to his own characteristic, caricatured interests.

J. S. PUGHE, *PUCK'S VALENTINES / J.S. PUGHE*, 1905. NY: J. OTTMANN LITHOGRAPHY COMPANY, PUCK BUILDING, FEBRUARY 8 (PHOTOGRAPH). RETRIEVED FROM THE LIBRARY OF CONGRESS, https://www.loc.gov/item/2011645674/.

An impressive bounty, to be sure! But the satisfied sighs from his compatriots did not move Reynolds; he looked crestfallen and gulped, "So much brown paper." The room was silent as they considered this enigmatic statement. When asked what he meant, he replied, "Brown paper is cheaper than white."[25]

Her securities busted and her credibility shot, the woman—Betty—wiled away in the Cuyahoga jail until her trial. When the fateful day came, she dressed in a splendid gown of black fitted velvet with a deep white collar and cuffs, topped with a black velvet hat with bird of paradise blooms and rings of pink and white roses. Her ensemble was fitting for the dog-and-pony show in its absurdity. In the back of the courtroom, a bearded man who had tried to stay out of sight and unobtrusive whispered to his seatmate, "So that's the woman. . . . She's handsomely gotten up." An ironic first impression from the Steel Master himself.[26]

The trial moved forward without inordinate fuss, and Betty, like she'd done in Toledo and Woodstock before, refused to take the stand. Her outfits never failed to amaze, however. C. T. Beckwith had died weeks prior, and none of the Bigley family had appeared at the trial. Emil remained steadfast and gripped his mother's hand when the jurors filed back into the courtroom to deliver their verdict of guilty on all seven counts of forgery and fraud. She wailed. On March 27, she was incarcerated on a ten-year sentence in the Ohio State Penitentiary. When being processed in the prison, administrators compared the Bertillon measurements of Madame De Vere with Mrs. Chadwick's, as if there was further doubt that they were the same woman.[27]

She had lived so long as other people that no matter who they thought they had, those she had swindled were never satisfied. Settlement from her case came to $14,000, which was split between her many creditors. The contents of the Chadwick mansion were sold in lots and the house razed soon after. It was said Dr. Chadwick moved east to play the organ for the remainder of his dotage.

Betty's third and final trial landed her in the Ohio State Penitentiary for a second time. She received visitors and reporters and mounted letter-writing campaigns on her own behalf. When her eyesight failed, followed quickly by her health, she sent Emil with their pittance of funds to purchase a headstone in her native Woodstock. It was already carved, cut, and erected when her coffin arrived there in October 1907.

The funeral for this mercurial, outlandish woman was befittingly absurd. Newspapermen overran the town and all its bars. Newsreel cameras made their first appearance in Woodstock. The family had hoped to keep the affair quiet and staid, but instead, hundreds flocked to see Cassie's . . . Lydia's . . . Betty's casket lowered into the ground. Even in death, she made waves.[28]

Betty Bigley had spent her life spending others' credit to boost her own. Not out of malice, it seems, but an undeniable urge to spend. She only wanted to get money so that she could use it to give. Certainly, much of the giving was directed toward herself, but to have scammed so

MRS. CASSIE L. CHADWICK.

Mrs. Leroy Shippen Chadwick poses for a portrait wearing a handful of her trademark jewels and inscrutable expression.

many wealthy men made her more a curiosity to the public than a villain. Sentiment remained bemused well past her death.

One man who remained blithely above it all while being the story's ostensible paterfamilias was Andrew Carnegie. Whether he meant it to be cruel, or ironic, or simply tone-deaf is unclear, but when asked if he would press charges against Mrs. Chadwick, Carnegie casually replied, "Why should I? Wouldn't you be proud of the fact that your name is good for loans of a million and a quarter dollars, even when someone else signs it? It is glory enough for me that my name is good, even when I don't sign it. Mrs. Chadwick has shown that my credit is A-1."[29]

CHAPTER SIX

Ways and Means

THE TIME:	1911–1936
THE PLACE:	Concord, NC
	Washington, D.C.
	El Paso, TX
	Hopewell, NJ
	Leavenworth, KS
THE TAKE:	At least $104,000, D.C. house, free food, drinks, and gambling, the Harding administration
THE PLAYERS:	Gaston Bullock Means
	Julie Means
	May Dixon Thacker
	William F. Burns
	Maude King
	Evalyn Walsh McLean
	Jess Daugherty
	Charles Lindbergh
	J. Edgar Hoover

"MR. FRANK HOGAN" REGISTERED AT THE PASO DEL NORTE HOTEL ON March 27, 1932.

The following day, March 28, "Mrs. Henry Kane, and secretary, of Wilmington, Delaware" also registered at the Paso del Norte Hotel in El Paso, Texas. The lady was immaculately dressed but obviously weary. Her secretary behaved more like a concerned nurse than one relegated to taking dictation. Both women were clearly tired from the journey and promptly retired to their rooms. They rested the whole day, neither making nor receiving any calls.

The telephone jumped off its receiver at 11 p.m.

A gruff but familiar voice growled, "This is Hogan. There's been a very important development. Hurry, at once, to the Clifton Hotel. Come alone."[1]

The elder, stately woman who'd registered as "Mrs. Kane" quickly donned street clothes that wouldn't draw attention to her presence, let alone her wealth. She was giddy from the call and what it might mean: Was there a development? Was she close to finding what she so desperately sought? Would her late-night trip across town by herself in an unknown city lead her to the stolen Lindbergh baby? She was practically skipping to the curb to hail a cab.

She climbed in. "Clifton Hotel!" she said, tired but cheerful.

As the cab moved down the El Paso street toward the Clifton, its passenger reassessed. It was nearly midnight. She was in an unfamiliar city. She was alone. And though there was speculation over the exact dollar amount of her net worth, she was the legal owner of both *The Washington Post* and the Hope Diamond. Evalyn Walsh McLean was the undisputed doyenne of the D.C. elite, and her spending power traveled with her. And now she was alone.

She was there to do whatever she could to help aid in the safe return of Colonel Lindbergh's kidnapped infant son, taken just a few weeks prior on March 1, 1932. Mrs. McLean was no stranger to tragedy and felt deeply for the Lindberghs as she was also a bereaved mother. She wanted to help and had already handed over $100,000 to the intermediary to the kidnappers to fund the ransom for the safe return of twenty-month-old Charles Jr. She was ready to go to the North Pole if it meant getting the baby home safe.

The cab continued toward its destination as an uneasiness started to grip Mrs. McLean. She was unsure of what awaited her at this latest location, having already traveled the eastern seaboard and points west in pursuit of the baby and gang of wily kidnappers. Maybe this late-night trip through the El Paso streets—a stone's throw from the Rio Grande and the Mexican border—was not prudent.

She began to mentally track the series of strange events that had landed her in the backseat of this taxi, when she realized she was being trailed. Perhaps the weeks sitting up late exchanging coded messages with go-betweens and ne'er-do-wells honed her radar for misdeeds, for there was no question she had spotted a dark touring car with two men in the front, following her closely.

"Driver, pull over to the right and slow down for a block. Go as slowly as you can."[2]

The car sat idling as other late night drivers passed along the street, headed for who knows where. Two cars passed. Then three. But not the touring car. McLean's nerves were frayed, and her patience was shot, and she was not willing to be the second high-society kidnapping after the Lindbergh baby.

She was scared but found her wits. She leaned forward and, breathlessly, said to the driver, "I want you to do as I say. Don't ask questions. I'll pay any fines, and there's ten dollars in it for you. Pick up a little speed. The first chance you get, make a complete U-turn."

They rejoined traffic, and the touring car reappeared behind them. The cab driver was able to put a half a block's distance between them when he jammed the wheel all the way around, flinging the car into a hairpin maneuver, McLean sliding along the backseat leather banquette and nearly onto the floor.

As the car was halfway through the turn, the driver shouted, "What do I do now, lady?!"

Highly sophisticated multimillionaire heiress, Hope Diamond owner Mrs. McLean gripped the seat for dear life and screamed, "GO LIKE HELL!"

———

Concord, North Carolina, had been home to generations of the Means family. "The General" W. C. Means had built and grown his antebellum plantation—Blackwelder's Spring—just outside Concord. The General's fifth son, "The Colonel" William Gaston Means, was a powerful lawyer, served as mayor of Concord and, later, in the North Carolina State Senate while his wife and seven children grew up in relative style a few blocks from Means Avenue in downtown Concord.

Gaston Bullock Means, born in 1879, was the eldest of the Colonel's sons. He and his siblings wanted for nothing; their pedigree all but guaranteed them good standing and easy advancement in Concord. But with the golden tickets afforded by their breeding came a predisposition for unpleasantness, one Concord resident describing the Means boys as "meaner than hell."[3]

Gaston's nose for mischief was genetically honed. He went through the motions of education and enrolled in the University of North Carolina in 1898 in a pre-law program, ostensibly in aid of the family business. He said he graduated in 1903—a "fact" oft-repeated but never verified. There were summer jobs and small stints between semesters, but Means really hit his stride as a salesman for the Cannon Mills textile firm, for whom his father was an attorney. From 1902 to 1913, Means was the overly friendly, too-pushy salesman for the Cannon Mills and tomcatted his way from Concord to New York to Chicago and back again. His towering, heavyset body supported his already balding pate and comically round babyface with a dimple so deep in his right cheek you could put your finger in it. He was big and bold. He quit the textile game in 1913 soon after marrying fresh-faced Julie Patterson, whom he met when peddling linens to her uncle's hotel goods supply. He was boisterous and loud and more than ten years her senior; she was polite and demure and had an as-yet-latent taste for excitement.

Three important notes about Means from this period:

First: Means found that customers were more willing to bend the rules, make allowances, and hand over cash when he presented himself as a son of the Cannon Mills's multimillionaire owner. Even if he only heavily implied that he was *in* with the boss, clients willingly handed over cash without the demand for a receipt for fear of angering their supplier's pride and joy.

Second: On a train trip between New York and Chicago, Means "fell" from a Pullman berth in a sleeper car. He hit his head. He was knocked out cold. A classmate claimed the fall altered Means's personality.[4] Means summarily sued the Pullman Company, which quickly launched an investigation that revealed the bed's supports had been sawed through halfway. Fortunately, Means had *coincidentally* taken out an accident insurance policy for this particular trip. Unfortunately for them, the investigators could not prove who had sawed the supports, so Means walked away unharmed and with a settlement. Though it's doubtful his head injury was real, Means was emboldened by this little scheme, and his trajectory likely forever altered as a result.

Third: Julie's uncle had left her to mind the store while he traveled in Europe. When she cabled him that she was engaged to the round-faced, towering salesman, her uncle looked into Means's background for Julie's sake. He called on Mrs. Maizie Melvin, Julie's unofficial minder, who had been a close friend of Julie's deceased mother. Maizie hired private detective William J. Burns to look into Means's background and prospects to determine if he was bona fide. Though he couldn't have known this, by enlisting help to protect Julie, her uncle facilitated an indeterminate number of Means's misdeeds by introducing Maizie and Burns into his soon-to-be-nephew's orbit.[5]

Julie was Gaston's "Sweetheart," and he was her "Bud." For all his schemes and lies, Means appeared to truly love Julie, and she him. He scared her, but Julie had a stomach for excitement. "And suddenly—I was in love with him. When I fell, I must admit I fell hard—I was wild about him! Have been ever since."[6]

No one could accuse Means of being lazy. He was always working. He had grown up in a town where his grandfather, father, and uncles all ruled with iron fists and mean-spirited winks. One might be tempted to diagnose Means's misdeeds as a plea for attention or cry for help from an emotionally repressive childhood or an unabating need for his father's approval. It is true he was likely damaged by the actions of the ruthless patriarchs—to claim otherwise seems inhuman. But therein lies the catch: Gaston Means was a deeply flawed individual who was unequivocally a product of his upbringing, but the very humanity that is therefore ascribed him is the same humanity—fear, love, approval, safety—he took advantage of in others. Means was likely a victim of trauma, but he spun that trauma into an all-out assault on trust. What a pitiful, horrible life he would have led had he any conscience to prick.

May Dixon Thacker, the author duped into co-writing Means's insidious yarn *The Strange Death of President Harding*, later wrote, "Comb the background of Gaston B. Means as finely as you wish. You will find in it only breeding and respectability—nothing to explain the man himself. Such common excuses as poverty, heredity, environment become impotent. For Gaston B. Means plunged into a career of evil for no reason that any man can, to this day, name."[7] J. Edgar Hoover, the infamous director of the Federal Bureau of Investigation, wrote of Means in 1936, "We regard him to be the greatest faker of all time."[8]

Whatever pathos was in Means's heart was perverted by his ethos. A story from his childhood invoked by every one of his biographers provides some insight, wherein Means stole from a coin bank on his mother's dresser and blamed it on the black servant girl working in the house (though "working" is being generous to the slave-owning Meanses, who were resistant to Reconstruction-era shifts in values and class). Means was a boy of seven, still in short pants, and when pressed by his mother if he had stolen the coins he answered, "No, mama. It never happened before." The little servant girl, barely older than Means, was immediately discharged, and as she left the house crying, little Gaston watched her through the window and muttered, "The damn fool! Let her look out for herself. I look out for myself."[9]

Without evidence, duress, or trying circumstances of any kind, Means had it in his head that the world was against him, and by hook or by crook and the grace of his bootstraps, he was going to come out on top. How lonely it must have been for him, moving through the world without ever finding his mental match, believing everyone to be mean-spir-

Gaston Means standing cockeyed in court. The imperfections on the photo seem to reflect Means's self-estimation: the sprays of light arching out from his head might be interpreted as angel's wings, or a divine hand, when they are, in fact, only superficial signifiers of age and deterioration.

"GASTON B. MEANS," MARCH 14, 1924, LIBRARY OF CONGRESS, PRINTS & PHOTOGRAPHS DIVISION, LC-DIG-NPCC-25464 (DIGITAL FILE FROM ORIGINAL), https://www.loc.gov/resource/npcc.25464/.

ited, empty-headed suckers that he had to get the best of before they could do the same to him.

Means's skewed morality, married with his abject inability to save money, produced violence. His hulking frame was imposing, and his tendency to drink was unnerving, and his logic was slippery, and his patience was unpredictable. He was a walking, talking powder keg without a moral compass, and he was combustible.

———

Maude King was considered one of the most desirable socialites of her day. She was pretty, tall, flighty, fond of drink, stylish, and reportedly worth over $4 million after the death of her second husband, James King, a lumber magnate. Maude's first marriage had ended ignominiously because, according to Julie Means, Maude's first husband was framed for adultery so she would be free to divorce him and marry King. When King died four months after the wedding, skeletons of various sizes threatened to erupt from Maude's mansion-sized closet. She left for Europe only to find herself in a string of tricky situations (e.g., the arms of lovers, fiancés, roués, etc.).[10] Her sister, Maizie Melvin, grew concerned so called on her friend, William J. Burns, and the services of his detective agency. Burns had just the man for the case.

After vetting him for Julie's uncle and allaying Maizie's misgivings, Burns had taken an interest in Means. He was offered an assistant's position, but Means quickly became one of Burns's top detectives, never shying from complications or getting his hands dirty. When Maude was in the thick of it, Means seemed uniquely qualified to man the case, given his familiarity with Maude's family and his penchant for gumshoe work.

Means freed Maude from the clutches and cruel intentions of her European suitors and brought her back to the States. She was exceedingly grateful to have someone on her side and looking out for her best interests. After Means was able to recover some money from yet another of Maude's nefarious suitors, her gratitude outweighed her sense; Maude made Means the manager of her money. She was happy to be relieved of the strain and confusion brought about by the finances, the will, and the probate. For Maude King had taken a settlement after James King's death while the rest of his fortune went to funding a charitable home in Chicago, as was written in the will. But Maude, with Means's helpful hints and suggestions, thought maybe there was a second will. Maybe one that confirmed her claim to the King $4 million? Maybe Means could find it?

And find it he did. But only after Maude had promised him a quarter share of the take (roughly $950,000). Means happened upon it while casually looking through some boxes and was delighted to "find" the document that would guarantee him nearly a million dollars.

By 1917, Means had spent two years with Maude and Maizie and was beginning to put forth considerable effort getting the second will validated while still managing the daily comings-and-goings of the two sisters. Means kept his eye on the prize as he grew tired of Maude's distractions; his job was to keep an eye on Maude, which he did through the filter of his self-interests.

In August of that year, as temperatures soared and his patience wore thin, Means took the whole group—Maude, Maizie, their mother, Julie, the two Means babies, and his brother Afton—on an outing to the Means family home in Concord. The town's diversions could not compete with those in Paris or Monte Carlo, but Maude's commitment to fun helped her embrace the local pastimes: mint juleps and shooting parties. On August 29, she got both.

Three miles outside town was a place called Blackwelder's Spring that Means touted as the locals' preferred shooting site, and near what was once the Means estate. After the oppressive heat of the day Maude was happy to get out of town and take in some local sport, and Means made sure she was in very high spirits that evening. She was glad to see some of the countryside, she was glad for the brief ride in the auto, and she was glad Means had thoughtfully brought along a recently purchased pistol that was just her size.

When their car stopped at a small clearing by the creek, Means and Maude walked toward the spring together. Means was thirsty, and he needed a drink. He didn't want to burden silly Maude with holding the gun while he leaned his face to the stream, so he shoved the pistol in the crook of a tree. He waved his lighter over the surface of the water to deter water bugs. He heard a commotion as he drank and so raised his head and turned to find Maude playing with the loaded gun. "Don't touch that!" he cried. She was startled and moved to put the gun back in the tree. But somehow, she tripped! The gun fell! It went off! Oh, the tragedy.

By the time Means claimed to reach her crumpling body, the bullet had gone in the back of her left temple and into Maude's brain. She died in the car as they rushed to a hospital. What an unfortunate accident to befall the merry widow just after discovering a second will that guaranteed her wealth!

However absurd Means's version of the day's events, the subsequent trial was an equal mockery. New York City prosecutors tried the case in Concord—a legal practice heretofore unheard of—with Means on full display for the jury and jam-packed courtroom gallery. Gaston Means, a scion in a Concord family that shored up a load-bearing pillar of the community, was assailed and vilified by the New York prosecutors. "Everybody wants to hear 'Bud' Means' trial. From the cotton and mills and foothills they have come bringing their dogs with them and, as the trial continues, canines of every description stroll unnoticed in and out among the witnesses."[11] The whole town, and their dogs, came to see the fate of Concord's own son.

After a grueling trial that took a visible toll on Means's health, closing statements were given on a Saturday. The jury adjourned to deliberate. For fifteen whole minutes, they deliberated. They returned with a not guilty decision and promptly left town to return to their rural homes before being charged for another night at the local hotel. The jury's decision was ultimately more a referendum on out-of-towners than a vindication of Gaston Means, but either way, Means was free to go.

In May Dixon Thacker's extensive serial on Means for *Liberty* Magazine in 1937, she asked him about Maude's death. His response was the following:

> *Now get this straight:* Her finger was on the trigger. . . . *I had just as much right to old man King's money as Maude had. Hell, she got it by fraud. Her divorce was crooked—crooked as a snake. What real right did she have to his money? . . . Maude King was no damned good. . . . What happened to her was the best thing that could happen. Best for her. Best for everybody else. . . . Maude was no damned good, I tell you. The world was better off without her. . . . If I ever meet this conversation again, I'll deny every word of it anyhow.*[12]

The stylings of an innocent man, for sure. Immediately after the trial, Means brought suit against the New York prosecutors for $1 million in damages. The case was almost immediately thrown out.

In 1929, the US Stock Market crashed. The Great Depression was born in misery, economic trauma, and political strife. The decade preceding had been marked by Prohibition, economic and class mobility, and rampant political corruption. For all the instability of the roaring twenties, the Depression meant average Americans knew what to expect each day when they begrudgingly rose from their threadbare mattresses. Senators debated long hours on the floor over who to blame and what to do. More than one mention was made of *The Washington Post*, but Senator George C. Norris of Nebraska pointed his finger squarely at Ned McLean, its owner. McLean had been a subject on the Senate floor before as he was implicated and embroiled in more than one political scandal in more than one administration (Harding, Coolidge, and Hoover!). But Senator Norris's direct link from the October crash to Ned McLean was more than the McLeans were willing to bear; as the leading society couple in Washington, they demanded restitution. But who could they hire for such a delicate operation? Who in Washington could have the connections, the wherewithal, the *means*?

Though he had been in the Atlanta Federal Prison from May 1925 to July 1928, Gaston Means remained the darling ne'er-do-well of Washington politicians and was quickly back to work upon his release. With a few scant months before the 1928 presidential election, the Republican Party was desperate for dirt on Democrats at all levels.

In prison, Means had met an Evangelical couple who were touring prisons to spread the Word and promote literacy. The wife, May Dixon Thacker, was a freelance writer specializing in true confessions who brought with her considerable credibility, being both a well-connected Democrat and sister to Thomas Dixon, author of *The Birth of a Nation*. Because Means's skills got ready use in prison—he quickly became the warden's spy and was often released for days at a time to consult on Department of Justice investigations—he baited Mrs. Thacker as he assessed just how valuable she might prove to be.

In October of 1928, both Means and Thacker were in Washington, D.C. Thacker and her husband were friendly with powerful Democrats like the head of the Anti-Saloon League and US Assistant Attorney General Mabel Walker Willebrandt who, incidentally, campaigned for Hoover—the Republican candidate—that fall. Willebrandt was no friend to Means as he'd been fired for being one of the worst enforcers of the Volstead Act, which she championed. But if Means could stay in Thacker's good graces, and by extension, her friends', then access to the dirt he was hired to unearth would be that much more easily gotten.[13]

Means's reputation as a man who could get information was re-gilded. So when Ned and Evalyn McLean wanted restitution for their perceived senatorial slander, there was but one man in Washington well-enough connected. Indeed, through cajoling, letter-writing, and frequent trips to Palm Beach, Florida, Means was able to get their mutual acquaintance, Mount Rushmore sculptor John Gutzon Borglum, to write Senator Norris and convince him to recant what he'd said about the McLeans. Means was very proud but, naturally, in a fix, so needed payment. For whatever reason, and despite Julie Means's repeated appeals, the McLeans never paid the $8,000 the Means felt they were due for greasing the various wheels.

The apparent debt did not keep Mrs. McLean from telephoning the Means's home on March 4, 1932, three days after the Lindbergh baby had been reported kidnapped. She wanted to help get the baby home safe and, apparently, figured that sometimes you need to hire a thief to catch a thief. Whether intentionally , or purposefully withholding, or genuinely flighty, Evalyn Walsh McLean was unbothered by the overdue remittance and, because Means had always been forthright about his sketchy past, she trusted Means to do the right thing while her interlocutor.

But Gaston Means never forgot a debt and always looked out for himself.

One of Means's most useful skills was keeping his fingers in as many pies as possible, often leveraging one pie into or against another. Just as William J. Burns had recognized Means's skills and sent him to save Maude King and her entourage, so too did his skills claim the attentions of another powerful set: Germany. In 1915, Captain Karl Boy-Ed was a German naval attaché in New York City who was secretly coordinating German wartime espionage. Boy-Ed found Means through the Burns Detective Agency, and Means found the relationship tantalizing. When Boy-Ed's espionage and true intentions were discovered by the US government in 1915, they found innumerable references to an "Agent E-13"

Mrs. McLean sits for a portrait wearing her favorite bauble—The Hope Diamond—almost twenty years before crossing Means's path.

who had provided them with any information they desired, no matter the veracity. If only they knew who Agent E-13 could be.

It was Means! He admitted to being Agent E-13 but explained that he, in turn, had information on every German operative in the United States. He also loudly explained that his work for the Germans predated the United States' entry into World War I and there was no need to mention treason or the like. So loyal was he that he would hand over the mountains of evidence he had collected on the Germans . . . in exchange for dismissing some of Means's pesky federal charges. Means's loyalty was often paid for but rarely bought.[14]

Despite Means's blockbuster testimony—he'd admitted to being a German operative while on the witness stand!—the fabricated second will of the late James King and his recently deceased widow's claim on the estate were being soundly discredited in the Chicago courts. It was in the interests of King's companies to prove the will a forgery given that the actual will kept the company intact. Expert testimony and the prosecution labeled Means a huckster and a forger—and a mediocre one, at that.

So Means took stock of his bargaining chips and did what Means did best; he leveraged one scam into another. He testified that Maude had been eager to partner with the Germans to sell them rubber during the Great War and that $167,000 was still due her estate after her untimely demise, essentially accusing Germany of being responsible for Maude's death. Bear in mind he had just been acquitted of her murder on his claim that her death was an accidental suicide.[15] Or maybe it was the theory he floated that Maude had been killed by a German operative who missed when intending to hit none other than Means himself! There was a flood of theories, most presented by Means, and often when on the witness stand. Confusion, misdirection, and theorizing aside, Means could feel the water rising. Now, it seemed, was the time for Means to access his "trunks of documents" on the Germans to hand over to the US Army in exchange for a letter of recommendation defending his character written to the Chicago judge overseeing the King will case. Means was always looking to nab as many birds with one stone as he could, no matter how fabricated or ephemeral the stone might be.

Means took his story to top Army brass and claimed he had reams of documents from his time dealing with and for the Germans—telegrams, codes, letters, receipts, spy reports, and so on—all of which he had stashed in a secret spot in North Carolina. The documents were in suitcases, and the suitcases were in a trunk buried in the hills. He would gladly retrieve this treasure if the Army did him the tiny favor of writing him a recommendation to the judge who ostensibly held Means's financial future in his hands. To sum up: Means wanted to trade the US Army a trove of documents obtained through treasonous subterfuge in exchange for a character reference to be sent to a judge who was presiding over a case to determine the validity of a forged document that would land Means with a payout of around $1 million. Means was nervy, to be sure.

There was a mad dash to retrieve his trove of documents. A military intelligence officer was waiting in Concord, North Carolina, when Means came into town with a giant trunk that he said he had retrieved from its hiding place in a monastery deep in the North Carolina hills. Means lifted the lid for a peek and verbally confirmed that these were the documents but that they needed to be examined in Washington. He escaped the intelligence officer's watchful gaze and sent the trunk to D.C., posthaste! But when senators opened the trunk once it arrived in Washington, it was empty. Not one single document. Means quickly blamed the Germans for perniciously stealing the papers en route—as if there were ever any documents to steal.[16]

Whatever good favor Means was currying with the military was gone with the wind, along with his reams of documents. The presiding judge soundly rejected the validity of the second will and said, "No fair consideration of this case can ignore the fact that Gaston B. Means is shown to be the controlling and dominating spirit in the attempt to establish this will. Indeed, the concluded is irresistible that Mrs. King and Mrs. Melvin were singularly under his influence and were largely dominated by his strong personality and inflexible will."[17]

❧

"The gang—there are about six of them—have the baby hidden on a boat off Norfolk. They've dyed its skin, dyed its curled hair, and even used a harmless liquid to change the child's eyes from blue to brown. When you see the Colonel, I want you to give him a message that will convince him that he is dealing with the proper gang. Tell him that the gang realized that the description of the baby's sleeping suit, released by state troopers to the newspapers, is an incorrect description."[18]

Means told this to Evalyn Walsh McLean on March 4, 1932, three days after twenty-month-old Charles Lindbergh Jr. was reported missing from the Lindbergh estate in Hopewell, New Jersey. The nation was aghast and breathless for information to help the Lindberghs. It was all anyone could talk of for days. Means didn't wait that long.

The Lindbergh baby was reported missing on a Tuesday evening. By Saturday evening of that same week, Means had secured permission from the Lindberghs to investigate, as well as a promise from Mrs. McLean to cover the ransom and expenses.

On Sunday, March 6, Means and Julie went to Far View, one of the McLeans' country estates. This was, Means said, to scope out the place as a potential handoff spot for the stolen baby. Means had styled himself as an intermediary for the kidnappers, and was selflessly walking the thin line between good and bad. Even Mrs. McLean said, "Gaston Means had sold himself to all of us, and I know that I was so tremendously excited by the thought of recovering the baby that I trusted him, unquestioningly."[19]

On Monday, March 7, Mrs. McLean mortgaged a block of her Washington, D.C., property and raised $100,000 cash. She put the cash in a box and gave it to Means, who acted unimpressed when receiving it but, upon getting it home, told Julie to never let it out of her sight, as if it might burst into flames. Once in the apartment, Means put the box on a shelf in a closet and set a bright-yellow costume wig on top of it. As if his methods weren't absurd enough already.

Means was smart enough to keep up appearances rather than scarpering with the cash right then and there. Though "smart" implies control over his actions; Means was pathological in his need for attention, and orchestrating a series of ridiculous schemes that drew directly on his experiences from both sides of the law was not something he could just walk away from. So, he set the stage and started directing.

The first planned exchange for the baby was at Far View, the McLean's country home in Maryland. Means had the money and would contact the kidnappers to arrange a drop-off. It would happen at midnight. Mrs. McLean was to follow his instructions to the letter for fear of inadvertently causing harm to be visited on the baby. Everything had to be coded. Mrs. McLean was "Number 11," the baby was "The Package," and Means was simply "Hogan."

By Tuesday night they were elbow-deep in the plan. Means was a master performer and knew his audience well, so he fed Mrs. McLean as much "top secret" pablum as he could. She was sick with anxiety but wanted nothing more than the safe return of the child. So, she submitted when "Hogan" instructed her to wait at Far View, with the lights off, until midnight when the Package would be delivered. To signal everything was alright, she was to listen for a series of twenty-one taps against a window, which would be repeated every five minutes, three times. If there was a pause longer than five minutes between the taps, she would know something was amiss.

At nearly midnight, a car pulled into the Far View drive and shut its lights off. Mrs. McLean held her breath as footsteps crunched through the snow toward the house. *Tap, tap, tap.* All twenty-one taps. Then there was an interminable five minutes of silence. All twenty-one taps came again at the window. There was another endless five-minute wait. Then six. Then seven. Then the car's engine broke the silence and slowly retreated from Far View. Something had gone wrong!

Mrs. McLean sat fretting in the darkness. She thought only of the Lindberghs. For half an hour, she sat in the dark, despairing. Then she heard the engine. The car had returned! With its lights off, it parked in the drive. Again, the footsteps. And again, *tap, tap, tap.* All twenty-one. Then five minutes exactly before the second set. Again, the full twenty-one. Again, she waited. But five minutes later, exactly, the taps made their final appearance. As soon as the twenty-first tap on the window echoed through the dark house, she burst out the back door to meet the car.

"Number 11, you come with me—at once."

It was "Hogan." Means. He and Mrs. McLean traveled back to Means's apartment, where he immediately poured himself a Means-sized drink and slumped in a chair.

"We were on our way to Far View in three cars, the baby in the middle car. I was leading. At the Maryland line I saw cops—a whole damned flock of 'em. I signaled. . . . [The other cars] turned around. I came through alone. I don't know where they are, but I've failed you."[20] Means was beside himself, but Mrs. McLean just wanted the baby back and was undeterred by this fall at the first hurdle. His performed distress was effective and recemented his good standing with Mrs. McLean, which meant he could keep her on the line for as many failed handoffs and near misses as he could contrive.

—◆—

Three days after being released from federal prison in 1928, Means was back in business. He was feeding May Dixon Thacker yarns about President Warren Harding and his wife, Florence. His lies were spun out of rumors or half-truths, making them both awkward and difficult to verify, but *The Strange Death of President Harding* was published in the spring of 1930. His lengthy airing of President Harding's dirty laundry, including a mistress, Nan Britton, and a baby, was capped with his accusation that Florence Harding had poisoned her husband to death out of jealousy. Not utter nonsense, but mostly.

Means had a singular skill for leveraging half-truths into whole cloth. Harding's mistress was indeed Nan Britton. And she did give birth to their child. But the rest was utter tosh. Further: Means later admitted he knew nothing of Nan Britton and whole-heartedly believed President Harding a staunchly monogamous man. This was doubly dastardly as his lies swept up scores of unwitting people—good and bad alike—into his house of cards, which they then had to support for fear of their own culpability when it all came crashing down. As J. Edgar Hoover, his onetime coworker but never a friend, wrote of Means: "He used the age-old trick of the confidence man in such deals—first involving his victims in a violation of the law. They would hesitate to make a complaint against him."[21]

Thacker repudiated and disavowed the book by the end of the following year, 1931; she'd experienced the full life cycle of one of Means's
cons but lived to tell the tale. Unlike Maude. For there was a rhythm to
his long cons. Whether syncopated or fluid or staccato, his moves were
practiced and always contributed to the overall flow of his set piece. But
he rarely got the ending right.

The lies he fed to Thacker were plausible when considered individu-
ally and downright sensational as a whole. Means was a disgraced former
Department of Justice official from the Harding administration so *must*
have had the inside scoop, right? Means didn't consider the personal toll
of his lies, only how to capitalize on them.

In prison, Means had continued playing both sides; he was a stool
pigeon for the warden, but was also often in cahoots with some of the
same people he'd put away when a DOJ agent. He lived his days convinced he was always the smartest person in the room and so was indiscriminate in finding his marks. "From his underworld friends he learned
much that was valuable to an investigator. Sometimes he played the game
straight on the side of the law; at other times the temptation of large
amounts of money was too strong for him and he switched his allegiance
to the outlaws. I never knew where he stood when he was working a case,
but it was a pretty good bet he was playing both sides for all they were
worth most of the time."[22]

The events that led to Means going to jail (the first time) came at a
breakneck speed. As his method required leveraging one lie into another,
his crimes started to meld in such a way that they became difficult to
pinpoint. He flooded courtrooms with wild accusations that were based
on rumors he himself had started. He would offer deals to bootleggers
and never follow up. He would make up calls from important people just
so he could later refer to them as "evidence."

His schemes started to seriously catch up with him in October of
1923. He had already been hired and fired within six months from the
Department of Justice, but he remained deeply involved in the Harding

administration's graft. The following twelve months, he was in and out of the courtroom as witness for the prosecution or the defendant, depending on the day. He feared jail and so lashed out whenever possible, throwing everyone in the administration under the bus, attorney general included. Despite his best efforts and worst instincts, Means was convicted of violating the Prohibition law in late September of 1924. He immediately appealed to the court to be held a pauper because he was flat broke.

Come October 1, though, he was taken to court for unpaid taxes. It was a total of $267,614.40 in unpaid taxes and fees. The Internal Revenue Service became aware of Means's delinquency only through Means's endless testimony on how much money had passed through his hands as an agent of graft during the Harding years. Oops.[23]

The expression on Gaston Means's perfectly round face accurately reflects his casual dis/interest in playing by the rules.
"GASTON MEANS IN COURT," BETWEEN 1909 AND 1932, LIBRARY OF CONGRESS, PRINTS & PHOTO-GRAPHS DIVISION, LC-USZ62-102198 (BLACK AND WHITE FILM COPY NEGATIVE), https://www.loc.gov/resource/cph.3c02198/.

While out on appeal—he was granted pauper's status—Means traveled to his home in Concord. There he claimed to be stricken with an acute gallstone attack and, therefore, unable to travel. He had his doctor write a note to that effect. He had implicated all his friends in high places so had nowhere to turn when he was soon arrested for failure to appear but also for faking the illness. He did not go quietly but was ultimately sentenced to two years and incarcerated in the Atlanta Federal Penitentiary on May 20, 1925. In 1927, all other pending prosecution of Means was dropped; he was given a second chance to move through the world with a hard-won tabula rasa. But in that mercy, Means saw only weakness.

—⁓—

Mrs. McLean sat panting in a chair in her room at the Paso del Norte while her nurse tended to her. She was extremely shaken after being in a high-speed car chase just north of the Mexican border. Her heart was fluttering, and her breath was short, but all she could think of was the Lindbergh baby.

Moments after catching her breath, Means burst into her room, his clothes covered in mud and his face drawn and pale. He spun her a story of being kidnapped and spirited across the border by gangsters who demanded he tell them where the Lindbergh baby was hidden. But he was stalwart and courageous and had wrested himself free of their dastardly clutches.

"What rotten breaks we're getting! That baby would have been in your arms right now. . . . First the police, now high-jackers!"

Mrs. McLean could only agree and then told Means of her harrowing car ride earlier that night.

"This is getting serious. If anything should happen to me, give this up and return to Washington. Don't risk trying to carry on alone. The money is in the safe at my home in Chevy Chase. Julie will turn it over to you at any time." Comforting words, however hollow.[24]

While on their goose chase they were missing the Lindbergh action back east, which now saw a $50,000 ransom being dropped in a Brooklyn graveyard. The FBI was on the case and lending all possible resources to local authorities to do whatever it took to get the baby home safe. (It must be noted that the child was already dead at this point, according to forensics performed upon discovering the corpse in early May, a half-mile from the Lindbergh farm.) The $50,000 was in marked bills and gold bonds and, therefore, un-spendable. "Luckily" for Mrs. McLean, Means could make contact with this other group of baddies and buy back the marked $50,000 at a discount of $35,000. What luck!

Mrs. McLean was desperate to help. She had been wiling away the days with worry in El Paso for over a week but couldn't sit still any longer, not when she could help the poor Colonel Lindbergh. Saving him $15,000 *and* getting his $50,000 returned was the least she could do, given the $104,000 she'd already given to Means needed to stay whole in case the ransom was called for. But she would get the money. She boarded a train for Washington the next day.

Mrs. McLean was genteel but human. She wanted to get the $35,000 in cash right away and so called a friend to meet her at her sumptuous home in Washington. She gathered a subset of her jewelry—not the Hope Diamond—and solemnly presented it to her friend. "I want you to pawn this. I must raise $35,000 on it, not a penny less. And I must get it at once."[25]

When a cheat is unmasked, victims can exhibit a host of emotional responses. Mrs. McLean's friend stared, gawping as Mrs. McLean described the whole unfortunate series of events. From Means's demonstrated grief over the taken child, to the details he used like breadcrumbs, to the $104,000 Mrs. McLean had given him for the ransom and expenses, to the car chase in El Paso. The friend—a true friend—refused to do anything with Mrs. McLean's jewels and told her to, instead, go immediately to her lawyers; Means was a cheat and a liar, and he was abusing Mrs. McLean's good nature and trust.

She had spent the better part of a month traveling with Means in pursuit of the baby, always one stop behind Means's contacts. Her days and nights were filled with codes and secrets and high-stakes excitement. "Previously I had interpreted every act of Means as part of an attempt to get the baby back. Now, interpreting these same actions as an attempt to get—and keep—my $104,000, they seemed a lot more credible and a lot less ridiculous."[26]

Even though he already had $104,000, Mrs. McLean knew Means couldn't resist a $35,000 payday. She wired Means to say she couldn't travel, and he should come to Washington to retrieve it. He happily obliged. She lured him back to his hometown jurisdiction, where he was followed by Department of Justice men every step of the way. Rather like the work he used to do.

Means strode into the McLean mansion all smiles and how-do-you-dos. He charmed her in his usual way: "Greetings, Number 11."

"Number 11 be damned! Now get this, Means: The little act is over. You don't know where the Lindbergh baby is any more than I do. I get my money back or you go to jail. Which is it to be? You'd better go home right now, get it out of your safe, and bring it here." Mrs. McLean had had enough. She demanded her money. Means was shocked but tried to recover with a show of repentance.

"I hid it in Concord—for safety's sake. I'll have to go down there to get it. . . . None of that money has been spent. You may be sure that it will be returned—to the last penny." His hulking frame was slumped and sad as he shuffled out the door. It would have been a pitiable scene had it been anyone else but Means.

The agents followed him to Concord, where they saw him retrieve a brown suitcase from the Means family home, which he tossed onto the seat of his car before heading back toward Washington. The agents lost sight of him until the following morning when they spotted him in D.C., heading to meet Mrs. McLean. She was waiting for him.

"How about the money, Means?"

He looked astonished. "What?! Do you mean to tell me you didn't receive that money?"

What followed would have sounded incredible to anyone who didn't know Means and his ways. He launched a tale of being stopped while crossing the Alexandria, Virginia, bridge. He was approached by a single man, waving a red lantern. This stranger announced, "Number 11 sent me; give me The Package." As the "Red-Lanterned-Man" knew Mrs. McLean's code name, why shouldn't he have trusted him? Means was apparently easily convinced to part with Mrs. McLean's $104,000 on that bridge. It was not his fault a clandestine stranger knew their code, was it?

On May 5, 1932, just over two months since Means's kidnapping chicanery began, he was arrested, and by June, he was convicted for larceny after trust and sentenced to fifteen years in prison. In 1933, two additional years were added to his sentence. He was transferred to Leavenworth, Kansas, in 1934, and his parole was denied in the summer of 1936. He was moved to the Hospital for Defective Delinquents in Springfield, Missouri, in 1938. The same illness—gallstones—he had faked to avoid going to jail in 1924 ended him on December 12, 1938. Julie was by his side when he passed. He used his dying breaths to confess something, but she couldn't hear.

Chapter Seven

If It Walks Like a Drake, and Squawks Like a Drake . . .

THE TIME:	1595–2003
THE PLACE:	Plymouth, England
	Berkeley, CA
	London, England
	Bloomington, IL
	Des Moines, IA
	Sioux City, IA
	Leavenworth, KS
THE TAKE:	$1.3 million, free drinks, first-class fares to/from England, the promise of $25 billion, the city of Plymouth, England, and all the gold in the Bank of England
THE PLAYERS:	Sir Francis Drake
	Professor Herbert Bolton
	Queen Elizabeth I
	Dr. Beckwith
	The Pantagraph
	Dr. W. D. Jones
	Mrs. Sudie B. Whitaker
	Mr. Whitaker
	Milo Lewis
	Mrs. Alma Shepard

Col. Drexel Drake
Mrs. Nina St. John Montague
Thomas Barnard
John Sparks
Carlos Goltz
Charles Challen
P. J. Cahill
Canfield Hartzell
Oscar Hartzell
anyone in America with the surname "Drake"

IN THE SUMMER OF 1936, A YOUNG MAN TOOK A SUNDAY DRIVE ALONG the California coast. He'd wended into the hills along the San Quentin ridge above San Francisco Bay when his tire blew. The day was so nice that he was unbothered by the unexpected pit stop and left his lamed vehicle by the side of the road while he hiked to get a better view of the Bay. He scrambled through thickets and under a barbed wire fence to reach a lookout point. He stopped and considered the natural vista as he casually rolled rocks down the steep hillside. He reached down for another rolling stone, but a small piece of dull metal sticking out from the dirt caught his attention. It wasn't shiny or visually compelling, but it was just the right size to patch a hole in the floor of his limping auto, so he casually pocketed it before calling it a day.

It was more than six months after his outing that the young man remembered the metal plate lying in his back seat, awaiting repurposing. As he held it to the hole in his vehicle's body, he noticed what looked like an inscription on the plate, mostly undecipherable but clearly ending with "cis Drake." He thought better of welding the object to his clunker and instead took it to Professor Herbert Eugene Bolton at the University of California. If anyone would know what to do with this artifact, it was Bolton, who had been professor and chair of the history department for twenty-five years. While there he'd forged his reputation as a scholar, founded the Bancroft Library, and moonlighted as a longtime leading member of the California Historical Society.

After the piece of metal was carefully scrubbed, the markings became clearer, and Bolton was able to decipher the following:

Bee it knowne vnto all men by these presents JVNE 15, 1579
   By the grace of god and in the name of herr majesty Qveen Eliz-
abeth of England and herr svccessors forever I take possession of this
kingdome whose king and people freely resigne their right and title in
the whole land vnto herr majesties keeping now named by me an to
bee knowne vnto all men as nova albion. Francis Drake.

As he held the crudely engraved metal plate, Bolton did all he could to contain his excitement. "My mind leaped to the conjecture at once, because for years I have been telling my students to keep an eye out for Drake's plate."[1] While he was globally recognized as a scholar of the Americas, Bolton's well-known pet obsession had been focused strictly on that scourge of the high seas, that buccaneer who felled the Spanish Main with grit and luck, Queen Elizabeth's pirate crown jewel: Sir Francis Drake.

The following April, in 1937, Bolton gave a speech at the California Historical Society. He began with a brief refresher for his audience, paraphrasing a well-known history lesson: Sir Francis Drake landed somewhere along the California coast to refit his global sailing voyage in 1579. After the six weeks it took for Drake and his crew to repair the *Golden Hind*, they marked their presence with "a large post, firmly planted, upon which he caused to be nailed a plate of brass, engraven with the name of the English Queen, the day and year of his arrival . . . and, underneath it all, his own name."[2] Bolton's fellow Historical Society members indulged him, but they audibly gasped when he said, "Here it is—recovered at last after a lapse of 357 years. Behold, Drake's plate—the plate of brass. California's choicest archeological treasure."[3]

With the willing assistance of a group of San Francisco residents and the president of the California Historical Society, Bolton purchased the plate from the waylaid motorist for the Society, which in turn gave it to the Bancroft Library's permanent collection at the University of

California. All of California's historians were electrified by the discovery, and to the naysayers, Bolton said, "If the Drake plate is bogus, the hoax was perpetrated by someone who had not only studied the history of his voyages minutely, but who also had knowledge of ship fittings of the sixteenth century and of spikes. . . . The evidence furnished by the plate itself and the circumstances of its discovery leave little room to doubt its authenticity."[4]

The size, shape, inscription, location, and hewn markings on the plate were tested and found consistent with sixteenth-century details before the Drake Plate was put on permanent display in the esteemed Bancroft Library. Until his death in 1953, Professor Bolton's excitement never dimmed that he was able to be near the invaluable artifact, that piece of Drake history he'd held in his own hands.

—◆—

When he landed on America's West Coast in 1579, Francis Drake was searching for the Northwest Passage to travel home to his beloved Queen Elizabeth with a pirate's payload worth of sacked Spanish treasure. His return to Plymouth with over eighty pounds of gold and twenty-six tons of silver weighing down the belly of the *Golden Hind* was celebrated for months, his journey being the first circumnavigation helmed by one captain, and only the second recognized after Magellan's historic voyage in 1522. The booty he brought to his Queen from raids in Panama and from any Spanish ship that dared get close to *El Draque*, as they called him, outstripped even Elizabeth's wildest dreams, and Drake was knighted in 1581.

Sir Francis continued sailing and fighting and pirating until succumbing to dysentery off the Panamanian coast in 1597, nearly ten years after defending England from the Spanish armada in 1588. Though he dabbled in politics, Sir Francis's heart was at sea. What time he spent on land was chiefly at Buckland Abbey, in Devon, which he purchased after his globe-spanning voyage in 1580. He and his wife were childless but happy. He was made mayor of Plymouth. He was briefly a member of Parliament. Drake's domestic life was only diverting for as long as it took him to get his land-legs; once on solid ground, the sea would call him back.

The Spanish, the Portuguese, everyone in Africa and South America, and probably North America, too, had a bone to pick with Sir Francis. He "found" treasure all over the world and claimed it all in Elizabeth's name. His success as a rover and pirate was legendary but only celebrated by those he was roving and pirating for. When his body was given to the sea in a lead-lined coffin in 1597, he was the only man on Earth who had a personally earned global reputation as a scourge and an evidence-based hero's welcome in England.

His problematic legacy did not sully his standing in Plymouth where, when mayor, he oversaw the construction of man-made rivers to provide badly needed fresh water. Beginning less than ten years after his death, Plymouth began an annual "Fishing Feast" in the summer to honor Sir Francis, who spent his life on the briny sea but brought potable water to little Plymouth. One of the English-speaking world's oldest secular festivals, the Fishing Feast, is still observed annually. To kick off the feast Plymouth's mayor and chamberlain drink from two goblets while declaring, "May the descendants of him who brought us water never want for wine."[5]

California was granted statehood in 1850, and Oregon attained it in 1859. When hashing out borders, Sir Francis Drake's brief stop at New Albion was remembered by American lawmakers who held their breath that England would not come knocking for Sir Francis's staked plot along the West Coast.

They were right to be anxious as there was activity in the courts that pointed to Americans' fervor for genealogy and windfalls coalescing into sustained legal battles over what people were entitled to versus what they were actually due. The distinction was subtle and under active debate in the American courts.

The progenitor of the contested estate mania was the Anneke Jans Bogardus fight over the sale of a tract of New Amsterdam land that later became the site of Trinity Church. Nine of Anneke's ten children signed on to sell the land in 1671, but the holdout's children felt slighted and filed a claim in pursuit of a fortune to which they felt entitled. For since England had purchased the land, the value had increased exponentially, and their descendant's glancing brush with future fortune chapped the Bogardus heirs. Between 1735 and 1850, over twenty lawsuits were filed, and every one of them was struck down. The scope and value of the claims increased with each generation. Associations were formed to hire lawyers to continue the fight.

Though the Jans Bogardus associations were unsuccessful in court, in practice, they set precedents for the kind of lawsuit (claim to an estate, frivolous), the enthusiasm for recompense (fortunes awaited, aggressive), and the length of time to pursue justice (unending) for future generations of slighted heirs. The Jans Bogardus associations failed in court, but their ardor produced a rich vein of followers.[7]

One thing must be made crystal clear: there was no Jans Bogardus estate to pursue. The family had sold the land. The descendants were entitled to resentment and regret but were due absolutely nothing. That the courts had entertained the Jans Bogardus claims for a hundred years only served to embolden future self-styled heirs, who would wrack their brains and raid their family trees for evidence of claims to estates "tied up" by the British Crown. One such estate, that of William Jennings, was advertised as unclaimed in American newspapers while soliciting anyone named "Jennings" to stake their piece of the £7 million pie.[7] To repeat, though: THERE WERE NO ESTATES TO CLAIM. From Jennings, Bogardus, or anyone else. The fortunes had already been meted out, and whatever was left was already well beyond the statute of limitations.

But the wave of inheritance enthusiasm had momentum. While lawmakers hoped Sir Francis's brief stop along the California coast would be conveniently forgotten by the Crown as state borders were being drawn, the mention of Sir Francis and his fabulous hoard appeared in 1850s American newspaper columns adjacent to those soliciting claimants to unclaimed estates. It did not take long for readers to connect the two.

"We hope our Mr. Drake will succeed in making good his claim to the immense property, now, like the 'Jennings' estate, in want of an heir. It is true that it was at one time doubted whether Drake was a Buccaneer or a law-abiding Englishman, but as the Virgin Queen solved that doubt by making him an Admiral and a Knight, we hope our Mr. Drake will have no conscientious scruples about taking the fortune founded by Sir Francis."[8]

This little notice in the *Weekly Raleigh Register* in October of 1858 was the first mention of the "Drake Estate" in American newspapers. The Reverend Caswell Drake of North Carolina took it upon himself to travel to London to investigate his claim, confidently believing himself to be on the receiving end of a long line of Drake descendants. By February of 1859, Mrs. Anna Cooper of Cincinnati was in all the papers for *her* claim to the Drake line.

While Rev. Drake was in England, another Drake—Samuel G. Drake, Esquire—wrote a letter to his brother in Raleigh, stating unequivocally, "That there is no shadow of ground on which to base his supposition that the Drake family in America can lay claim to any portion of the estate of Sir Francis Drake."[9] This letter was printed in the *Raleigh Christian Advocate* in May of 1859.

In October of that year, *The Sunday Delta* of New Orleans wrote of Mrs. Cooper's claim to the estate: "The recovery of this stupendous property is doubtful; but that lady, or any other lady, or any gentleman, who forward . . . $10, $5, or $2.50, will insure their chances of drawing a prize of $50,000 or its proportion. This sum drawn is paid down, and not subject to the litigations and doubts attending lawsuits in England to recover doubtful estates and fabulous fortunes."[10] Or, in other words: Suckers beware, for the only sure thing in the Drake bet is that money put in never pays out.

The Civil War broke out in April of 1861, which forced the Drake machinations to take a backseat. But in the two years preceding the Drake Estate seed had been sown in the fields plowed by the Jans and Jennings' Estates, and the roots grew fast and wide.

———

New York City was a pulsing, energetic collision of people in 1870, and on August 24, in Brandreth House's Parlor A on the corners of Canal Street and Broadway, fifty disparate souls gathered.

The lobby of the hotel was littered with trunks and bags, bivouacked in inelegant heaps. The entire building was abuzz. A *New York Herald* reporter was on the scene.

"What part of the building is Parlor A?" he asked a hotel employee.

"So you want to go there, too, do you?" This was a strange reply.

"That is my intention."

"I suppose you're one of 'em?"

The reporter was otherwise professional but was literally dumbstruck as to how to answer.

"Your name is the same as the rest, I suppose?" the hotel man pressed.

The reporter paused.

"Oh! It's the like of you don't know at all, and you goin' to Parlor A. Why, I know your name."

Again, the reporter paused, silent.

"Isn't your name . . ."

"What?"

"DRAKE?!" The worker slapped his thigh and doubled over with laughter. The reporter remained bemused while the man laughed himself silly. When he replied that no, his name wasn't Drake, the laughter faded. The worker steadied himself and extended a hand to show the reporter the way to Parlor A. As they trudged into the hotel the worker muttered, "'Pon my soul I'm glad to hear it; for I've had nothing but Drakes here all the day." Parlor A's double doors were propped open, and the room was teeming with people. "They're all there, every mother's son of 'em," the worker said soberly. He considered the room another moment before disappearing.

What lay before the reporter was a picture-perfect cross-section of the broad spectrum of 1870 (white) Americans. There were men, women, and children; there were hayseeds, indigents, and upper-crust; there was deaf, dumb, and talkative—and all of them Drakes.

Though Drake news was scarce in the papers during the war, grass-roots communication kept humming. By 1870, word of the claim had spread, and the Drake Estate heirs were assembling to hash out who was which Drake and what was due to whom. There were Jersey Drakes. Michigan Drakes. New York Drakes. Ohio Drakes. North Carolina

Drakes. Maine Drakes. And, of course, England's Drakes, whom their American cousins had collectively supposed to be pretenders to the estate and the Crown their greedy, silent partner.

From the thrumming chatter of Parlor A rose a clear voice. The Drakes quieted themselves as Dr. Beckwith stood to address the hopeful, expectant faces of the would-be millionaires, all of whom were hungry for information on their claim.[11]

Beckwith was prepared and all too happy to wade into the minutiae. He had come armed with copies of Sir Francis's will, as well as those of Sir Francis's brother, Thomas, and Thomas's eldest son, Francis. He explained the matter as follows: Sir Francis had no children, so he bequeathed his estate to his brother, Thomas, who bequeathed the estate to his sons, the eldest being called Francis. Upon his death Francis (the younger) was to will the estate to his male heirs, and absent heirs, he was to will it to the next eldest brother to pass to *his* male heirs. However, upon Francis's death, his will had been amended such that his daughters would inherit the estate rather than his nephews. One of these nephews, also named Francis, came to America, and those in Parlor A who could prove a link to Sir Francis Drake's grand-nephew, Francis Drake, should start preparing their genealogical materials in anticipation of a payout.

Sir Francis Drake had willed an annuity to the city of Plymouth (£20) and an annuity to the poor and almshouses (another £20). The proceeds from his estate (once his corporeal debts were settled) went to his wife, Dame Elizabeth, and management of his estate and ultimate ownership to his brother, Thomas. This included nearly all his properties in Devon, many of which were mills or tenant houses that would continue bearing profit long after Sir Francis's death, thereby assuring his family's comfort. The actual value of the estate would have been practically impossible to determine, but even a conservative estimate of the value of the 8,000 acres of landholdings in 1870's dollars was close to a billion. That's Billion-with-a-B. Even conceiving of this amount of money would have been difficult for the Drakes in Parlor A. The figure Beckwith quoted was $125 million.[12]

Beckwith's biased view of the Drake family tree—he was married to one of the many Drake heirs—was both incomplete and incorrect. To repeat: there was no unclaimed Drake Estate. Beckwith's version claimed the Crown had $125 million salted away, Drake's (imagined) hoard having accrued interest in the preceding 275 years. This was in addition to the 8,000 acres and all the rents and profits deriving therefrom since *their* Francis was denied his inheritance, amounting to over two hundred years' worth of back rent with interest. As Beckwith told it, the returns for a small amount of the Drakes' time, money, and effort were dizzyingly high; for just $1 paid to the cause, Beckwith was hawking a return of $5,000—a life-changing sum in 1870.[13]

As Beckwith happily gave the odds to the gaggle of Drakes in Brandreth House, a sister meeting was held in Philadelphia. Drake Associations were forming in pockets around the country and all after a common goal: Sir Francis's nonexistent unclaimed fortune. There was a prescribed rush to raid family trees and heirlooms for evidence of Drake lines to shore up the claim. But as one association was growing its research, so too were others, and in practice, there would have been at least five competing suits for the same (unmerited) claim. Luckily for Beckwith—and unlucky for the flock of Drakes—there was little in the way of accountability, so whatever bits of genealogical information the eager claimants fed to him, Beckwith could spoon back out as breadcrumbs. How dastardly of Beckwith to fleece the people of their money and their family histories; how pitiful the people paying to be fleeced while trying to take care of their own, as Sir Francis had done for his family through his will.

When the Brandreth House meeting was drawing to a close, the *Herald* reporter felt the excitement and avarice grow in the room. The "Drakers" were dutifully lining up to give Dr. Beckwith their money to help defray any costs that he might incur bringing their suit to court, while hopefully securing their positions on the ground floor. Each of them had big plans. A young lad—Charley Drake—when asked what he would do if he got all that money, proudly announced, "Buy 'lasses candy!" which would have been a safer investment than the illusory estate.

They gave Beckwith their money and their family secrets; he kept the former and spun the latter. The Drakers ransacked their own houses and hope chests for documents and family Bibles to use as evidence to establish lineal lines. They clamored to whisper long-held secrets to Beckwith in hopes that it would serve their common cause. One of Beckwith's fellow Drake Estate salesmen placed an ad in Brooklyn newspapers to solicit knowledge and artifacts related to the Drake Estate. One member of the Long Island Drakes consulted a clairvoyant who tapped into the ethereal plane and the Drake vibrations—perhaps she communed with Sir Francis himself—to reveal that the long-lost family Bible was under a pile of dust in a cubby in the side of the chimney in their family farmhouse. As fate would have it, this Bible held the "best" and "most accurate" history of the family such that all signs pointed toward the legitimacy of the Long Island claim. What kismet![14] Beckwith was selling a wildly warped story, rooted in an untruth, so likely had zero qualms about receiving evidence with questionable integrity. It's not like he was actually trying to prove their claim in court.

But the appearance of legitimacy—no matter how contrived—was what Beckwith and his fellow organizers were actually selling; with each new genealogical item they expanded the narrative so that the intel became a key to the final link in the family chain, rather than the link itself. For two years following his pitch to the Brandreth House Drakes, Beckwith continued this cat-and-mouse game with the Drakers' information, all while collecting fees. After one of his last documented meetings, held in Jersey City in 1872, Beckwith was thus described: "When the descendants of the great Sir Francis grow lukewarm to contributing to the expenses of the investigation, Mr. B fans their ardor judiciously by revelations of important discoveries. . . . Though it's our first acquaintance with him, Mr. Beckwith impresses us as an artist. This rich-ancestor-in-England business has been sadly botched, and the sight of a man like Beckwith affords us a welcome relief from the contemplation of confidence games vulgarly played."[15] A glowing endorsement indeed.

Beckwith exited the game after two years on the scene. Perhaps he was found out. Perhaps he bowed out. Whatever the nature of his exit, Beckwith's was not the final Midas touch upon the Drake narrative; he'd lined his pockets while greasing the wheels, but he did not have ownership of the Draker momentum.

The paterfamilias of an ever-growing number of select few: Sir Francis Drake.
"PORTRAIT OF SIR FRANCIS DRAKE," FROM *THE WORLD ENCOMPASSED*, FROM THE KRAUS COL-
LECTION OF SIR FRANCIS DRAKE. ENGRAVING WITH HIS COAT OF ARMS AND MOTTO, *SIC PARVIS
MAGNA*–"THUS GREAT THINGS FROM SMALL THINGS COME." PUBLIC DOMAIN, https://commons.
wikimedia.org/w/index.php?curid=1507923.

The Draker game was so irksome to lawmakers that three successive US ambassadors to London issued official correspondence to dissuade credulous Americans. In 1892, Ambassador Robert Todd Lincoln echoed the warning against "putting any money with persons claiming to have any interest in any so-called Sir Francis Drake Estate."[16] Ambassador Lincoln's statement was tacitly underscored by a quote often attributed to his late father: "You can fool all of the people some of the time, and you can fool some of the people all of the time; but you can't fool all the people all the time."

The Draker game was so deeply rooted in America that—like the invasive kudzu plant introduced to US soil at the 1876 Philadelphia Centennial Exposition—as soon as one branch of the game was pruned, two more grew in its place. And without legal action taken by those who'd been swindled (the Drakers themselves) newspapers and politicians were loath to wade into the fray beyond issuing warnings and occasionally poking fun at the so-called heirs. That is until the game came to Bloomington, Illinois and the reporters of *The Pantagraph*.

In 1911, the briefly dormant Drake game was picking up speed between Bloomington and St. Louis, Missouri. There were new players in a slightly different configuration, but the central components were the same: local people were allowed to pay for the privilege of being a once-and-future Drake. Whereas Beckwith and his compatriots had made themselves the nexus points through which all-things-Drake needed to pass, this new iteration had layers of agents. Potential Drakers were more receptive to investing when the details were expressed by someone they knew, someone local, who would also act as the clearinghouse for the money and the information. What the agent collected in $1, $10, $50, and $100 installments was remitted to the higher-ups, while they would feed him information piecemeal, which he would then feed back to the local Drakers. This new setup was twofold genius because it gave the head grifters an added layer of plausible deniability and safety, and was inherently effective as the local promoters were usually themselves investors—a true believer is more convincing when preaching to potential converts.

Mrs. Sudie Whitaker, her husband, and Chicago attorney Milo Lewis were the brains behind this generation of the Drake swindle. The Whitakers were out of St. Louis, 250 miles from Bloomington, but their Draker territory extended up to Chicago and over to Sioux City, Iowa. Whereas Beckwith had pinned his operations on the missing Drake heir, this crew assigned Mrs. Whitaker—Sudie—the leading role of "rightful lineal descendant." She was selling shares of her Drake inheritance before-the-fact to fund the research and litigation required to prize the contents of the Estate from the English pretenders. The Whitakers and Lewis had local agents in towns across their territory. In Bloomington, it was Dr. W. D. Jones.

When the Drake game came to Bloomington in 1911, Jones was the local salesman but he had nothing but vitriol for the paper's reporters and their questions. "Now, I refuse to talk for publication," published *The Pantagraph*, "and I don't want my name connected with this matter. When I get something authentic on this question I will tell you about it, but until then I have nothing to say."[17] Jones's attitude and *The Pantagraph*'s search for information clashed savagely; lines in the sand between the Drakers and everyone else were being drawn in Bloomington. *The Pantagraph* continued to report, and Jones had the paper branded an "enemy of the people" amongst the Drakers in return. The Drakers believed Jones, and Jones hated *The Pantagraph*, so the Drakers hated *The Pantagraph*. That the transitive nature of their opinions was determined from the top down made the Drakers that much harder to convince of the facts of the matter, let alone that their claims were rooted in fraud.

In January of 1912, Bloomington was anxiously awaiting the arrival of Mr. Whitaker. Jones had promised him a dozen times before, and the local investors were starting to sweat. There were theories surrounding his delay that flew among the faithful: some said the Drake castle had been sold for $1.5 million so time was needed to apportion; others said a literal boatload of Drake Estate money had been held up en route from England. Amid the rumors were the first whispers of anxiety from Drakers over the integrity of their investment. But Bloomington's unconverted did not mince words, which only deepened the Drakers' us-versus-them mentality. One newly immigrated Englishman met a particularly chilly reception in Bloomington when he said, "In my country promoters sell shares in Alaskan gold mines and here they sell stock in old estates."[18] Meanwhile, children in the street were pronouncing, "We are going to get a whole lot of money pretty soon. . . . Mr. Drake is going to give it to us."[19] These were the two sides in the binary—haughty arrogance versus wholesome worthiness—with no shades of gray in between.

On January 8, 1912, *The Pantagraph* tried, again, to settle the matter. The paper's managing editor wrote for an authoritative answer for the people of Bloomington as to whether they should hold their breath for a golden flood. *The London Times*'s pithy, if exasperated, reply should have been the end of it: "There are not $600,000,000, as once claimed by the American promoters, nor $25,000,000, nor 25¢ remaining of the estate of the lamented Sir Francis awaiting distribution to claimants." The editor went on to express sympathy for those who had unfortunately handed over their coin and demanded the perpetrators answer for their deception.[20]

But less than a week later a group of over two hundred Drakers met in the basement of the Unitarian Church in downtown Bloomington. Dr. Jones had rented the room especially. The Whitakers had finally arrived, and they were ready to address the flock. The Drakers, Dr. Jones, and *The Pantagraph* were all eager to learn where things stood. But the rift between Dr. Jones and the newspaper had widened into a chasm, and the meeting started off with absurd fanfare as Dr. Jones forcibly ejected a *Pantagraph* reporter from the room. The imbroglio was cheered by the Drakers, and horrified the two *Pantagraph* reporters who remained in the room undetected. The meeting was officially called, and Dr. Jones used his opening remarks to again rail against *The Pantagraph*'s incessant meddling and compared this perceived persecution to that which Jesus Christ suffered in his final days. The Drakers ate this up.

Whitaker took the lectern. His large frame and balding pate and purple necktie and tawny mustache and oversized jade pinky ring made him a sight to behold. The church basement was in a frenzy. Whitaker announced he had information that there would be court action on the Drake Estate in six weeks, with the whole matter to be settled by 1913. He explained that he had been doing his own genealogical research on his wife's ancestral line and that everyone heretofore had gotten it wrong by focusing on the wrong Drake. Why, he had certified copies of a host of wills to prove it! Whitaker held a sheaf of papers aloft like Moses presenting the stone tablets as the Drakers strained to see. He let them drink in the enormity of his stack of papers before getting to the good stuff; Whitaker's research had determined that the Drake Estate would pay out upwards of £350 million, or, in plainer terms, nearly $1.75 billion—a healthy bump from the measly $125 million (of imaginary money) Beckwith had offered forty years prior. Whitaker said he would return to England in February in further pursuit of their cause.

The Drakers' furor sometimes gave way to strained anxiety. When pressed on how they were to receive information, Whitaker deftly passed the buck: "Have you confidence in our local representative [Dr. Jones]? If so, talk to him and he will tell you all, for he will be in touch with my movements." Shoot the messenger, please.

Whitaker pressed on, flooding the Drakers with numbers, dates, family names, amounts, and places. He got into the weeds of real estate values (high!) and inheritance taxes (too high!) and British parliamentary procedures (tedious and expensive but necessary!). According to him, the English kept moving the goalposts such that the Drake heirs always found the estate just out of reach, and that this was further evidence of England's designing plot to keep the Drake hoard through clever and devious schemes. (Pot, meet kettle.)

Whitaker emphasized that it was going to take a little more faith and a little more money to realize their aims: "When I go over there again, I'll not wire for money unless it is absolutely necessary, but when I do wire I want to have $500, or $1,000 or whatever amount I ask for . . . it is necessary and I am sure of results, for my signature on a cablegram means business." Even amid the mammoth dollar amounts flying across the room, Whitaker was sure to emphasize that it was up to the Drakers to give him their money so he could spend it to try to get them their money. Oy.

Before the meeting adjourned, there were a series of pointed questions about Mr. Lewis, their Chicago partner, who was conspicuously absent from the meeting. (Remember, there were at least two incognito reporters still present.) The questions did not comfort Whitaker, who sputtered more than once as Sudie rushed to fill in the blanks with vague answers about Lewis's arrest record. One of the final questions was particularly incisive: "Were you ever arrested for fraudulent use of the mails in connection with the Drake estate?" The Whitakers ended the meeting in response. The final order of business was to pass the hat for a collection to reimburse Dr. Jones the $10 he'd spent securing the room—a remarkably fitting end to the meeting.

The evening's coda was the arrest of Dr. Jones. His manhandling of the reporter had induced assault charges, and two officers arrived at the meeting as the Drakers were starting to disperse. As the policemen approached the doctor, Jones greeted them with a barked question: "Are you from *The Pantagraph*?!"

"No, I am an officer. I have a warrant to serve on you."

"I will come to the police station tomorrow morning."

"No, you will not, Doctor. You will have to come with us now. You are under arrest."

The two officers escorted Dr. Jones to the police station, followed by a small gaggle of incensed Drakers. Jones was booked on a charge of assault and paid his bail of $10—which he borrowed from a friend—before he was released into the Bloomington night. The Whitakers were not present, having slipped from the church basement with the arrival of the arresting officers.[21]

～⌣～

Bloomington's Drake mania came to an end not with a bang but with a whimper. "Case lost. House of lords decides against us. –LEWIS." This brief, loaded message was conveyed to the Bloomington Drakers on November 15, 1912. It came swiftly on the heels of, "Send $200 at once. Whitaker and I want to come home. –LEWIS." Since the heady days of Dr. Jones's basement rally in January of that year, he, the Whitakers, and Milo Lewis had been ostensibly hard at work furthering the claim's cause. They all traveled to London in February where research and fancy footwork had revealed that—shocker—they were going to need more money.[22]

A week after the cablegrams, a group of a dozen Drakers went to Jones's office to demand the list of all of Bloomington's shareholders to begin investigating where things went south. Jones flatly refused. This was mostly for show, given the Bloomington Drakers were well-known to each other, but Jones's unwillingness to engage with anything or anyone who questioned the veracity of the claim spoke volumes. It turned out that a federal investigation into the higher-ups in the Drake game—namely: The Whitakers—was undertaken the same day as the basement meeting. Jones knew about this. So, whether he was protecting himself or the Whitakers, his message was clear: complaints not welcome.[23]

The Drakers had spent 1912 awaiting news. They had sunk their fortunes into what was purported to be a safe bet. The shares the Whitakers had been selling at $5 to $500 a pop were supposed to float the operation until the Drake ship came in. "In all I would say we have taken in more than $30,000. Most of this has gone to defray the expenses of my research, but, of course, a man has to live, you know. I have taken my percentage for a living all the time."[24] From Mr. Whitaker's lips to God's ears. There was a functioning cash flow in the operation, but it flowed from Drakers' bank accounts through the local promoter (i.e., Jones) and into the Whitaker's pockets. The reams of papers they continued to brandish as evidence of a job well done had cost something, but the overwhelming bulk of the funds remained in Mrs. Sudie Whitaker's bank account. Sudie's genealogy had been seen as the conduit through which the Drakers could realize their claim but, of course, the inverse was the reality: the Drakers were the easy marks from which Sudie could rake in a fortune—their belief in the Drake windfall only further fattened Sudie's Draker take.

There was a collective groan in Bloomington when the November cables came. The Drakers were crestfallen, but *The Pantagraph* had no interest in schadenfreude. *The Pantagraph* showed remarkable restraint by not printing "TOLD YOU SO!" splashed across every page of the morning edition. They did print, however, a statement from one Draker who'd made a beeline to the paper's offices after hearing that the Drake bubble had burst: "*The Pantagraph* was right and I was wrong. Your paper cannot be too strongly commended for the [stance] it has taken in the matter and I cannot understand now why I did not recognize this fact long ago."[25] The people of Bloomington had been swindled, and *The Pantagraph* was more relieved than vindictive.

Except, that is, when it came to Mr. Whitaker. Three months after the House of Lords' cable, Whitaker sent a statement to *The Pantagraph* concerning the voyage to England the preceding year. "The statement of Whitaker in its entirety would occupy about three columns in *The Pantagraph*, but as most of it is made up of what might be considered unimportant detail of a hard luck story, it is useless to give it all." Ouch. *The Pantagraph* related the contents of Whitaker's letter, which amounted to a hard-luck story, indeed. Whitaker claimed he was broke because Sudie held all the money. While in London, Dr. Jones only occasionally lent money to Whitaker but freely spent the Drake funds Sudie readily gave him. Milo Lewis met them later, and only after months of Whitaker ducking the London solicitors demanding payment on Lewis's trail of debts. Whitaker said that Lewis spent his non-Drake time selling stocks in American land (supposedly) rich with coal and timber to unsuspecting Brits. In his letter to *The Pantagraph*, Whitaker took the opportunity to chastise the Bloomington Drakers for not sending him money when he'd demanded. Especially since Dr. Jones was dutifully sending money to Lewis. To the state of the Drake claim, he only mentioned that he'd seen a solicitor who told him they were waiting on an American attorney to make out the claim. Meanwhile, Sudie and Lewis sailed home in first-class cabins without him, leaving Whitaker broke and friendless in London. And only after repeated cajoling did they wire him money to book passage home. Whitaker had been cut out, and his bitterness was unrestrained. "Whitaker closes his statement by appealing to the Drake stockholder to learn from them what they want him to do and whether they want him to proceed with the prosecution of the claim, and if so, he will have to have more money." Though *The Pantagraph* hadn't printed Whitaker's statement in full, they'd certainly made a meal out of it; there was no honor among thieves and no pity for them neither.[26]

Bloomington leaned into accepting the Drake Estate was a scam, and the whole town breathed a sigh of relief.

On June 15, 1915, a familiar scene was unfolding in Parlor H of the Chamberlain Hotel in Des Moines, Iowa. A *Des Moines Register* reporter had been given a scoop "on a wonderfully good story" that there was a woman offering a $1 million return within four weeks on a $500 investment. The reporter, and over forty others who had been "tipped off," were filing up to the designated parlor, one at a time.

The *Register*'s reporter went to the room and was greeted by a plain, if pleasant, young woman—Mrs. Rees, an erstwhile Sunday school teacher—who escorted him to sit facing a small woman of indeterminate age with a thin, pale face and glamorous black silk dress. Perhaps her black garments were to indicate that she was a widow, given her husband was not mentioned. Whatever her situation, Mrs. Rees presented the reporter to the imperious Mrs. Whitaker. Yes, *that* Mrs. Whitaker—dear Sudie. The reporter said a friend had sent him. This was good enough for Sudie, and she solemnly addressed the reporter with a speech so smooth and complete it was clear she'd given it a hundred times before:

> *I am one of eighty-five heirs to the estate of Sir Francis Drake. The estate is located in Devon county, England. It includes the city of Plymouth, with about 200,000 population. The lands, buildings, money, bonds, and the like belonging to the estate are worth about $400,000,000. . . . It cost a great deal of money to trace the line of inheritance and to trace back all the records to get proof of the claims of the heirs to the estate. Finally we reached a point when we were out of funds. We were about to give up, when I proposed that it would be better for us to get half a loaf than no loaf at all. So I said that if all the heirs would give me power of attorney and right to sell part of their shares I would raise the money to carry on the work of searching the records. They did that, and I have been offering to my relatives and friends a percentage of the various shares.*

The *Register* reporter absorbed the facts of the monologue before posing the $400 million question: "I suppose there is a chance yet that the arrangement for your getting the estate might not go through?" The woman had a rote response for this, too: "No . . . My Chicago lawyer is in London now. . . . I have been working for fifteen years to get the estate settled and I will be supremely happy if I can only live for one day after it is all done and I can see how fortunate all these people are who have put their money into it. I expect then to give the rest of my life to do all the good I can." Well, bless her heart.

Her speech was measured, but she rattled off facts and figures in rote fashion. The room was strewn with stacks of papers; there were contracts and certificates with which the people of Des Moines could pledge their financial support to the Drake castle in the air. Mrs. Rees kept quiet and observant as Mrs. Whitaker laid out the terms.

Suddenly, the door burst open. Into the room strode two giant men with mania in their eyes. They shouted and gesticulated and rumbled the reporter's subterfuge, identifying him as one of the *Register*'s own. They were incensed that he'd had the temerity to try to trick them into spilling their secrets! How dare he?!

"My goodness! Are you a reporter? Now if you are, I ask you not to put a word of this in the paper. . . . Not but that it wouldn't be the truth, all right, but I don't want to put anything in the paper until the estate is all settled up and what I have said is proved." Mrs. Whitaker chided the young man, though her surprise and consternation struck his ear with the same rote tones as her Drake facts. Standing menacingly behind her were the two men, one of whom had just recently lost the election for Polk County sheriff, Oscar Hartzell. The reporter demurred and said he had come to better understand her business proposition and that he would mull it over but with the aside that the deal looked too good to be true. Hartzell glared. Mrs. Rees chimed in that she was herself an investor and wouldn't give anyone the bum steer. Hartzell dutifully announced he was also an investor to the tune of $2,100. "You're young, and it's a big chance. You could afford to lose a little if it should turn out badly on as big a chance as this," was Mrs. Rees' helpful parting thought.[27]

The reporter escaped the room without signing a contract or handing over his cash, but could not shake the feeling he'd been set up. No other reporter or editor had gotten an interview with Mrs. Whitaker, she'd said, but it was not as if the *Register* reporter had been *that* sneaky. And the two men had certainly chosen just the right moment to burst on the scene. It was almost like they'd rehearsed it.

Whether the reporter had escaped the Drake clutches or been ensnared in a scheme-within-a-scheme hardly mattered twenty-four hours later when the script was flipped; Sudie was mid-spiel when an imposing man burst through the door of Parlor H. He was a deputy and was there to arrest Mrs. Whitaker. Bedlam ensued. The room was crammed with investors who immediately started shouting and jostling in confusion. Sudie yelled to Clint Hartzell—Oscar's brother and fellow Drake agent—to grab her purse and skedaddle. He had the small bag in hand, stuffed with $2,100 cash and a stack of contracts both blank and signed, when he, too, was arrested. Oscar Hartzell tried to block the door when the sheriff and county attorney arrived. Even as Sudie was being led away by the lawmen, Mrs. Rees continued filling out contracts.

The arrest party marched to the court of Justice John T. Conroy—who had invested $100 just days prior—where Sudie was charged with obtaining money under false pretenses, and Hartzell with assault. The president of the Corn Belt Land and Loan Company—himself a true-believer Draker—posted Sudie's $2,000 bond, as well as Hartzell's for $750. They were released.[28]

Just as with *The Pantagraph* in Bloomington not five years before, the article in *The Register* had drawn and deepened the Drake Estate's line in the sand in Des Moines. The morning after the arrest, at least fifteen anxious investors came to (fellow investor) Justice Conroy's office in search of refunds or guarantees against further fleecing. "The persons . . . admitted they had been carried away by the proposition set up by Mrs. Sudie M. Whitaker of St. Louis, Chicago, Bloomington, Des Moines, etc., and that the deal 'still looks good' to them. But, they added, 'under present conditions' and 'in view of prevailing circumstances,' etc., etc., they 'guessed it would be better,' etc., etc."[29] As these investors were talking out of both sides of their mouths, Sudie and the Hartzells were back at work in Parlor H, doing what they did best.

Sudie's court appearance had been set for June 28, 1915, and County Attorney Wilson had summoned the county grand jury in the meantime and would need to call witnesses to testify against Mrs. Whitaker.

Drakers were in high demand by everyone, but finding one willing to either speak against the cause, or admit to being conned, was no mean feat. One investor received a postcard that further convinced him not to pursue legal action:

> *Owing to business reverses I find it necessary to dispose of 106 gold bricks, and as I find your name on a list of easy marks furnished me from the office of the Federation of Con Men of the World, will call upon you next week. Can't sell you but 27, however, as I want to favor as many as possible.*—*"I Will Skinnum"*

Sudie's court appearance was postponed, and she and her entourage went to Chicago at the end of June while Oscar Hartzell was left to mind the store in Des Moines. When asked about Sudie's travel plans, he dutifully replied, "I don't know exactly, but I'll have a bunch of contracts all right." A true prince of the Drake Estate.[30]

Sudie and her entourage were in Des Moines for her hearing on August 9, all comfortably installed at the Chamberlain Hotel, where they huddled and planned for the coming court proceedings. Dressed in black with a white feather boa around her neck and her usual placid expression, Sudie and company reported to the courthouse for the 10 o'clock hearing. The grand jury handed down an indictment minutes before, rendering the hearing unnecessary, but Sudie was on-site to hear her indictment for obtaining money under false pretenses (duh) from W. A. Alstrand, who had grown tired of waiting for the promised $100,000 return on his two $50 investments. This complaint was one of hundreds and, once lodged with the county attorney, opened the sluice gates on a reservoir of Drake estate claims, contracts, and broken promises. This was not welcome news to Sudie and company.[31, 32]

Instead of answering these charges, Sudie, her trusty right-hand man Oscar, and Chicago attorney Milo Lewis immediately left for England. In the midst of their hurried departure, Sudie found the time to give a statement to the papers: "All my trouble in Des Moines is the result of a clever plot on the part of enemies of mine whose names I cannot reveal at present. . . . [T]he name of W.A. Alstrand, which appears on the indictment as preferring the charge, was forged according to positive information which I received from Des Moines by phone today. . . . Reports to the effect that the estate is a myth and that I have been using the story as a means of obtaining money are absolutely false and unjust."[33] The lady doth protest too much, methinks.

Before the hammer fell again, the Drake cabal was bound for England.

In the ten years from 1916 to 1926, the world changed: World War I (1914–18); the resulting Depression of 1920 and historic deflation (1920–21); Prohibition (1920–33); President Warren Harding's Tea Pot Dome Scandal (1923; Gaston Means, hard at work); and Iowan farm boy Oscar Hartzell's wrest of control from Sudie and Lewis.

The Drake party arrived in England at the beginning of 1916. Once there, Milo Lewis took the lead. In 1917, he filed a suit in British Chancery court on behalf of Ernest Drake, of Missouri, claiming that he was entitled to the Drake baronetcy and should henceforth be known as Sir Ernest Drake. Lewis had recast himself as the chief of operations, Oscar as the lackey, and Sudie as the powerless passenger. Such was the dynamic when all three rushed back to the States so Lewis could appear before the Supreme Court of Illinois as they tried to disbar him for his connection with the Drake game—as well as for bigamy—in 1919. Sudie remained stateside and was indicted by the Cook County grand jury a year later, though she slipped the charges. Lewis and Hartzell returned to London to tend to Draker operations and their ever-growing string of girlfriends. But by 1922, they were again back in the States for Lewis to again appear before the Illinois court. This time, they disbarred him.

When Lewis was receiving his legal dressing-down in Chicago, Hartzell was laying the groundwork to move himself and the headquarters of the Drake game to London "officially." Oscar had spent the better part of a decade watching Sudie and Lewis slink from scrape to scrape, and now he was going to take control of operations and do it correctly. He met with his siblings, a fight broke out, one brother left, and the three remaining Hartzells sketched out how things were going to work from there on out: They were no longer selling shares but would instead receive "donations" that would pay out once the estate was settled—a legal side-step that guaranteed Hartzell's income and all but shielded him from having to account for how he spent other peoples' "donations." Oscar next went to Des Moines to deprogram the local Drakers from Sudie's sway and convert them to his. His chief agent was Mrs. Alma Shepard. He enlisted her to hire sub-agents to pound the pavement to bring in the $2,500 a week he declared necessary to pursue settlement of the estate in London. It was organized. It was a crime. It was organized crime, or "racketeering," on top of fraud.

The schism that Hartzell created between himself and Sudie and Milo was extreme. Hartzell's growing legion of agents on the ground was dutiful in its charge to send him money, disseminate his correspondence among the faithful, and keep to his credo of "Secrecy, Silence, Nondisturbance." The Drakers were told of Sudie and Milo's untrustworthiness as Hartzell branded them "crooks." He spilled Milo's secrets of infidelity and unraveled Sudie's scheme by "disproving" her genealogical research.

Hartzell's airing of his former partners' dirty laundry was extremely effective. By 1923, the Drakers were firmly in his camp. So when he cabled to his flock, "Know that it's all a question of wheels within wheels and wheels within those wheels and the inside wheels are the ones that succeed. . . . Just remember that O.M. Hartzell is top dog," they took his word as gospel. Oscar had gotten in front of the Drake bandwagon and was now steering it into territory all his own.[34]

Hartzell's apostles/agents on the ground were unfailing in their $2,500-a-week charge, which they wired to Hartzell via American Express. He had the funds but needed to establish his competing claim to the nonexistent Drake Estate. No one could accuse Hartzell of not being creative, for the yarns he spun played directly into the Drake zealots' appetites for intrigue surrounding the estate and their adopted family name. The story he settled on was that he had been approached by the wife of the man assumed to be Britain's next prime minister. She wanted to help Hartzell's Sir Francis Drake cause without scandal, so furtively pointed him toward a long-buried second will by glancing her eyes skyward during service in a Devon church. Hartzell returned at midnight to follow the lady's gaze and found, buried under six inches of dust in a small cupboard in the church belfry, Sir Francis's second will. Just like the miraculously discovered family Bible that had so conveniently filled in the blanks for Beckwith's cause fifty years prior, the dusty cubby armed Hartzell with a missing link. This super-secret second will was written after Sir Francis's super-secret third marriage that produced a super-secret heir whose line could be traced to an aging Colonel Drexel Drake, currently living in London. Hartzell had retrieved this will from the Devon church in the dead of night and had since received Col. Drake's blessing to pursue the estate because, naturally, the Colonel's niece had fallen in love with Hartzell and they wanted to keep the estate in the family. Hartzell had fabricated a paper trail to his own legitimacy. And though he kept mum on how exactly the Drakers' donations were being used, he happily tallied their settlement account:

Figure up all the land in Missouri, Kansas, and Iowa at an average of $125 an acre, and all of the stocks, and all the bank deposits, all the railroads and cities in those three states and add them together and the combined amount would not be as large as the Sir Francis Drake estate here in England, of which I am the sole owner, and to which I hold the sole title, which the British parliament is now conveying to me in cash, and which I am going to bring to America to distribute among the men and women who have advanced me money with which to carry on the money to win this estate.

I will put it before you in another form: it has been said by people of high finance here in London that the amount I am to receive from the sale of the Drake is considerably more than the combined debt of Britain to the United States, and the debts of all other countries to Great Britain, and that, as you can read for yourselves, is over four and a half billion pounds sterling, or some 20 billion dollars, a stake worth fighting for and working for and waiting for.

[Drake estate transfer was delayed due to "drawing up the balance sheet" and assessing the value of] "all rock quarries, brick yards, pottery clay, mineral ores, such as tin, etc., fishing rights in rivers, income off railroad land, and all the rents from properties, which have been

accumulating all these years," including land in Africa, Alaska, Australia, Europe, South America, Virginia, California, England, all the important buildings in London and the Muir Valley redwoods. To get everything settled will take "reams and reams of special parchment."[35]

It seemed the Drake estate had grown considerably since Beckwith's measly $125 million promise in 1870; Hartzell promised not just a castle in the sky but an entire sovereign nation. By 1925, he had unequivocally cabled his flock, "I am Sir Francis Drake"—man, myth, mountebank.

Hartzell had set his wheels-within-wheels in motion, and the money kept rolling in. Honest Oscar's clothes, apartments, lady friends, and drinking habits reflected this. His daily schedule consisted solely of walking to the American Express offices to collect that morning's take, and from there, directly to the Savoy and his designated table, 101.

Mrs. Shepard's credulity was wearing thin back in Des Moines, though, and she traveled to London to see Hartzell's evidence in the flesh. "He could not show me Col. Drexel Drake, nor Drake's niece, nor any evidence that there was a Drake estate. He did take me into the vaults of the Bank of England and show me big bags, like potato sacks, filled with coins, which he said were Spanish doubloons and pieces-of-eight which Drake had captured and that belonged to the Drake estate, but I did not believe him." Hartzell cabled to Des Moines that Mrs. Shepard, who had sent him $166,775 in donations, including $5,000 from mortgaging her own home, was undesirable, a troublemaker, and a thief. Such was the price of disloyalty to Honest Oscar Hartzell.[36]

As Oscar went on "gathering evidence" and preparing documents on "reams and reams of special parchment," his bluster reached from London to Des Moines and all points in between, which included both the British and American authorities. Using cables kept Hartzell's correspondence and money transfers out of the federal government's hands; "using the mails to defraud" applied to a wide swath of crimes but only those committed using the US Postal Service. Like a payout from the Drake Estate, Hartzell was forever *just* out of authorities' reach.

The crash of the American Stock Market in October of 1929 shifted life in America but had little effect on Hartzell. Draker devotees continued scraping together his increasingly frequent demands for increasing amounts of money while Hartzell continued living high on the hog in London, spending more freely than ever before. For over a decade, he'd been telling Iowans to expect a $22.5 billion payout but not to bother him about it. Now, with Americans out of work and their fields blowing away as dust in the wind, the onus was on him to show them the money. Instead, he doubled down and showed London twice as many of the Drakers' hard-earned dollars. Hartzell's ledger, kept by his assistant/accountant in London, shows he received $6,000 in November of 1929, the month immediately following Black Friday. This was a low take for Hartzell but an enormous sum for the newly impoverished Drakers, who had already raided their savings for "Honest Oscar." By December, he'd browbeat them into sending him $9,000, and over the following two years, he received over $200,000 from the Drakers.[37]

His extravagance drew attention. More than one tip was sent to Scotland Yard, to whom Hartzell was no stranger; he'd been slipping through their grasp and the still-forming US/UK extradition laws for nearly ten years. One of these tips was signed by a man who had recently hosted Hartzell for the weekend. "He mentioned that he was connected with the Sir Francis Drake estate but did not approach me in connection with any financial transaction. Hartzell gave the impression that he was a man of wealth. But there was something suspicious about him, something strained and not quite right."[38] More significant than the meeting itself was that Hartzell, when traveling back to London from the weekend, was thrown from his car and sent flying twenty feet before landing unhurt. The self-proclaimed new Sir Francis considered this divine intervention, or a miracle, at least, so quickly consulted a London psychic—the dramatically named Mrs. Nina St. John Montague.

In 1930, mediums and clairvoyants were far from their turn-of-the-century heyday but were still a staple of any urban center—no hustle and bustle was complete without a dash of spiritualism to raise up the indigent and smite down the unworthy. Hartzell called at Mrs. Montague's for solace, direction, and affirmation. Or perhaps he was hoping she would sniff him out and free him from living a lie. Or maybe he just wanted to ogle her winsome assistant. In any case, he was in her sights.

Two months after the stock market crash and just a few weeks after his own, Hartzell was crazed. The global financial chaos had only inflamed the Drakers' mania, and they were pouring money into their holy cause and their faith into Hartzell, who was their alpha and omega. This unhinged adulation was not great for Hartzell's mental state; if he didn't truly believe himself to be the new Sir Francis Drake, the Drakers' god-like worship, at the very least, warped his already skewed perspective. So, by January of 1930, whatever time he didn't spend cashing his American Express cablegrams or consulting with Mrs. Montague, Hartzell spent looking for solace deep in his cups.

On January 7, he was at the Savoy Bar, downing drinks with abandon. Hartzell was all bluster and boldness and had no problem making friends—or, drinking buddies, at least—wherever he went so was naturally engaged when an American in the bar struck up a conversation. He was a Texas oil man on vacation, and he asked if Hartzell minded if he joined for one drink. Or three? Or nine? Hartzell (already drunk) had an immediate rapport with this fellow larger-than-life American. They drank and laughed and reminisced until the bar closed at 3:00 p.m. In between being served countless drinks, the oil man had used the restroom, and perhaps this was why he was faring so much better than Hartzell. Utterly soused, their next stop was Hartzell's lavish Basil Street apartment and more drinks. But, bathroom first.

The oil man was happy to find a kindred spirit, too, and confided to Hartzell that his dealings with business had been from the shadier side of the tracks, and that he was not so much an oil man as a stock promoter—like Hartzell's agents in Iowa—or, when down to brass tacks, a con man. Hartzell was bleary-eyed from drinking but something within him clicked and, for a brief moment, he remembered his roots. He fell forward and clutched the Texan as he slurred his memories of his early days with Sudie and Milo—whom he still called "crooks"—and that he now worked exclusively on the Drake Estate and that the claimants were awaiting billions. The Texan asked why the authorities didn't come after Hartzell and this obvious skin game? Drunker still, Hartzell said he'd given the American Feds the slip and that it was Scotland Yard that was genuinely troublesome. "It is, of course, merely a racket, but based on an old legend. . . . I am making money out of it, but I can't say that they will." With this, the Texan again excused himself to the toilet. They had been drinking for something like ten hours at this point.

When the Texan reappeared, he was visibly relieved. But not from the restroom. The oil man had been excusing himself throughout the afternoon to run to the toilet to furiously scribble down notes and tran- scription. For the oil man had a secret, too: He was not a stock promoter, nor from Texas, nor even American. He was Thomas Barnard, of Barnard & Howarth Detective Agency of London, and was there on assignment from his then-employer—Mrs. Nina St. John Montague.

Hartzell's next visit to Mrs. Montague was enlightening, indeed.[39]

Hartzell's wheels-within-wheels-within-wheels were indeed spin- ning, but he was drifting from the axle.

——•——

Later that year, in 1930, Hartzell received a letter: "Dear Sir, I am a farmer living near Alton, Iowa, and some of my farmer friends have asked me why I did not donate something to the Drake Estate, which is to be settled through you. . . . Will you please write to me relative to the matter, so that I may know what to do. . . . Respectfully yours, H. W. Jansen." This was just one of 5,000 letters he received from potential investors that year alone. For all his bluster and brass, Hartzell was sometimes brilliant, and in this case, his prescience served him well because these letters, on the whole, were not simple folks earnestly looking for guidance. Rather, they were an expansive sting operation by US Post Office Inspection Service Agent John Sparks. Hartzell recommended "Jansen" consult with a local agent. Remember, Hartzell's code of conduct for the Drakers was "Silence, Secrecy, Nondisturbance," so even if this "Jansen" was genuine in his inquiry, he was jumping the chain of command and violating all three governing principles. And Hartzell had little patience for rebels.

The US Post Office Inspection Service had, just ten years prior, taken down a certain Mr. Ponzi and his elaborately pyramided hustle and could boast a 90 percent conviction rate for all cases the F (for "fraud") Division brought to trial. Agent John Sparks had been working Hartzell's case exclusively since 1928, and the Inspection Service was anxious to nab Hartzell as the American and British governments passed the buck on how to bring down top-dog Honest Oscar.

By January of 1931, Sparks had secured signed affidavits from five of Hartzell's agents in America, all copping to the racket but escaping convictions as they had "acted in good faith," or, were suckers themselves just following their scion's marching orders. Hartzell seized upon these heretical Drakers and excommunicated them by "red-inking" them. One agent in particular, Otto Yant, bore the brunt of Hartzell's rage and was so thoroughly scolded that some Drakers stood behind him out of compassion or empathy. There was a brief "Yantism" schism in the flock, but Yant himself denounced his confession and was allowed to return to the Draker fold as a warning example of what *not* to do. When the flock was reunited, enthusiasm surged; Hartzell was now taking in $15,000 a month. For penance for their flirtation with apostasy and out of fear that he would punish them by docking their expected payout, Hartzell issued a new order to his flock: "[W]rite a registered letter to the proper people at Washington to the effect that they want all these disturbances, and all this putting out of false statements and misrepresentations of our matter stopped at once. . . . I expect them to pour the letters into Washington like buckshot into a chicken thief. I would not trust one of the whole bunch down east in my chicken house in broad daylight."[40]

In December, Hartzell received a visit from Scotland Yard's chief inspector, who had been receiving Drake-related complaints for years. He'd come to assess whether Hartzell was worth deporting using the extradition laws between England and the United States that had been signed and ratified just that August.[41] For all his volume and brass, Hartzell was slippery, too. When asked for details on the Estate and the Drakers, he slithered around reason.

"Are you the heir?"
"No."
"Are you the supposed heir?"
"That I cannot divulge."

"Where is the Drake Estate?"

"I cannot tell you offhand."

"You had time to find out."

"I know, but I cannot divulge."

"On 15th of November last . . . one of your agents in America, addressed a large body of citizens at Winnebago and said that you had established the identity of the one person who was entitled to the whole of the Sir Francis Drake property. Who is that person?"

"I cannot divulge. I think you will get that at the Home Office."

"Is it you?"

"No. I have the assignment of the heritage from the proper man whose name I cannot divulge."

"Have you ever seen this person?"

"No." (Remember, he'd claimed to meet the fictitious Drexel Drake many times and was supposedly engaged to his niece.)

"How do you know he exists?"

"From people who have done business for me."

"Who are these people?"

"I cannot divulge. It is a great mystery."

"You are getting plenty of money from this mystery."

"Certainly I am . . . I do not give a damn for all the officials. The American government has treated me very badly and I have no use for Americans or America. The American government has done some mean things, including interfering with my mail . . . I am practically British. Someone at the Home Office arranged this for me and when all this is ended my name will suddenly become Drake and I will be a British subject."

Well, la-de-da.

Though the interview was not very helpful to Scotland Yard for fact-finding, it was a telling character reference for Hartzell, who was dangerously close to being branded an "undesirable alien."

This interview was still on Hartzell's addled mind when he dined at Table 101 at the Savoy on New Year's Eve 1932. Not twenty feet from him sat the American Ambassador to London and former Secretary of the Treasury, Andrew Mellon. Hartzell later recalled, "He got the information from the head waiter about which was my table and ordered his so he could face me directly. He wanted a table so he could get a good view of me. The head waiter said, 'Andrew Mellon must be interested in you.' Mellon stared at me for a long time." Of course he did—Hartzell was both an undesirable alien, and a wanted man.[42]

On January 13, 1932, the *Globe-Gazette*, out of Mason City, Iowa, ran the headline: "FRAUD INDICTMENT, 17 YEARS OLD, DISMISSED."[43] Sudie was now free to return to Iowa. She never did.

Scotland Yard returned to Hartzell's Basil Street apartments less than a month after their first visit and arrested him. He struggled and then slumped. Once processed in at Brixton police station, they found $5,000 cash on his person. They informed him of his pending deportation. He seemed almost relieved, but perhaps his anxiety was masked by the lavish meals and bottomless drinks he was served—even behind bars, his swagger held sway. After a month of fine dining and a brief appearance before Whitehall's Aliens Deportation Advisory Committee wherein his only statement was, "All I have to say is that I am ready to go," Honest Oscar Hartzell was put in a first-class cabin aboard the *SS Champlain* on a one-way ticket to America.

A week later, on February 16, 1933, John Sparks motored out to meet the *Champlain* in New York harbor. With him were an officer of the post office, a district attorney, a US Marshal, and the Vice-Consul of the American Embassy in London (who had been keeping tabs on Hartzell from his own first-class stateroom). The group descended on Hartzell, who was genuinely shocked and confused by what was happening. Sparks brandished letters he'd seized from a Draker agent, and a flustered Hartzell admitted to writing and sending them. When asked where the Drake Estate was, Hartzell waved his arms in a wide circle and said, "All over." When asked where the Drake suit was filed, Hartzell said, "The Ecclesiastical Courts and the powers that be." When asked the status of the unclaimed Drake Estate, Hartzell said, "There is no such thing as an unclaimed Drake estate." At this point, Sparks arrested Hartzell, and the whole party went immediately to the district attorney's office. An unfortunate welcome home for Honest Oscar.[44]

At the heart of the matter, the Drake Estate claim subverted generally accepted history and prompted legions, generations of Americans to ask, "But what about . . . ?" Sure, the overwhelming majority could look at facts contained in documents, testimony, and tradition and arrive at a consensus of what is reality. But a minority chorus of cheekily posed what-ifs, demanding a reexamination of this reality and demanding revision to right perceived wrongs, wears away the integrity of the otherwise accepted state of being. This construct creates an us-versus-them mentality, and the combination of sectarian community-building, as well as the defensiveness springing from the perceived affront from actual reality, further entrenches each side. There are few things as unifying as a common enemy, and for the Drakers (i.e., "us"), the enemy was England, America, and recorded history (i.e., "them"). For non-Drakers, the enemy was collective delusion. But how do you use facts and logic to convince someone who has rejected those same facts and logic?

When Hartzell was trucked into Sioux City for his trial, he was steeled for a chilly reception. Instead, he was welcomed home as a conquering hero. In Hartzell's cult of personality—worship of Drake, then by extension and fiat, Hartzell himself—there was no question that veneration was due the man who would lift America from its depressed station. The train arrived on February 19, 1933, to throngs of Drakers straining for a glimpse of the preternatural, modern-day Drake.

The prosecutors saw the challenges of proving charges "beyond a reasonable doubt" to a community that had, apparently and evidently, lost all sense of reason. Hartzell's hero's welcome did little to convince them otherwise.

Five days after arriving in Iowa to face the music, Hartzell was released on $10,000 bail. He met with over a hundred Drakers that very night. A collection was taken up, and a fund was established to raise money for his legal expenses. Nearly $70,000 rolled in that summer, in addition to the standing tithe of monthly donations.

As Otto Yant and his brethren had discovered when they met John Sparks, intent was paramount in cases of fraud. Their signed affidavits were proof they had entered into Hartzell's good graces with the genuine belief that the retroactively corrected Drake Estate would pay out dividends to the rightful heirs. And that they were among those rightful heirs. They didn't believe they were scamming people by soliciting donations, because they didn't think it was a scam.

Hartzell's trial was a veritable circus. Hartzell took up an entire wing of the Martin Hotel—the sequestered jurors in another, just down the hall—and dined on a raised dais in his rooms where eager Drakers congregated to catch a glimpse of their man and savior. Yes, Hartzell was there to answer for his gargantuan lie but, also, yes, Hartzell liked the limelight—these two states of being were not at odds in his mind.

Hartzell was indicted on fifteen counts, twelve of which were tried. The prosecution's uphill battle included satisfying three central points: First, Hartzell used the mail. Second, money was exchanged as a result of this use of the mail. Third, Hartzell willingly and knowingly engaged in a fraudulent scheme. The cast of characters that appeared at the trial was long and involved, but the leads were Prosecutor Harry Reed, Defense Attorney Carlos Goltz, Judge George C. Scott, witness for the prosecution Charles Challen, defense consultant P. J. Cahill, and a "Mr. X." The trial began at 10 a.m. on October 23, 1933.

Sioux City had never seen such mania, and the courtroom was bursting with the defense and prosecution entourages, and seemingly every Draker in the state was jostling for a seat in the gallery. The press had rows of benches for themselves.

John Sparks was the first witness on the stand, and he easily and incontrovertibly proved the first point: Hartzell had admitted to sending letters to Sparks on the deck of the *SS Champlain*. The second point was also easily proven by any one of the Drakers called to the stand who, one by one, proudly announced their donation levels as testimony to how much they trusted Sir Oscar. That the first two mandates were so easily met probably was very encouraging to the prosecution, but the third point put truth on the docket: they had to prove Hartzell had dishonest intentions through establishing, supporting, and restating the facts and recorded history of the last 337 years.

A history professor took the stand to give an overview of the original Sir Francis, the Drake line, and English history. Defense attorney Goltz conjured a what-if and interrupted the professor with, "All history is inaccurate. All history is badly written." Or: Just because it's written down doesn't make it true. (Much like Hartzell's supposed belfry will.) The prosecution continued with a reading of the Scotland Yard Basil Street interview wherein Hartzell displayed his mastery of deflection. A minor furor followed when a representative from the Manuscripts Division of the Library of Congress produced a photostat of Sir Francis Drake's will, heretofore the oldest document produced in an American court of law. The document was impressive on its face and further . . . again . . . once more established that Sir Francis had died childless and his estate had been handed down according to his wishes.

Next on the stand was the star witness for the prosecution: Charles Challen. He was key to the government's case because he was a London barrister with unassailable knowledge of British probate law, but also because he really looked the part. Hartzell was well-groomed and put together and had a generally bored attitude throughout the trial, making him appear a less-than-compelling British heir. Challen, however, mounted the stand in his black robes, powdered white wig, upper-crust accent, and minus an arm from his time in the Royal Field Artillery in the Great War—a period during which Hartzell had been drinking in London and getting girls "into trouble." Challen's Anglo tones filled the room as he systematically refuted Hartzell's wild legal claims. Hartzell had cabled the Drakers that he'd been fighting in the King's and Lords' Commission, the Ecclesiastical Courts, and against all the powers that be in England. Challen duly informed the anxious courtroom that, in addition to there being no such thing as the King's and Lords' Commission and no such thing as the Ecclesiastical Court, that even if by some miracle Hartzell's claims were true, the statute of limitations on Drake's will expired twelve years after his death. Hartzell was about 325 years too late. Furthermore, there was an English law that forbade thieves, or their heirs, from recovering stolen property. Finally, assuming Col. Drexel Drake was real and his Drake line proven, there was no legal way for him to transfer the "billions upon billions" of the estate to anyone else, let alone an American. This was damning stuff. Oscar "I am Sir Francis Drake" Hartzell was being lambasted by one of his would-be chums.

Then, Mr. X was called. There was no shortage of speculation over just who would appear when the mysterious witness was called, but when the man showed up, only one person outside the prosecution knew him. Hartell had met Mr. X on a cold January afternoon in 1930 when they'd become friendly, had a few drinks, and retired to Hartzell's place. Yes, Mr. X was actually the Texas oil man, who was actually Thomas Barnard, P.I. He'd peddled his intel to the seer Nina St. John Montague, and his frequent trips to the toilet that night were again paying off. He quoted Hartzell's confession to knowing the Drake game to be "a racket."

Goltz's defense of Hartzell was predicated on Hartzell's good intent. Over twenty Drakers were called to the stand to profess their utter support for Hartzell's belief in their claim, and their ardor was evident. He recalled Challen to the stand to press him further on facts and figures of English probate law, for Goltz was driving at establishing—or at least emphatically suggesting—that the English laws Challen quoted, some less than ten years in effect, had actually been passed in anticipation of Hartzell's Drake claim. Or, in other words: England saw Oscar coming and closed all the loopholes before he could rob the Banks of England of their pirate hoard. This line of reasoning clearly resonated with the gallery of Drakers who believed their savior had been thwarted by unfeeling, secret powers. That these laws had been passed with Hartzell in mind was going to make it that much more difficult for him to file his petition of right to the Drake Estate in Chancery.

To drive his point home, Goltz finally called consultant for the defense, immigrated Irish, Chicago-based lawyer P. J. Cahill, the defense's answer to the prosecution's spit-spot Charles Challen. Goltz posed his first question, "What is the basis for a petition of right?"

"OBJECTION!" Prosecutor Reed took exception to the relevance of the question because, as he raised his voice for the packed room to hear, Hartzell had not filed a petition of right and had never even begun the process—the only process through which legal action could be taken. The enormity of the implications took a moment to settle on the people in the courtroom, but when they did, the conclusion was clear: Oscar Hartzell had taken in over $1.3 million in donations from Iowans over the course of eighteen years to put toward the legal battle for the Drake Estate in British court, but after eleven years in England, he had never even started to file suit. The bluster was blown, and Hartzell was shown to be nothing but hot air.

Goltz and Reed each gave impressive, far-reaching closing arguments that compared Hartzell to the likes of Columbus and Lindbergh in vision, and Scheherazade in creative duplicity. Reed punctuated his parting words to the jury: "Promises! Promises! Promises! Fraud from start to finish and he knew it. If this man goes out of here with the endorsement of this jury the state of Iowa will pay millions more tribute to him."

The jury was given its charge at 2 p.m. on November 14 and adjourned to deliberate, later retiring to their rooms at the Martin Hotel, down the hall from Hartzell. By 9:05 the following morning, they had their verdict. Hartzell repeatedly dabbed his sweaty forehead, his first sign of worry after the three-week trial.

Guilty on all counts.

Judge Scott immediately sentenced Hartzell to ten years in Leavenworth state prison and a $2,000 fine. Goltz shouted desperately about appeals and bail, but Judge Scott was through with Hartzell and directed the marshal to take him away.

The press clamored and strained to get a quote from Honest Oscar as he was being led out of the room, but all he gave them was, "I have no statement to make. I'm in jail. I'm through."

Or was he?[45]

The air of intrigue Hartzell had cultivated in America during his eleven years in England served him well. Much of this aura was concentrated on misdeeds by, and mistrust of, government—both American and British. So, when Hartzell was put on trial and found guilty while defending himself from said governments, the Drakers' fervor was only further inflamed.

Carlos Goltz raced to Omaha, Nebraska, after the verdict and secured a federal judge to review Judge Scott's denial of bail. This time, Goltz won, and Hartzell's bail was set at $25,000, which was met in a matter of hours. Hartzell was back out and returned to doing what he did best.

With operations relocated to Chicago, Hartzell moved into the Croydon Hotel—Croydon being a town in England abutting London, so perhaps it was a whiff of "home" for him. For Hartzell, 1934 was a madcap combination of secret Drakers meetings—now held at night and in fields and far from the prying eyes and ears of nonbelievers—and fundraising—over $150,000 for his appeal, on top of the $68,000 he'd received for his first trial—and extensive drinking.

At this point, Hartzell's drinking was probably as much a cure for anxiety as it was a cause for concern. His life had been spent peddling another man's name, and it had gotten him upwards of $2 million, an unhinged mind, and an unsettled soul. He had spent eleven years promising the imminent settlement of the Drakers' long-awaited claim if they could just hang on a little longer, send just a little more money. But now the bloom was off the rose: he'd been rumbled, was going to jail, and the opportunity for him to stay a free man was as close, and as far, as his promised Drake Estate. Not to mention his myth had outstripped his mortality as Drakers continued pouring money into the coffers in spite of, or because of, his situation. He still held a central role in the play, but Oscar Hartzell was no longer writing the story.

In August, a circuit court of appeals upheld the Sioux City conviction. Hartzell responded by demanding to take his matter all the way to the Supreme Court, then went on a bender with his new bosom friend, P. J. Cahill. Hartzell would rant and rail and pontificate when drinking and let loose impressive ravings. Cahill later recalled, "He told me that the Pope was tying up the Drake Estate and that the Pope was trying to steal his gold and had gold belonging to him in the Vatican; he told me that the Pope and the King of England had joined hands and were stopping the final determination of the settlement; he told me that President Roosevelt had been compelled to gather in all the gold in America for the purpose of paying him."

It was Cahill that Hartzell called when the Supreme Court declined to take up the case and determined he needed to report to Sioux City to be processed into Leavenworth. It was Cahill that answered the phone when Hartzell wanted a last hurrah. And it was Cahill that turned him down: "I did not accept the invitation. His condition was such that I did not want to be with him. He was then utterly and hopelessly incapable of realizing the seriousness of his position or anything else serious at all." The police arrived at Hartzell's door at midnight on January 12, 1935, and dragged him from his rooms.[46]

On January 16, 1935, Oscar Merrill Hartzell was processed into Leavenworth state prison in Kansas. The Drake game was running hot in Chicago. Sudie was out west someplace.

On April 8, the Chicago Police led a raid on the Drakers' headquarters and recovered nearly $60,000 on the eve of them closing up shop for good. The raid prompted another trial, this one with forty-one agents indicted.

Canfield Hartzell had collected upwards of $300,000 since 1933, but he was nowhere to be found. The story was that he had sailed to England with a bag filled with $150,000 to use to settle the estate, which he would then escort back to its rightful owners in America. A fine set, the Hartzell brothers.

Honest Oscar was called to appear at the Chicago trial in November of that year. Challen was there, as was the Scotland Yard inspector. The Drakers showed up in droves. The wide net cast for defendants brought to the trial a cast of thousands. Over the course of eleven weeks of restating facts and truths and reality, the judge acquitted thirty-three of the defendants, determining they had "acted in good faith." To them, he said, "To defendants who are going to be found not guilty: if you have sinned, go ye and sin no more, and don't be sinned against any more. Go back to your hamlets, villages, your cities, highways, byways and farms, and tell all those people, the donors and contributors, that the court has judicially found that there is no pot of gold at the end of the rainbow. . . . There never was a goose that laid a golden egg. Sir Francis Drake is dead. Let him rest in peace." With that, he sentenced the eight remaining defendants to five years in prison, including Canfield Hartzell, and Oscar made his first and last statement in court. "I'm responsible for all this. All they did was take the money. The people who worked for me are all innocent." The judge probed Hartzell a bit, and when he asked Hartzell how big the Drake Estate is, Hartzell's response of "It's beyond anyone's imagination. If I disclosed anything about it now I'd be a traitor. . . . I'm sworn to secrecy by the highest powers. They run the country over there," was enough to prove to the judge that madness was king and the heir-apparent its prodigal son. The judge reduced the sentences of all defendants—except Honest Oscar—to one year and one day.[47]

Oscar Hartzell spent the rest of his life in prison: first Leavenworth, then Springfield, Missouri's Hospital for Defective Delinquents, which was brand new when Hartzell was admitted. He was monitored by Dr. Clark Mangun, head of psychiatry, who submitted annual reports to Hartzell's judges to certify and recertify Hartzell's paranoid state and pervasive delusion. He was obsessed with the Drake Estate, was a swindler, and was insane. Any one of these would be burdensome, but in total, they fueled Honest Oscar from Iowa, to London, back to Iowa in search of something that didn't exist.

On August 27, 1943, Oscar Hartzell died in his hospital bed. The records showed the contents on his person at the time of death: one wallet containing 10¢. It is unclear whether he left a will.

"Research isn't just finding facts, it's finding fiction and learning how to separate the two," said the director of the California Historical Society at

The storied plate of brass, fortuitously snatched from the dirt and spared the igno-
miny of remaining unrecognized on America's shores.

a press conference at UC Berkeley in 2003. He was addressing a gaggle of reporters, a tranche of jacketed academics, and a huddle of men in bright-red sweaters. They listened intently while an ancient man scowled from the front of the room. "You should be ashamed of yourselves," he hissed to the crowd. The bitter, spitting curmudgeon was the grandson of Dr. Herbert Bolton, a longtime fanboy of Sir Francis.

His beloved grandfather's beloved Drake Plate of Brass, rescued from the roadside in 1936 and cornerstone of white history on America's Western shores, was a fake.

The plate had been tested in the 1970s, and its electrochemical properties were found to be inconsistent with those of Elizabethan-era copper, but the backstory was a mystery until 2001. Like Hartzell reaching into the Devonshire belfry or the New Jersey Drake who found her long-lost Bible in the side of her chimney, historians at UC Berkeley came upon a dusty box of sepia-tinged notes from a member of a group of history-and-liquor enthusiasts, E. Clampus Vitus, or "Clampers." This still-active fraternal order, whose mission is "dedicated to the erection of historical plaques, the protection of widows and orphans, especially the widows, and having a grand time while accomplishing these purposes" has attracted fans of Western lore and ribaldry for over 150 years. Professor Bolton was a member. The red-shirted men at the press conference were members. It is unclear whether the curmudgeon was a member. Or a fan of ribaldry.

Professor Bolton's love of all things Drake was well-known by his fellow Clampers in the 1930s, all of whom were prone to pranking. There may have been some barely contained professional resentment in the group, as well. Whether out of malice or merry misrule, the Clampers had a grand time conspiring to play the joke on their fellow member. They prepared to have a right old laugh with Bolton when he found the plate. They prepared to have a fight with Bolton, should he not take kindly to their ribbing. What they were not prepared for, however, was for Bolton to take it seriously.

The Clampers continued to produce historical japes that should have prompted Bolton to reexamine the Drake Plate, but the pranks-upon-pranks did not inspire deeper examination. The Drake Plate was purchased, prominently displayed, and became a central jewel in California's historical crown by the 1940s, making the truth that much harder to reveal. The narrative had gotten away from the tricksters. Bolton's enthusiasm embarrassed them as he confidently broadcasted his good intent. Hartzell and Sudie and Beckwith would have been easier to call out as their faith in the cause was biased from the start: they leaned into the benefit of the doubt to use as a cudgel, but for Bolton, it was an opportunity and an offering.

The joke was a fiction that was authenticated into fact before being declared a fiction again. The 2003 announcement snuffed out any speculation that the Bancroft Library's Drake Plate was *that* Drake Plate, which, ironically, reignited speculation over the *real* Drake Plate. As historian Edward P. Von der Porten said, "There is still a plate of brass out there."[48]

Acknowledgments

Many thanks to my patient readers: Nora, Rachel, and Marian.

Newspapers.com, for its ever-deepening bench of archives.

The Library of Congress, for remaining my favorite resource-cum-pastime.

Eugene at Rowman, for his patience.

Clara and Gwen, for continually raising the bar while reinforcing sisterhood.

Tim, for leading by example.

Mom, for being supportive while keeping it real.

Chuck, for being a true-blue partner.

And to Peter Bogdanovich for *Paper Moon*, which sparked my love for Americana, film theory, and hustlers.

Notes

Chapter One

1. Manitoba Historical Society's MHS Transactions, Series 3, 1950–51 Season by J. L. Johnston
2. August 6, 1874, *Ottawa Daily Citizen*, Ottawa, Ontario: GORDON GORDON'S SUICIDE
3. April 12, 1872, *New York Herald*, New York, NY: WHO IS GORDON?
4. Manitoba Historical Society's MHS Transactions, Series 3, 1950-51 Season by J. L. Johnston
5. Ibid.
6. Chambers' Journal, "Glencairn, A Dramatic Story in Three Acts," Ser. 4: v.12, 1875, pp. 721–23, 738–41, 755–59
7. Ibid.
8. January 3, 1893, *New York Sun*, New York, NY: JAY GOULD ONCE OUTWITTED
9. Chambers' Journal, "Glencairn, A Dramatic Story in Three Acts," Ser. 4: v.12, 1875, pp. 721–23, 738–41, 755–59
10. October 10, 1905, *The Minneapolis Journal*, Minneapolis, MN: THE CAREER OF LORD GORDON GORDON
11. Ibid.
12. Manitoba Historical Society's MHS Transactions, Series 3, 1950-51 Season by J. L. Johnston
13. Aug. 17, 1874, *Boston Daily Globe*, Boston, MA: GORDON GORDON
14. Ibid.
15. March 23, 1870, *The Lawrence Tribune*, Lawrence, KS: THE NORTHERN ROUTE
16. August 5, 1874, *The New York Times*, New York, NY: "LORD" GORDON GORDON
17. Chambers' Journal, "Glencairn, A Dramatic Story in Three Acts," Ser. 4: v.12, 1875, pp. 721–23, 738–41, 755–59
18. August 5, 1874, *The New York Times*, New York, NY: "LORD" GORDON GORDON
19. November 22, 1871, *The Philadelphia Enquirer*, Philadelphia, PA

20. August 5, 1874, *The New York Times*, New York, NY: "LORD" GORDON GORDON
21. April 12, 1872, *New York Herald*, New York, NY: WHO IS GORDON?
22. Ibid.
23. January 3, 1893, *New York Sun*, New York, NY: JAY GOULD ONCE OUTWITTED
24. Chambers' Journal, "Glencairn, A Dramatic Story in Three Acts," Ser. 4: v.12, 1875, pp. 721–23, 738–41, 755–59
25. January 3, 1893, *New York Sun*, New York, NY: JAY GOULD ONCE OUTWITTED
26. Ibid.
27. March 13, 1872, *New-York Tribune*, New York, NY: JAY GOULD SURRENDERS
28. March 15, 1872, *New York Herald*, New York, NY: THE ERIE ACT
29. August 14, 1874, *The Boston Globe*, Boston, MA: GORDON GORDON
30. Ibid.
31. Ibid.
32. Chambers' Journal, "Glencairn, A Dramatic Story in Three Acts," Ser. 4: v.12, 1875, pp. 721–23, 738–41, 755–59
33. January 3, 1893, *New York Sun*, New York, NY: JAY GOULD ONCE OUTWITTED
34. Ibid.
35. May 18, 1872, *The Sun*, New York, NY: THE GOULD-GORDON FIGHT
36. January 3, 1893, *New York Sun*, New York, NY: JAY GOULD ONCE OUTWITTED
37. Ibid.
38. Manitoba Historical Society's MHS Transactions, Series 3, 1950-51 Season by J. L. Johnston
39. Ibid.
40. Ibid.
41. Ibid.
42. Ibid.
43. Ibid.
44. Chambers' Journal, "Glencairn, A Dramatic Story in Three Acts," Ser. 4: v.12, 1875, pp. 721–23, 738–41, 755–59
45. August 13, 1874, *The New York Times*, New York, NY: LORD GORDON GORDON
46. Ibid.
47. February 12, 1879, *Manitoba Free Press*, Winnipeg, Manitoba, Canada: GORDON GORDON

CHAPTER TWO

1. Samuel Emmons' Field Notes, "The Diamond Discovery of 1872," R.G. 575, National Archives.

2. Woodward, Bruce A. *Diamonds in the Salt*. Boulder, CO: Pruett Press, 1967. p. 5.
3. Ibid., p. 6.
4. Harpending, Asbury. *The Great Diamond Hoax and Other Stirring Incidents in the Life of Asbury Harpending*. The James H. Barry Co., 1913.
5. Woodward, Bruce A. *Diamonds in the Salt*. Boulder, CO: Pruett Press, 1967. p. 18.
6. Alter, J. Cecil. *James Bridger, Trapper, Frontiersman, Scout, and Guide: A Historical Narrative, With Which is Incorporated a Verbatim Copy, Annotated, of James Bridger, a Biographical Sketch by Maj. Gen. Grenville M. Dodge*. First published 1925; reprinted Columbus, Ohio: Long's College Book Co., 1951. pp. 356, 384.
7. January 30, 1871, *Times*, London, England: STOCKS and RAILWAY and OTHER SHARES
8. February 6, 1871, *Times*, London, England: MONEY-MARKET & CITY INTELLIGENCE
9. Harpending, Asbury. *The Great Diamond Hoax and Other Stirring Incidents in the Life of Asbury Harpending*. The James H. Barry Co., 1913. pp. 176–78.
10. December 16, 1872, *Courier-Journal*, Louisville, KY: PHILIP ARNOLD'S MONEY
11. Woodward, Bruce A. *Diamonds in the Salt*. Boulder, CO: Pruett Press, 1967. p. 24.
12. December 19, 1874, *Times*, London, England: COURT OF EXCHEQUER
13. Harpending, Asbury. *The Great Diamond Hoax and Other Stirring Incidents in the Life of Asbury Harpending*. The James H. Barry Co., 1913. p. 147.
14. Ibid.
15. Woodward, Bruce A. *Diamonds in the Salt*. Boulder, CO: Pruett Press, 1967. p. 34.
16. Harpending, Asbury. *The Great Diamond Hoax and Other Stirring Incidents in the Life of Asbury Harpending*. The James H. Barry Co., 1913.
17. Raymond, Rossiter W. "Biographical Notices: Henry Janin," *Bulletin of the American Institute of Mining Engineers*, No. 53 (May, 1911), xxxii–xxxiii.
18. Woodward, Bruce A. *Diamonds in the Salt*. Boulder, CO: Pruett Press, 1967, p. 37.
19. Ibid., p. 38.
20. December 18, 1874, *Times*, London, England: COURT OF EXCHEQUER
21. December 10, 1872, *Los Angeles Daily Star*, Los Angeles, CA: THE GREAT DIAMOND FRAUD
22. December 24, 1874, *Times*, London, England: COURT OF EXCHEQUER
23. December 16, 1872, *Courier-Journal*, Louisville, KY: PHILIP ARNOLD'S MONEY
24. Ibid.
25. September 11, 1875, *Daily Union*, Sacramento, CA: THE RALSTON MEMORIAL MEETING
26. George D. Lyman, *Ralston's Ring: California Plunders the Comstock Lode*. New York: C. Scribner's Sons, 1937. p. 191.
27. December 16, 1872, *Courier-Journal*, Louisville, KY: PHILIP ARNOLD'S MONEY
28. Woodward, Bruce A. *Diamonds in the Salt*. Boulder, CO: Pruett Press, 1967. p. 80.

29. Letter of Clarence King to Brigadier General A. A. Humphreys, November 27, 1872, Records of the Office of the Chief of Engineers, R.G. 77 (Envelope 2442 Eng., Letter 2468), National Archives.
30. Samuel Emmons' Field Notes, "The Diamond Discovery of 1872," R.G. 575, National Archives.
31. Ibid.
32. Letter of Clarence King to Brigadier General A. A. Humphreys, November 27, 1872, Records of the Office of the Chief of Engineers, R.G. 77 (Envelope 2442 Eng., Letter 2468), National Archives.
33. Woodward, Bruce A. Diamonds in the Salt. Boulder, CO: Pruett Press, 1967. p. 112.
34. Samuel Emmons' Field Notes, "The Diamond Discovery of 1872," R.G. 575, National Archives.
35. Report of David O. Colton, November 25, 1872, printed in the *Daily Alta California* (San Francisco), November 26, 1872.
36. December 19, 1872, *Courier-Journal*, Louisville, KY: DIAMONDDOM.
37. April 4, 1873, *Courier-Journal*, Louisville, KY: THE GREAT DIAMOND SUIT.
38. Quoted in December 23, 1874, *Courier-Journal*, Louisville, KY.
39. August 29, 1878, *Courier-Journal*, Louisville, KY: ELIZABETHTOWN.
40. April 24, 1921, *Denver Post*, Denver, CO, magazine section.
41. August 29, 1878, *Courier-Journal*, Louisville, KY: ELIZABETHTOWN.
42. July 30, 1896, *White Oaks Eagle*, White Oaks, NM: AN HONORED CITIZEN GONE.

CHAPTER THREE

1. Feb 19, 1890, *The Boston Globe*, Boston, MA: FEAFRUL TEST.
2. Ibid.
3. September 26, 1866, *Hartford Courant*, Hartford, CT.
4. January 27, 1883, *Boston Globe*, Boston, MA: A WILY DOCTOR.
5. October 20, 1865, *Bangor Daily Whig and Courier*, Bangor, ME.
6. January 27, 1883, *Boston Globe*, Boston, MA: A WILY DOCTOR
7. Ibid.
8. January 11, 1867, *The United Opinion*, Bradford, VT: (advertisement).
9. February 19, 1890, *The Boston Globe*, Boston, MA: A FEAFRUL TEST.
10. November 20, 1874, *Vermont Farmer*, Newport, VT: SOME MORE HUMBUGS.
11. January 26, 1876, *The Boston Globe*, Boston, MA: (advertisement).
12. February 4, 1876, *The Boston Globe*, Boston, MA: "OXYGENATED AIR."
13. February 19, 1890, *The Boston Globe*, Boston, MA: A FEAFRUL TEST.
14. November 23, 1878, *New York Daily Herald*, New York, NY: THE VAULT ROBBERS.
15. https://boundarystones.weta.org/2015/10/28/george-christians-shipping-ring.
16. February 19, 1890, *The Boston Globe*, Boston, MA: A FEAFRUL TEST.
17. Blood, C. L., M.D., Physician for Disease of the Head, Throat, Lungs, and the Kidneys. *A Century of Life, Health and Happiness, or A Gold Mine of Information, For*

One Dollar: A Cyclopedia of Medical Information for Home Life, Health, and Domestic Economy. Published by The Author, 38 West Thirtieth Street, New York—A FIVE DOLLAR BOOK FOR ONE DOLLAR.

18. Ibid.
19. October 26, 1880, *The Sun*, New York, NY: CHAS. L. BLOOD'S PRACTICE.
20. February 1, 1881, *The Brooklyn Daily Eagle*, Brooklyn, NY: GUDGEONS.
21. October 26, 1880, *The Sun*, New York, NY: CHAS. L. BLOOD'S PRACTICE.
22. December 23, 1880, *The Philadelphia Inquirer*, Philadelphia, PA: (section heading missing).
23. December 30, 1880, *The New York Times*, New York, NY: SUBORDINATION OF PERJURY.
24. March 31, 1881, *The Kansas City Times*, Kansas City, MO: DEAN BUCHANAN GIVES AWAY HIS WICKED PARTNERS.
25. June 14, 1883, *Evening Star*, Washington DC: "THE "OXYGENIZED AIR" CASE.
26. May 28, 1884, *The Boston Globe*, Boston, MA: BLOOD AND BLACKMAIL.
27. December 18, 1884, *The Fall River Daily Herald*, Fall River, MA: MORNING NEWS.
28. February 19, 1890, *The Boston Globe*, Boston, MA: BORROWERS AND SPONG-ERS.
29. January 28, 1885, *The Boston Globe*, Boston, MA: THE BLOOD-EVANS CASE.
30. June 3, 1886, *Detroit Free Press*, Detroit, MI: THE JUDGE CALLED FOR BLOOD.
31. February 19, 1890, *The Boston Globe*, Boston, MA: A FEAFRUL TEST.
32. Ibid.
33. February 17, 1890, *The Boston Globe*, Boston, MA: HIS BIRTHRIGHT.
34. October 29, 1890, *The Boston Globe*, Boston, MA: FOR HEALTH AND RECRE-ATION.
35. October. 3, 1908, *Turner's Public Spirit*, Ayer, MA

Chapter Four

1. April 20, 1888, *The Evening World*, New York, NY: ANN SHOW UP.
2. April 21, 1888, *The New York Tribune*, New York, NY: MARSH AFFIRMS HIS FAITH.
3. May 1, 1888, *The Sun*, New York, NY: PRINCESS OF GHOST LAND.
4. Ibid.
5. July 10, 1870, *Chicago Tribune*, Chicago, IL: A BOGUS PRINCESS.
6. Ibid.
7. Ibid.
8. June 6, 1870, *Chicago Tribune*, Chicago, IL: THE SPIRIT OF LOLA MONTEZ. *From the New York Herald, June 3.*
9. June 24, 1870, *New York Daily Herald*, New York, NY: THE ROYAL PRE-TENDER.
10. June 29, 1870, *Buffalo Morning Express and Illustrated Buffalo Express*, Buffalo, NY: TELEGRAPHIC BRIEFS.

11. November 10, 1870. *The Brooklyn Union*, Brooklyn, NY: EDITHA.
12. December 29, 1870, *The New York Herald*, New York, NY: PRINCESS EDITHA. Hopelessly Insane—Committed to the Lunatic Asylum.
13. March 30, *The Sun*, New York, NY: SHE BEATS MME. BLAVATSKY.
14. March 25, 1880, *Memphis Daily Appeal*, Memphis, TN: OLD MOTHER SHIP-TON'S.
15. March 25, 1880, *The Times-Picayune*, New Orleans, LA: GOTHAM GOSSIP.
16. August 20, 1884, *The Sun*, New York, NY: MRS. DEBAR AGAIN.
17. June 30, 1881, *St. Louis Post-Dispatch*, St. Louis, MO: LOLA MONTEZ REDI-VIVUS. *New York Letter to Buffalo Courier.*
18. Ibid.
19. July 15, 1887, *Narragansett Times*, Narragansett, RI: To the Editor of the Times.
20. March 29, 1888, *The York Dispatch*, York, PA: UNDER THE INFLUENCE OF MEDIUM.
21. April 1, 1888, *The New York Times*, New York, NY: SLID DOWN THE BANIS-TERS.
22. March 30, *The Sun*, New York, NY: SHE BEATS MME. BLAVATSKY: Lawyer Marsh's Princess Has a Grip on His Real Estate.
23. April 1, 1888, *The New York Times*, New York, NY: SLID DOWN THE BANIS-TERS.
24. March 30, *The Sun*, New York, NY: SHE BEATS MME. BLAVATSKY.
25. April 2, 1888, *New-York Tribune*, New York, NY: MME. DISS DEBAR DRA-MATIC.
26. April 5, 1888, *San Francisco Chronicle*, San Francisco, CA: A CHALLENGE ACCEPTED.
27. January 1, 1888, *The Leavenworth Times*, Leavenworth, KS: HERRMANN'S LAT-EST TRICK.
28. April 7, 1888, *The Evening World*, New York, NY: INCENSED AT ANN O'DE-LIA
29. April 21, *The New York Tribune*, New York, NY: MARSH AFFIRMS HIS FAITH.
30. April 12, 1888, *The Sun*, New York, NY: GOOD EVENING, DISS DEBAR.
31. April 21, 1888, *The New York Tribune*, New York, NY: MARSH AFFIRMS HIS FAITH.
32. June 24, 1870, *New York Daily Herald*, New York, NY: THE ROYAL PRE-TENDER.
33. April 24, 1888, *The Evening World*, New York, NY: NOT SPIRIT PAINT.
34. April 19, 1888, *The Evening World*, New York, NY: CORNERED AT LAST.
35. April 26, 1888, *The Evening World*, New York, NY: PRESTO! HERE IT IS!
36. May 1, 1888, *The Sun*, New York, NY: PRINCESS OF GHOST LAND.
37. May 28, *The New York Times*, New York, NY: MAKING SPIRIT PICTURES: HERRMAN'S WAY OF DOING THE DISS DEBAR PERFORMANCE.
38. October 22, 1888, *The Inter Ocean*, Chicago, IL: MRS. FOX-KANE'S BIG TOE.
39. Houdini, Harry, *A Magician Among the Spirits*, 1924, p. 77.

Chapter Five

1. http://teachingcleveland.org/category/industrial-revolution-1865-1900/million-aires-row/.
2. December 2, 1904, *Chicago Tribune*, Chicago, IL: MYSTERY SHIELDS CHADWICK RICHES.
3. December 13, 1904, *The Berkeley Gazette*, Berkeley, CA: MAN OF MILLIONS WANTED.
4. Abbot, Karen. "The High Priestess of Fraudulent Finance," *Smithsonian Magazine*, June 27, 2012. https://www.smithsonianmag.com/history/the-high-priestess-of-fraudulent-finance-45/.
5. January 1, 1939, *Daily News*, New York, NY: JUSTICE AND LADY BOUNTIFUL.
6. December 12, 1904, *The Province*, Vancouver, BC: HER FAMILY TREE IS RATHER SHADY.
7. April 25, 1927, *Press and Sun-Bulletin*, Binghamton, NY: REPORTER RAN FEMALE CROOK TO TRAIL'S END.
8. January 1, 1939, *Daily News*, New York, NY: JUSTICE AND LADY BOUNTIFUL.
9. December 12, 1904, *The Province*, Vancouver, BC: HER FAMILY TREE IS RATHER SHADY.
10. December 8, 1904, *The Inter Ocean*, Chicago, IL: MRS. CHADWICK ARRESTED; CASE REACHES A CRISIS.
11. January 1, 1939, *Daily News*, New York, NY: JUSTICE AND LADY BOUNTIFUL.
12. April 26, 1936, *Chicago Tribune*, Chicago, IL: QUEEN OF SWINDLERS.
13. Abbot, Karen. "The High Priestess of Fraudulent Finance," *Smithsonian Magazine*, June 27, 2012. https://www.smithsonianmag.com/history/the-high-priestess-of-fraudulent-finance-45/.
14. January 1, 1905, *El Paso Times*, El Paso, TX: THE SIREN'S EARLY LIFE—*Pittsburg Dispatch*.
15. November 29, 1904, *The Buffalo Times*, Buffalo, NY: CLEVELAND WOMAN WHO BROKE MEN AND BANKS.
16. January 1, 1939, *Daily News*, New York, NY: JUSTICE AND LADY BOUNTIFUL.
17. December 7, 1893, *The Cincinnati Enquirer*, Cincinnati, OH: DE VERE.
18. Crosbie, John S., *The Incredible Mrs. Chadwick*, Whitby, Canada: McGraw-Hill Ryerson, p. 149.
19. April 26, 1936, *Chicago Tribune*, Chicago, IL: QUEEN OF SWINDLERS.
20. November 16, 1907, *The Morning Call*, Paterson, NJ: MRS. CHADWICK'S VAGARIES.
21. Crosbie, John S., *The Incredible Mrs. Chadwick*, Whitby, Canada: McGraw-Hill Ryerson, p. 180.
22. January 1, 1939, *Daily News*, New York, NY: JUSTICE AND LADY BOUNTIFUL.

23. Ibid.
24. November 29, 1904, *The Buffalo Times*, Buffalo, NY: CLEVELAND WOMAN WHO BROKE MEN AND BANKS.
25. April 26, 1936, *Chicago Tribune*, Chicago, IL: QUEEN OF SWINDLERS.
26. January 1, 1939, *Daily News*, New York, NY: JUSTICE AND LADY BOUNTI-FUL.
27. December 31, 1904, *The Salina Evening Journal*, Salina, KS: CHADWICK ARRIVES.
28. October 24, 1907, *Monmouth Democrat*, Freehold, NJ: CONDENSED DIS-PATCHES.
29. Crosbie, John S., *The Incredible Mrs. Chadwick*, Whitby, Canada: McGraw-Hill Ryerson, p. 223.

Chapter Six

1. "Gaston B. Means—Master Bad Man", *Liberty Magazine*, April 17–June 12, 1937, by May Dixon Thacker.
2. Ibid.
3. Means, Gaston Bullock, by D. A. Yanchisin, 1991, excerpted from, *Dictionary of North Carolina Biography*, 6 volumes, edited by William S. Powell. Copyright ©1979–1996, found: https://www.ncpedia.org/biography/means-gaston-bullock.
4. Ibid.
5. "Gaston B. Means—Master Bad Man", *Liberty Magazine*, April 17–June 12, 1937, by May Dixon Thacker.
6. Sept. 10, 1939, *Phildelphia Enquirer,* Phildelphia, PA: "My Life with Gaston Means", by Julie P. Means, serial running 9/10—10/1/39, across four Sunday editions.
7. "Gaston B. Means—Master Bad Man", *Liberty Magazine*, April 17–June 12, 1937, by May Dixon Thacker.
8. "The Amazing Mr. Means," J. Edgar Hoover, with Courtney Ryley Cooper, *The American Magazine*, 1936, v. 122, n. 06
9. "Gaston B. Means—Master Bad Man", *Liberty Magazine*, April 17–June 12, 1937, by May Dixon Thacker.
10. September 10, 1939, *Philadelphia Enquirer*, Philadelphia, PA: "My Life with Gaston Means", by Julie P. Means, serial running 9/10—10/1/39, across four Sunday editions.
11. September 25, 1917, *The Marion Star*, Marion, OH: MEANS IS HELD TO GRAND JURY
12. "Gaston B. Means—Master Bad Man", *Liberty Magazine,* April 17—June 12, 1937, by May Dixon Thacker
13. September 10, 1939, *Philadelphia Enquirer*, Philadelphia, PA: "My Life with Gaston Means", by Julie P. Means, serial running 9/10—10/1/39, across four Sunday editions.
14. "The Amazing Mr. Means", J. Edgar Hoover, with Courtney Ryley Cooper, *The American Magazine*, 1936, v122 n06

15. July 20, 1918, *The Des Moines Register*, Des Moines, IA: HUERTA CAME TO UNITED STATES TO STIR UP TROUBLE TO AID GERMANY.
16. April 12, 1922, *St. Louis Post-Dispatch*, St. Louis, MO: MEANS' SUSPENSION AS INVESTIGATOR PROVING A MYSTERY.
17. December 10, 1920, *The Charlotte News*, Charlotte, NC: GASTON B. MEANS LOSES FIGHT IN KING WILL CASE.
18. "Gaston B. Means—Master Bad Man", *Liberty Magazine*, April 17–June 12, 1937, by May Dixon Thacker.
19. Ibid.
20. Ibid.
21. "The Amazing Mr. Means", J. Edgar Hoover, with Courtney Ryley Cooper, *The American Magazine*, 1936, v122 n06
22. September 10, 1939, *Philadelphia Enquirer*, Philadelphia, PA: "My Life with Gaston Means", by Julie P. Means, serial running 9/10—10/1/39, across four Sunday editions.
23. October 1, 1924, *The Weekly Kansas City Star*, Kansas City, MO: SOME OF MEANS'S TALK COSTLY.
24. "Gaston B. Means—Master Bad Man", *Liberty Magazine*, April 17–June 12, 1937, by May Dixon Thacker.
25. Ibid.
26. Ibid.

CHAPTER SEVEN

1. April 6, 1937, *Oakland Tribune*, Oakland, CA: BRASS PLATE LEFT BY DRAKE FOUND BY OAKLANDER, HINTS BRITTON DISCOVERED S.F. BAY.
2. Ibid.
3. Ibid.
4. Ibid.
5. November 4, 1900, *Detroit Free Press*, Detroit, MI: MEMORY OF A BENEFACTOR TOASTED. *–Pearson's Weekly*.
6. Anneke Jans, http://homepages.rpi.edu/~holmes/Hobbies/Genealogy2/ps13/ps13_018.htm.
7. December 17, 1846, *New York Tribune*, New York, NY: JENNINGS' ESTATE.
8. October 20, 1858, *Weekly Raleigh Register*, Raleigh, NC: REV. CASWELL DRAKE, OF NORTH CAROLINA.
9. May 5, 1859, *Raleigh Christian Advocate*, Raleigh, NC: SIR FRANCIS DRAKE AND HIS ESTATE.—*Pacific Methodist*
10. October 16, 1859, *The Sunday Delta*, New Orleans, LA: ENGLISH AND AMERICAN FORTUNES.
11. August 25, 1870, *The New York Herald*, New York, NY: THE WHEEL OF FORTUNE.
12. December 2, 1870, *The Times-Picayune*, New Orleans, LA.
13. https://www.officialdata.org/us/inflation/1870?amount=5000.

14. November 14, 1870, *The Brooklyn Daily Eagle*, Brooklyn, NY: SIR FRANCIS DRAKE.

15. October 17, 1872, *The Inter Ocean*, Chicago, IL: GENERAL.

16. Rayner, Richard, *Drake's Fortune: The Fabulous True Story of the World's Greatest Confidence Artist*, New York: Doubleday, 2002.

17. January 3, 1912, *The Pantagraph*, Bloomington, IL: DRAKE ESTATE INVESTORS ANXIOUS.

18. Ibid.

19. January 2, 1912, *The Pantagraph*, Bloomington, IL: TO BUY A FARM.

20. January 8, 1912, *The Pantagraph*, Bloomington, IL: THE DRAKE ESTATE.

21. January 12, 1912, *The Pantagraph*, Bloomington, IL: DRAKE ESTATE INVESTORS IN SECRET SESSION.

22. November 16, 1912, *The Pantagraph*, Bloomington, IL: FINAL BLOW-UP OF THE DRAKE ESTATE BUBBLE.

23. November 25, 1912, *The Pantagraph*, Bloomington, IL: LOCAL PROMOTER REFUSED.

24. January 17, 1912, *St. Louis Post-Dispatch*, St. Louis, MO: ST. LOUIS COUPLE PROMOTING FAMOUS SIR FRANCIS DRAKE ESTATE INVESTMENT CONCERN.

25. November 16, 1912, *The Pantagraph*, Bloomington, IL: FINAL BLOW-UP OF THE DRAKE ESTATE BUBBLE.

26. March 11, 1913 *The Pantagraph*, Bloomington, IL: TELLS HARD-LUCK STORY.

27. June 16, 1915, *The Des Moines Register*, Des Moines, IA: SHARES IN DRAKE ESTATE ON MARKET.

28. June 17, 1915, *Evening Times-Republican*, Marshalltown, IA: WORKS ANCIENT GRAFT.

29. June 17, 1915, *Des Moines Tribune*, Des Moines, IA: DRAKE INVESTORS NOW ARE IN DEADLY FEAR OF PUBLICITY.

30. June 26, 1915, *Des Moines Tribune*, Des Moines, IA: COMING BACK FOR ANOTHER DRAKE WHIRL.

31. August 9, 1915, *Des Moines Tribune*, Des Moines, IA: THE BILL IS FOUND AGAINST DRAKE'S HEIR.

32. August 10, 1915, *Ottumwa Tri-Weekly Courier*, Ottumwa, Iowa: WOMAN IS ARRESTED ON CHARGE OF SWINDLING SUPPOSED HEIRS.

33. August 11, 1915, *Des Moines Register*, Des Moines, IA: HEIR-IN-CHIEF SCENTS PLOT.

34. Rayner, Richard, *Drake's Fortune: The Fabulous True Story of the World's Greatest Confidence Artist*, New York: Doubleday, 2002, p. 67

35. Ibid, 84-88, 91

36. June 9, 1929, *The Kansas City Star*, Kansas City, MO: FAKE "ESTATE" OF SIR FRANCIS DRAKE STILL REAPS A GOLDEN HARVEST FROM AMERICAN SUCKERS.

37. Rayner, Richard, *Drake's Fortune: The Fabulous True Story of the World's Greatest Confidence Artist*, New York: Doubleday, 2002, p. 118
38. Ibid. pp. 121-23
39. Ibid. p. 125
40. October 30, 1933, *Des Moines Tribune*, Des Moines, Iowa: HARTZELL SOUGHT TO PUT PRESSURE ON U.S. OFFICIAL.
41. https://www.loc.gov/law/help/us-treaties/bevans/b-gb-ust000012-0482.pdf.
42. Rayner, Richard, *Drake's Fortune: The Fabulous True Story of the World's Greatest Confidence Artist*, New York: Doubleday, 2002, pp. 132-37
43. January 13, 1932, *Globe-Gazette*, Mason City, IA: FRAUD INDICTMENT, 17 YEARS OLD, DISMISSED. Des Moines, January 13 (AP).
44. Rayner, Richard, *Drake's Fortune: The Fabulous True Story of the World's Greatest Confidence Artist*, New York: Doubleday, 2002, pp. 137–50.
45. Ibid., pp. 161–68.
46. Ibid., 172–73.
47. Ibid., 185–88.
48. "Who Made Drake's Plate of Brass? Hint: It Wasn't Francis Drake," Edward Von der Porten, Raymond Aker, Robert W. Allen, and James M. Spitze, *California History*, Vol. 81, No. 2 (2002), pp. 116–33.

Index

Page references for figures are italicized.